"This is a valuable guide for anyone with unfinishea *especially like the many examples of men who have] 'Great Dads' themselves! This book will help any ad tionship with father and grow as a parent and person. ...spiring!*

– Harold H. Bloomfield, M.D.
Best-selling author of *Making Peace with Your Parents*
and *Making Peace with Yourself*

"My Father, My Self *is a powerful reminder of the unique contributions that fathers give their children. Whether you are an adult child who wants to resolve issues from your past, a father who wants to heal your relationship with your children or a parent who wants to be a positive force in your own children's lives, this book will assist you.*"

– Gloria G. Harris, Ph.D.
Co-author of *Surviving Infidelity*

"Anyone whose father has been missing from their lives will find this book to be of profound benefit in coming to terms with the past and moving on.*"

– Erhard Vogel, Ph.D.
The Vogel Institute

"My Father, My Self *is refrehsing, inspiring and wise. This is a 'must read' for adult children – and if you are a father, treat yourself. You will be enriched.*"

– David McArthur, J.D.
Author of *The Intelligent Heart*

"A straightforward, compassionate, father-positive book about why good dads are vital and how to become one.*"

– Warren Farrell, Ph.D.
Author of *Why Men Are The Way They Are*
and *The Myth of Male Power*

"If you are a man or woman who longs for a closer relationship with your father or simply wants to understand yourself better, these are the powerful stories and guidelines that will help you rebuild generational bridges with insight, compassion and love.*"

– Charles E. Nelson, Ph.D.
Family Treatment Institute

Also by Dr. Masa Aiba Goetz

Books

Getting Back Together
   Bettie Youngs Bilicki, Ph.D., and Masa Goetz, Ph.D.
   Holbrook, MA: Bob Adams, 1990.

Audiotapes

Visualization: A Healing Process

Understanding Your Mental Images

Deep Relaxation

Love Potion Visualization

The Answer Tree Visualization

The Magic Pillow—
   relaxation for children ages three to ten

Relaxation for Young People—
   ages ten to twenty

My Father, My Self

Understanding Dad's Influence on Your Life

*A Guide to Reconciliation and Healing
for Sons and Daughters*

by
Masa Aiba Goetz, Ph.D.

E L E M E N T

Boston, Massachusetts • Shaftesbury, Dorset
Melbourne, Victoria

© Element Books, Inc. 1998
Text © Masa Aiba Goetz 1998

First published in the USA in 1998 by
Element Books, Inc.

This edition first published in the UK in 1998 by
Element Books Limited
Shaftesbury, Dorset SP7 8BP

Published in Australia in 1998 by
Element Books
and distributed by Penguin Australia Limited
487 Maroondah Highway, Ringwood, Victoria 3134

The Publisher gratefully acknowledges permission to
reprint excerpts from:
"Cats in the Cradle" by Sandy Chapin and Harry Chapin,
Copyright © 1974, Story Songs, Ltd.

British Library Cataloguing in Publication Data available

First Edition
10 9 8 7 6 5 4 3 2 1

Printed and bound in the United States by Edwards Brothers

ISBN 1-86204-291-8

Contents

DEDICATION

In loving memory of my father,
George Chusaku Aiba,
whose example inspired
and who always understood

Acknowledgments

Hundreds of men, women, fathers, and children have played a role in creating this book. Almost two hundred people generously shared important parts of their lives as they talked about how their relationship with their father had affected them. Countless numbers of clients opened their hearts over the years and taught me more than I could ever have imagined.

Heartfelt gratitude to my cousin Leonore Baeumler and my daughter-in-law PJ Hess Goetz, whose active encouragement helped bring the project to completion; and to Jackie McQuade Lancaster and Guru for their invaluable support and insightful comments. Thanks to Adrien Gordon for her enthusiasm, Lisa Bach for her many thoughtful and valuable suggestions, and Rosana Francescato for helping bring it to life. I especially want to thank Roberta Scimone, Editorial Director of Element Books, who believed in this work and put her considerable energy behind it.

Special appreciation goes to my three sons, Matthew, Nick and Mike, who have consciously dedicated themselves to being Great Dads and have shown how good fathers are created as well as born.

Above all, I want to thank my father, Chusaku Aiba, whose understanding and love was a presence so tangible it did not need words.

Without them, this book could not have been written.

Introduction

- Do you have unfinished business with your father?
- Have your relationships been affected by unresolved issues with your father?
- Do you have difficulty committing to a relationship?
- Are you still carrying pain, anger or resentment from your childhood?
- Do you avoid letting anyone know the "real" you?
- Do you constantly feel that you need to prove yourself?
- Are you comfortable expressing your sexuality?
- Do you have difficulty with authority figures in the workplace or elsewhere?
- Do you want a different relationship with your own children?
- Do you want to make peace with the memory of a father who has died or is unavailable to you?

You may not realize it, but these and countless other areas of vital personal concern are directly linked to the kind of relationship you had with your father—a powerful bond that has rarely been closely examined until recently. For years, it was taken for granted that the major influence on a child's life was their mother. Today, we know that is not true. Fathers also have an enormous and long-lasting influence on their children's development that continues through-out adult life.

Whether you are able to sustain satisfying, committed relationships; whether you find gratification in your work life; whether you are comfortable in your expressions of sexuality; whether you are effective as a parent; even whether you are at ease speaking up and asserting yourself, at work or in relationships, is in large part dependent on your relationship with your father.

If your father was what I call a "Great Dad" (which I'll define later in the book), his love, support and attention gave you a foundation of self-confidence and optimism about your future, as well as the skills to form deeply rewarding personal relationships of your own. But if you had a troubled relationship with your father, it may have resulted in difficulty committing to relationships, a nagging doubt that you can ever be "good enough," or fears that the person you love will leave you.

When I first started my counseling practice, about twenty-five years ago, I suspected that fathers played a key role in determining the later happiness of their adult sons and daughters—but I was not prepared for the extent to which that proved to be true. I never questioned that my father loved and cared about me. Like many good things in life, it seemed natural. I took it for granted that most fathers were like that until I experienced the opposite in an abusive marriage. Those years made up what I now call the "tenderizing process." That experience gave me insight when working with the women and men who came to me for assistance, and it led to the writing of this book.

During my work with clients and in the close to two hundred in-depth interviews I conducted for this book, I met people of all ages and from all walks of life. Some had advanced degrees; others had less formal education. Some had grown up in urban areas; others were raised on farms. There were students, retirees, those just starting careers, others at the peak of professional accomplishment. Artists, nurses, engineers, social workers, sales people, physicians, clerical workers, construction workers, mechanics—almost every type of profession was represented.

Most of the interviewees had never been in therapy. Telling the story of their relationship with their father was extremely helpful to them. There were many "Aha!" experiences as the reasons for personality traits and preferences that they had not previously examined suddenly became clear. Husbands, wives or significant others who sat in on the interviews invariably found they developed an entirely new level of understanding of their partners.

The problem that came up most frequently with my clients and in the interviews was relationship difficulties stemming from unresolved father issues. Problems with Mom don't seem to affect relationships in the way that problems with Dad do. The biggest problems in relationships are usually the inability to commit, fear of abandonment and lack of communication. Inability to commit and fear of abandonment are two sides of the same coin. These problems usually stem from experiences with fathers who walk out on their families, disengage after divorce, or are emotionally detached even though physically present. Emphasis on communication is a relatively new development. The John Wayne "strong, silent type" was a male role model for years. Expression of emotion was viewed as womanly and weak. The tide is slowly turning, but for many adult men, easy, open communication is still a problem area.

Women whose fathers had left their families, either emotionally or physically, were fearful of being abandoned by the men they fell in love with. Men often reacted to their father's leaving by seeking the fulfillment of a relationship but then fleeing when faced with a commitment. Sexuality was another issue that frequently surfaced. Women who had received negative messages about their bodies felt ill at ease sexually and reported marital difficulties. Men whose fathers were unfaithful to their mothers found themselves repeating the same pattern.

Lack of self-confidence was also a common issue. Men and women who had been constantly criticized and expected to meet unreasonably high standards of performance frequently felt that they didn't measure up to expectations—no matter how well they did. Their distorted self-image and fears of being exposed as impostors frequently prevented them from achieving to the potential of their talents.

In reaction to these anxieties, women and men often set up their own obstacles—unconsciously sabotaging the attainment of the very goals they most desired.

To help clients resolve these issues, I evolved the method of therapy that is presented in the Path to Healing workbook at the end of this book. The method involves gently confronting the past in order to resolve it. Clients are guided back to the time when their current problems originated. They identify the decisions and coping mechanisms made as young children that work against them when acted out in their present lives as adults. Using imagery and other metaphorical techniques, they are able to reexamine early experiences from an adult perspective. Reexperiencing the past from another vantage point leads to release of the earlier pain and creates a new world view—one that allows people to lead the fulfilled, joyful lives they are capable of.

When presented with this method, clients protested, worrying that they would be unable to successfully negotiate difficult emotional terrain. They questioned whether revisiting the past could be of any help—especially since most had spent a great deal of time, money and energy trying to forget it.

I reassured them that in my experience, no matter how troubled the past has been, it *can* be healed. We carry all of our life experiences with us, whether we acknowledge them or not. It is impossible to leave behind anything that still carries an emotional charge. The only way to truly leave the past in the past is to confront it and resolve it. To come to peace with yourself in the present, you must come to peace with what has happened in your past.

This book will inspire you, inform you and assist in your healing using three elements. The first element, covered in each chapter, is the background information on various areas of your life that are affected by your father. The second, which forms the heart of this book, is the "Dad Stories" and the principles they illustrate. These are the stories you might hear if you were sitting around the kitchen table late at night exchanging confidences with your best friends. They are intimate, eye-opening glimpses of father-child relationships that will stay with you.

If you didn't have the kind of father you desired, these stories show you there are alternative ways of doing things. They will help you to see how you can be guided by the stories in your own life. If you did not have a Great Dad, you can read about the experiences of others who had Great Dads and discover just what made them so great. Those stories will deepen your appreciation of the blessings you received. Above all, the stories demonstrate that there is always hope. No matter what the current situation is with your dad, it is possible to resolve or repair it—even if your dad is dead or his whereabouts are unknown.

Some of these stories will strike home. You will feel that they are your story. If you have a flash of recognition, give yourself time to sort out the feelings and thoughts that arise. The exercises provided in the workbook and elsewhere will help you do this.

The stories in this book tend to highlight the extremes—either Great Dads or fathers with obvious flaws—in order to illustrate a point. In ordinary life, most fathers try their best and succeed more often than not. In the middle ground where most of us dwell, good points and bad points overlap in a constant state of flux.

There will be stories that parallel your life so closely that they seem to be written about you. Other stories may contain elements that are totally foreign. Almost all the stories will contain important parts that you can identify with and that will help you better understand yourself and those you are close to.

The third element in the book that will help in your healing is the Path to Healing workbook, found at the end of the book. This section is like a series of therapy sessions with information, exercises, and stories that illustrate the concepts described. Each one will work on a different level of your awareness to help you along your own path of healing. They are designed to assist you in perceiving in a new way the influence your father had on your life, giving you a view that allows you to see the previously hidden positive aspects as well as the negatives. Each step carefully guides you to the next to help you resolve the old hurts.

As you make your way through the workbook section, be gentle with yourself. Take time between each of the exercises and allow yourself the space to process the feelings that arise. You may want to share some of your reactions with a trusted friend or work through them in the safety of a therapist's office. For more information, a bibliography of additional suggested reading is provided after the workbook section.

Above all, know that as you read the book, do the exercises, and understand your relationship with your father more completely, you will free yourself of the past and open your life to living more fully in the present as a joyful, liberated, empowered being.

SECTION I

Fatherhood

CHAPTER 1

Longing for Dad:
Why Fathers Are So Important

*By profession I am a soldier and take great pride in that
fact. But I am prouder—infinitely prouder—to be a father.*
— GENERAL DOUGLAS MACARTHUR

"Maybe He Didn't Get the Invitation"

"I wonder if he's coming? Maybe he didn't get the invitation." Patty's
thoughts cast a momentary shadow as she heard the special music
she and Bill had selected. Giving one last glance into the mirror, she
made a final adjustment to her veil. "Oh, well, it doesn't matter if
he's not here," she comforted herself. "Grandpa has always been like
a father to me. There's no one I would rather have walk down the
aisle with me. Besides, Bill is everything I've ever wanted in a husband. We've worked so hard to make our wedding perfect—I'm not
going to let anything spoil it. I just wish my father were here to see
me get married."

"Patty, they're waiting for you," her matron of honor gently
reminded her. Brushing thoughts of her father aside, Patty placed
her hand on her grandfather's arm and, taking a deep breath, smiled
up at him radiantly. As the organ swelled with the familiar wedding
strains, Patty and her grandfather started to walk down the aisle.

Why Are Fathers So Important?

Whether you are a man or a woman, Patty's story captures a theme that is all too familiar—the pain that results from the loss of fathers as significant figures in our lives. Just as Patty wanted her father to share in the momentous occasion of her wedding, you too may have longed for your father to be there during times when his presence would have made a vital difference. Those times might not have been such pivotal events as a wedding; they might have been simply the small, everyday happenings such as the father-son or father-daughter night that your father didn't attend, the after-the-game gathering where you envied other kids whose dads were there, the time you desperately needed help with a problem but were afraid to approach him or got brushed away when you did. Above all, you wanted him to be a meaningful part of your life.

Why is this so? What makes the presence of fathers in our lives so important? Why do we still long for them years after we have lost contact? How does that affect our other relationships and our own families? Is there something we can do to repair the losses we feel?

The stories, guidelines, and exercises in this book will help you find answers to these and other questions raised by adult children. They will clarify how your relationship with your father creates a prism through which you view yourself and those you love, how it colors your relationships with others—from loved ones and family members to colleagues—and how it influences important decisions about who you are, your life goals and your deepest values.

No matter how great the time or distance, the effects of your father's influence and any unresolved issues regarding your father do not diminish. Whether dad was present in the home or not, whether he was a loving *Father Knows Best* type or a harsh disciplinarian, whether he was involved with you or held himself aloof, his influence remains and continues to affect you.

If he was warmly loving, the self-esteem you developed from his acceptance played a vital role in developing your present confidence in yourself. His example of affection and respect is a major factor in your own ability to create satisfying relationships. His encouragement of your abilities helps you believe you can attain your goals.

If he rejected you, the feelings of loss and the frustrating struggle to win his love and approval can create feelings of emptiness or anger that harm other relationships. Self-doubt and the inability to believe that others can love or accept you may prevent you from enjoying the fulfilling relationships you deserve. Or, you may fail to attain the successes that your abilities could enable you to achieve.

Recognition that fathers play such an important role is very recent. For years the focus was on Mom and how she affected her children's physical, emotional and spiritual well-being. If she was a "good mother"—able to provide the correct balance of love, attention, discipline, and ultimately, detachment—her children turned out well. If not, she was blamed for their failings. She was labeled as too passive and dependent or conversely, too controlling and all-consuming, and her inadequacies were thought to lie at the root of most family problems.

The parental role of fathers was omitted from this equation. They might be warmly affectionate or sternly uncommunicative, aloof or supportive, harsh in their judgments or fair, but little thought was given to the effect they had on their children. The importance of fathers as emotional nurturers was largely neglected.

The primary responsibility of fathers was to be a good provider, capable of supplying their families with financial security and a comfortable living environment. In their dedication to succeed in this role, many fathers in the past became shadowy "men in gray flannel suits" who disappeared into the corporate world at dawn before their children awoke and returned long after they were asleep. Historically, men were responsible for their family's survival. Currently, a second income is a necessity for most families. Although women still generally have lower-ranking and lower-paying positions, as they achieve greater economic and social equality it will be interesting to see how this changes.

These "good fathers" focused on the careers that supported their families. They assumed the part of ultimate authority in matters of discipline, but their role in their children's development was incidental to other concerns.

In contrast to Mom, whose success was historically measured in terms of her family's achievements, Dad's success was judged by his own personal career advancement, occupational prestige or financial status. His ability to form satisfactory relationships with his children was considered irrelevant. A child's high grades, sports achievement or career accomplishments were matters of pride that enhanced Dad's image—but they did not determine it.

We know now that leaving fathers out of the parenting loop is like trying to maintain balance when one-half of the whole is missing. This has nothing to do with whether men or women are superior as parents or whether either can adequately fulfill the role of both parents. Millions of single and noncustodial parents devote all their efforts to ensure that their children are not shortchanged, and they do magnificent jobs of child rearing.

But mothers and fathers have different and complementary approaches to parenting children. "Dadness" is an expression of the more outwardly directed way men relate to their children. They tend to be less protective, more casual, freer in the way they hold and play with children, quicker to let them experiment. Their matter-of-fact, brisk manner encourages children. It implies that they are competent and able to handle novelty and challenge and builds future self-confidence. Mothers tend to be more protective and containing in the way they handle children. Both approaches are necessary in order for children to learn to take care of themselves while also developing the sense of competence that allows them to try new challenges.

Whatever the quality of the relationship between you and your dad, it forms an emotional foundation that pervades your entire life—especially in the six major areas that dictate how much success you achieve, the degree of satisfaction or difficulty you encounter in your relationships, your choice of career path and the extent of personal fulfillment you attain. His role, and the unique influence of fathers in these areas, will be discussed in the chapters to come.

Six Ways Your Father Influences Who You Are

Self-Esteem and Self-Confidence

Self-esteem and self-confidence provide the foundation for success in every area of your life. When you believe that you are a worthwhile person who deserves success and possesses the inner resources needed for accomplishment, you can set your sights as high as your vision will take you. But when these vital elements are lacking, self-doubt may keep you from setting goals that reflect your potential, or it may engage you in a constant struggle to achieve fulfillment despite your negative belief that you are not good enough.

Sexuality and Personal Identity

A strong identity and healthy appreciation of yourself as a sexual being are essential in fostering your ability to form satisfying relationships. If early conditioning distorted your natural appreciation of your body and sexual feelings, it is likely that you doubt your sexual attractiveness and have difficulty feeling at ease in intimate situations.

Relationships and Marriage

Commitment to a deeply fulfilling relationship is one of the main satisfactions in life. Role modeling and relationship skills learned during childhood are major factors in making relationships work. Seeing your father's love, respect, and appreciation for your mother leads to a desire to seek the same kind of relationship. If there was coldness, lack of communication or abuse, however, you may have difficulty creating satisfying relationships—either submerging your identity in deference to another's needs or fearing to commit to them.

Personal and Professional Achievement

Fathers are traditional role models for career achievement. Their encouragement and ability to guide your academic and job training plays an important role in preparing you for success. If Dad could not help you plan your education or prepare for a career, you may feel that you were at a disadvantage in getting the start in life you needed. Or, anger at authority may cause conflict at work or in other situations in which people have control over you.

Being a Parent to Your Own Children

One of the most important influences on your parenting style is the example you absorbed growing up. Whether you are eager to give your children the same happy experiences you enjoyed or vow that *your* children will have a more positive childhood, your own background is the key element in determining your attitudes and actions when you become a parent.

Values and Beliefs

Fathers are the traditional upholders of community standards and beliefs. If your father had strong religious, political, or philosophical convictions, they undoubtedly have been instrumental in shaping your own faith—whether you agreed with his ideas and followed in his footsteps or reacted against his doctrines and adopted other ways of believing and living.

| | | |

Influences such as these start early. Do you remember running to your father, arms raised, clamoring to be picked up when he came home from work? Do you recall how proud you were when you showed him your first report card? Can you recollect your dad sitting in the bleachers, cheering you on, when you played in a Little League team or other sports event?

When your father played with you, praised you, cheered your accomplishments and consoled you when you met disappointment, he gave you a great start in building self-confidence. The good feelings you got from Dad's approval when you were small play a major role in your positive appraisal of yourself today.

But perhaps you didn't get the love and attention you craved. Being deprived of your father, or growing up in a home where Dad was physically present but emotionally unavailable or abusive, can result in feelings of inadequacy and resentment and can make it hard for you to trust that others can love or accept you. Anger at not receiving your father's love, and fear that perhaps you weren't worthy of it, can undermine the quality of your life. You keep asking yourself, "Didn't he love me?" "Why wasn't he there for me?" "Wasn't I good enough?"

The truth is, his actions had nothing to do with you. Your father's ability to show his love for you or even to have the experience of love within himself was his own responsibility, not yours.

Although your father seemed so omnipotent when you were small, there are many possible reasons why he was unable to give you the love and affection you craved. The most likely is that he did not receive love or approval himself as a youngster and therefore didn't know how to show it. Perhaps he had secret worries that he kept to himself, or external pressures that sapped all his energy. His early upbringing might have taught him that men suppress their emotions and limit their communication to what is necessary.

Perhaps your father came from a generation in which the prevalent definition of a good father was someone who worked hard to provide a comfortable standard of living for his family. If this was the case, your father might have often been away at his job, and when he was home, he may have been too tired to pay attention to you. Possibly he felt overwhelmed by the demands of family life and sought refuge behind a newspaper or in his hobbies. Or he found escape from his own personal demons in alcohol or drugs—either isolating himself from his family or terrorizing them.

| | | |

Why do the effects of a father's rejection linger so long? Why is a father's love and approval so important? One reason is because traditionally, Dad had higher status than Mom. And his approval usually had to be earned, in contrast to Mom's praise, which was more freely dispensed. Despite mothers' career advancement, in many households the father is still the family's chief representative to the outside world. It is a position reinforced by thousands of years of tradition, although it is rapidly being reshaped by today's realities.

You may remember hearing, "Wait till your father gets home," "You'll have to ask your father," "Is the head of the house in?," "Let's not tell your father about this" or "I'll have to talk to my husband."

All of these were messages that Dad was the most important member of the household and that the real power and prestige in the family resided with him.

Yesterday: The Mythic Father

To understand how fathers arrived at this preeminent position and the accompanying mystique that still makes us long for their love and approval, we have to take a look at the traditional patriarchal structure upon which Western society is based. It is a powerful blend of social, religious and legal tradition that has made the longing for Dad's love and approval so enduring.

The larger-than-life attributes found in age-old legends and stories of the heroic king, prophet, protector, lawgiver and warrior are embodied in the concept of the Mythic Father. The heroic figure who protected and cared for his people relegated his status to the human father in his function as family patriarch and tribal elder. Assumptions that present-day fathers will provide for their family's needs, protect them from danger, transmit the skills necessary for physical and economic survival and act as final arbiters in important family and community decisions are rooted in our society's ancient legends. Whether taken from the Bible, Greek and Roman mythology, or the deeds of the Knights of the Round Table, echoes of these earlier archetypal myths are buried in our unconscious and still form part of our expectations.

Today we still have Mythic Fathers, but they come from television, movies and other public arenas. Countless men and women formed their ideal of fathers from television programs such as *Cosby*, whose overwhelming appeal stemmed from its emphasis on commitment to family, mutual respect between parents and children, and firm but insightful parental authority. *Leave It to Beaver, The Brady Bunch, Father Knows Best, My Three Sons, Little House on the Prairie* and other popular programs that defined an era also made their mark.

Like his predecessors, the new "ideal father" possesses inner strength and resolve. However, there is an important difference in the kind of relationship he has with his children. As society has evolved and changed, so has the role of fathers. In contrast to the ideal of physical prowess, unquestioned authority over family members and stoic sacrifice celebrated in ancient times, today's image of the ideal father emphasizes open affection, mutual respect and attention to the needs of his family.

Other traditional masculine functions were never explicitly stated in those TV programs but still remain part of our expectations. They are to exemplify the role of men as husbands and fathers, to provide a model for work and business success, to instill community traditions and values and above all, to serve as an example of manhood.

Today: The Disappearing Father

In recent times, these age-old assumptions have been badly shaken. Urbanization, the massive influx of women into the workforce, the easing of divorce laws and the availability of more effective birth control methods, which overturned sexual mores, have created far-reaching changes that have ruptured existing social standards. These changes have propelled the family into uncharted territory and altered fundamental assumptions about the viability of the two-parent family.

How did this happen? What shattered the seemingly unchangeable structure of father-mother-children and caused it to deteriorate so severely?

Answers can be found in the social upheavals that marked the end of World War II and the growth of suburban "bedroom communities" that isolated women and children from fathers. The work-driven "commuter fathers" of the 1950s and 1960s who remembered the Depression Era hardships of their own childhood were determined that their children would have a better life. Togetherness and conformity to community standards were promoted as the ideal, but the only time many children saw their fathers was during the weekend. Dad's absence and the unmet longing for his attention became one of the defining features of the father-child relationship.

The 1960s and 1970s saw a dramatic reaction. Viewing their father's lives as narrow, empty, joyless and driven, young people were determined to avoid the same fate. In their rebellion against the pressures to conform to their father's standards, they proclaimed a new age whose motto was "Do your own thing."

This social revolution was exacerbated by the bitter divisions caused by the Vietnam War, which intensified youthful distrust of authority and established institutions. It was further fueled by women's drive for equality and experimentation with new types of living arrangements. Drug use became socially acceptable, and its widespread availability led to often catastrophic consequences for individuals and society.

Despite the drawbacks of the 1950s, the yearning for family and stability has cast a golden glow around that era. It evokes a nostalgic image of home, family, school, church, PTA meetings, softball games, and backyard barbecues—memory snapshots of an age when most children had fathers in the home and divorce was still comparatively rare.

The past cannot be recaptured, however. Increasingly, fathers are permanently out of the home, absent not because of work demands but because divorce is so frequent. Childbearing outside marriage is increasingly common, and for many people, personal fulfillment instead of personal responsibility is the highest priority. Couples frequently enter marriage with unrealistic expectations and with little preparation for the hard work of creating a successful family.

The effect on children has been devastating. In his landmark book, *Fatherless in America*, David Blankenhorn revealed that in 1990, more than 36 percent of all children were living without their fathers—more than double the number in 1960; and that before age eighteen, more than half of all children in the United States will live without their father for a significant part of their childhood. In fact, according to statistics from the U.S. Bureau of the Census, the United States is now the world's leader in fatherless families. Estimates of a first marriage ending in divorce are approximately 50 percent; for second marriages the divorce rate rises to more than 60 percent—giving rise to a trend in which more couples are expected to be living in second and third marriages than with their original partner.

What do these numbers mean in human terms? In most divorces, mothers receive primary custody of children. If they do not remarry, mothers usually raise the children alone. Although this is changing, fathers are still too rarely considered to bear a vital responsibility for their children's emotional and psychological well-being. About 40 percent of children whose parents are divorced have not seen their fathers in at least a year. Ten years after divorce this figure rises: more than two-thirds of these children have no contact at all with their father for a year or more.

Although millions of single mothers are successfully raising their children alone, children of disrupted families are much more likely to experience emotional, behavioral, and educational problems. Loss of fathers is especially hard on adolescent boys. The National Longitudinal Study on Adolescent Health reports that teenage boys who get involved in violence at school are eleven times more likely to come from fatherless homes. In contrast, children who reported close family relationships were the least likely to engage in risky behaviors, underscoring previous studies indicating that children whose fathers are involved with them have stronger self-esteem, are less susceptible to peer pressure and are more self-reliant.

No one wants to go back to the days when husbands and wives endured years of misery together in unhappy marriages and women's options were severely limited. But as an ever-widening gulf separates biological paternity from the role of involved father, a trend has emerged that has put us in danger of becoming a nation of mostly fatherless children—with the attendant consequences of increased emotional, educational, and behavioral problems.

With more than one-half of all marriages ending in divorce, the loss of fathers and the results of that deprivation cannot be shrugged off as just another regrettable statistic. We need to understand just why fathers are so important in our lives, strengthen the bonds that connect us and heal the father-child relationships that have fallen by the wayside.

In the pages that follow, you will learn about the kinds of relationships other adults have had with their fathers and how those relationships affected their self-image, sexual identity, marriage, career and values. You will discover what other women and men have done to resolve father issues that have haunted them well into adulthood. And you will find new information to help you better understand the relationship you have with your own father and how it affected you—a discovery that can help you make the bond even deeper or allow you to take the first steps toward a longed-for resolution.

Recommendation

You will notice that you experience a variety of feelings and thoughts as you read this book. Some are expected; others may take you by surprise. To process your reactions, I encourage you to buy yourself a notebook for recording a journal. This will be a record of your journey to understanding the connection between your father and yourself. Here you will write down what resonates for you, the questions that arise and the answers that you ultimately find. It is also an excellent place to record your experiences doing the various exercises.

Be prepared for surprises along the way, and keep yourself open to whatever surfaces. Allow your thoughts to flow without judgment. This is a journey of inner growth that will free you from the past and allow you to create your own future.

CHAPTER 2

Finding Our Fathers:
When Dad Is Emotionally or Physically Unavailable

My son turned ten just the other day.
He said, "Thanks for the ball, Dad. C'mon, let's play.
Can you teach me to throw?"
I said, "Not today, I have a lot to do."

.   .   .

He said, "When you comin' home, Dad?"
I said, "I don't know when,
but we'll have a good time then.
You know we'll have a good time then."

—FROM "CAT'S IN THE CRADLE"
by Sandy Chapin and Harry Chapin,
© 1974, Story Songs Ltd.

Poignant images of a boy's repeated and futile attempts to engage his father resonate for millions of adults who have grown up without the attention they desired from their father. "Play ball with me, Dad," "Talk to me, Dad," "Spend time with me, Dad"—children want to know they are important to their father. They want their father to pay attention to them and be interested in them. But too often the response they get is, "Not now," "Don't bother me," "I'm too busy." Sometimes these words are said out loud; other times a child understands them from body language or tone of voice. But they always hurt.

Divorce and visitation schedules often compounded the problem by providing even less opportunity for those precious moments of spontaneous play. Children pack their bags with their favorite toy, stand at the window in eager anticipation of Dad's car and fight the knots in their stomach if the clock ticks past the time when he was supposed to arrive.

Children need their father's attention. They find security in his presence and the knowledge that he is interested in them. Whether it takes the form of sitting together companionably at the neighborhood ballpark watching a soccer game, accompanying him to the local hardware store to pick up a new tool, or just having their hair tousled as Dad passes by, children want recognition and will do almost anything to get it.

In this chapter you will read about adults who did not have the closeness with their fathers that they yearned for. Emotional distance, physical absence, or permanent deprivation due to abandonment or death all left their personal mark. Each loss is different in the details, but each demonstrates the creativity and determination that children exhibit in their attempts to strengthen the bond between themselves and their fathers.

"If I'm Good Enough, Will You Love Me?"

"No matter how hard I tried, I never could seem to get my father's attention," Brad said. "It was like he was living in another world. He would come home and drop his briefcase down and go to the den, and we'd never see him again except for when he was eating supper with us—and even then, most of the time he was reading something. He never talked to us; we never had those cozy dinner table chats that you see on TV. He never asked me how school was going. It was like he just didn't care.

"I tried a lot of different things to get his attention. I told him what I was doing in school, how I got elected president of the Science Club, how I thought I had a chance to make the football team—but it all seemed to go over his head. I always got the impression that he thought we kids were a big drag on his life and if we weren't around he could have been doing the things he *really* wanted—

like concentrating more on his business and making more money.

"I never knew whether he resented us because he thought we tied him down to my mother, or whether he didn't like kids in general, or if it was just us he didn't like. He was always Mr. Jovial with my cousins, so for a long time I thought he just didn't like us. Now, I think he really didn't want kids, and when he found himself saddled with the three of us, he dealt with it by ignoring us."

If you grew up in a home like Brad's you know how painful it was to try to find some way to get your father involved. It seemed that no matter how hard you tried there was nothing that could ignite his enthusiasm and get him to show that he was proud of you. It's only when you become an adult and you begin to understand things from an adult perspective, as Brad did, that you discover *why* your father was so detached and realize that his aloofness, even though hurtful, had nothing to do with you. It helps to know that it wasn't you he disliked but the situations he found himself in—and probably felt powerless over. Distancing himself from his family was the only way he knew how to manage.

Fathers who detach themselves from their children usually fall into one of the following categories.

The Emotionally Distant Father— He is physically present but emotionally detached.

The Alcoholic or Addict Father— His addiction alienates him from his family.

The Overt Rejecter— He openly repudiates his children.

The Divorced Father— He divorces not only his wife but also his children.

The Abandoner Father— He disappears and rarely makes contact.

Two other types of missing fathers are not distancers, but their loss has profound effects on their children.

The Deceased Father— He leaves a legacy of unfulfilled promise that his son feels compelled to live up to and leaves his daughter with the fear that men will leave her.

The Captive Father—   He is separated from his children by
                      career requirements or physical barriers
                      such as frequent travel, tours of duty,
                      political boundaries, hospitalization or
                      incarceration.

Each of these fathers leaves a unique imprint on your emotions that
may still affect you in adult life.

The Emotionally Distant Father

Being in the same room with an emotionally distant father is like
having your nose pressed against the candy counter, staring long-
ingly at the display and knowing you can't have any. His physical
presence holds out the hope of availability, but his demeanor shuts
you out. Although he acts removed, he is not necessarily disinter-
ested. He may be pleased when you get good grades, be concerned
if you are sick, and provide money for your education. But this dad
has just never learned to enjoy his children, who experience his
withdrawal and lack of affection as disinterest and unavailability.

"Buffer zones" bolster this impression. Some dads isolate themselves by spending long hours at the office or bringing home
briefcases full of work that allow them to disappear even when they
are at home. They create psychological barriers by burying themselves behind a newspaper, immersing themselves in television, or
secluding themselves in their workshops. They usually spend leisure
time in the company of their friends or business associates rather
than with their family, which leads their children to conclude that
they are not very important to their father.

Children have such a strong need to connect with their fathers,
however, that despite such discouragement, they often go to remarkable lengths to create opportunities for interaction. Some of them
become proficient in hobbies their father enjoys, even if they themselves have no interest in these areas. If Dad enjoys woodworking,
they take shop so they can participate in projects with him. If he
spends his weekends watching sports, they become familiar with
his favorite teams and join him in front of the television set. If he

collects stamps, they start educating themselves about rare issues. Whatever the effort, these children feel that the reward is worth it.

"I Even Took a Class in Auto Maintenance"

Miriam, a chemistry major and talented amateur chef, followed this route in order to get closer to her father. "My dad has always worked very hard," Miriam said. "He got up early in the morning and wouldn't come back till late at night. Most of the time, I didn't see him during the week. But if he was home, I would wait till he sat down to read the newspaper, then creep into his lap very carefully so I wouldn't disturb him and pretend to read along with him.

"I desperately wanted to get his attention; so as I got older, I took courses I knew he would approve of that would also allow us to spend time together. I have no mechanical ability at all, but I even took a class in auto maintenance because I figured he'd be proud of me for doing something so practical. Also, I could be with him while he was working on the cars.

"I don't think my father ever realized how much I wanted his attention. He really felt that he was fulfilling his role by working hard and being a good provider. Now that I'm an adult, he's more comfortable with me and we've gotten much closer. I know he really loves me. He just had so much trouble growing up with his own father that he didn't know how to relate to kids."

Miriam found a very creative way to connect with her father. Even though his hobbies held no real interest for her, she was rewarded by the opportunity to work together with him—thereby setting the stage for a better relationship. Working on cars together gave them an easy way to connect in companionable silence without the necessity of talk.

The Alcoholic or Addict Father

When fathers engage in more destructive activities, however, attempts to bond with them can have disastrous consequences. "If you can't beat 'em, join 'em!" can become the motto of a desperate child. If a youngster has tried in vain to win his father's attention, this might mean engaging in self-destructive activities—for example, connecting with an alcoholic father by drinking with him.

"You're Old Enough to Drink Now"

The first time fifteen-year-old Brian ever felt close to his father was when he was given his first beer.

"I was eleven years old the first time my dad poured me a beer and invited me to sit down in front of the TV to watch a football game with him and my grandfather," Brian said. "He told me I was old enough to drink with them now. It made me feel good that he was treating me like a grownup. I felt accepted, and happy that we were finally doing something together. By the time I was thirteen, I was a full-blown alcoholic. I'd steal liquor from my father's cabinet, I'd go to school drunk and get into fights, and I'd drive even when I was blind drunk. I've been in three treatment centers now, and I'm praying I'll stay sober because I'm afraid I'll end up seriously hurting myself or somebody else."

Brian's case is extreme but not unusual. When it seems there is no other way, we grasp at whatever we believe it takes to make a connection with Dad. Sometimes that means doing things he enjoys that we hope will bring us closer. Other times, anger at Dad takes us in the opposite direction: we'll prove that we don't care.

The Overt Rejecter

Even harder to deal with than fathers who distance themselves are those who openly reject you. Unlike emotionally distant fathers, who set up psychological barriers to keep their children at a distance, overt rejecters openly repudiate them.

Most people find it completely unfathomable that a father would blatantly disavow his children and refuse to participate in their lives in any way. But it does happen. Sometimes these fathers live a great distance away; sometimes they live in the same house. In either case, such fathers make it brutally clear that they want nothing to do with their children and disown them psychologically, if not legally.

Daughters and sons of overt rejecter fathers must cope with the pain of being rebuffed through repeated attempts to communicate. They endure the heartbreak of their father's refusal to attend major coming-of-age rites such as graduations, weddings, award ceremonies or other significant milestones at which Dad's non-attendance creates a conspicuous and painful void. His absence at these ceremonies is especially wounding because, by tradition, a father plays a major symbolic role in them as the patriarch whose presence acknowledges and legitimizes his child's newly attained status.

Because the desire for connection is so strong, children usually make repeated attempts to create even a limited relationship with their father. When rejection follows, the feelings of emotional abandonment inflict overwhelming psychic pain. Most adult children eventually resign themselves to accepting this loss, but their anguish usually keeps them searching for the love they never experienced. Wanting resolution, they may repeat the pattern of seeking love from emotionally unavailable partners. Or they may transcend their pain and find an inner strength they never knew existed.

"I Realized I Was All Alone"

"When my husband and I broke up, I was utterly devastated," Christy, a young elementary school teacher in a small midwestern city, explained. "I felt so completely alone and lost. I had a three-year-old son, I didn't have a job, and I was in a strange town where I knew hardly anyone. I was so desperate that I called my father, who had refused almost all contact with me for several years, hoping that at least I could talk to him and get some moral support. Instead, he cut me off and said he never wanted to hear from me again. I don't think I've ever felt so alone in my life. I sent him a long letter asking what I could do to get him to stop being angry with me, and I called him several times after that, begging for a chance to talk to him, but he just said, 'No.'

"In that moment, the last time he said, 'No,' I finally knew that I was really alone; there was no one I could go to. I lost my mother as a child, and I realized that I would never be able to go to my father for *anything*. I had been abandoned by my husband, I had been abandoned by my father—I knew it was all going to be *me*.

"I remembered a story I'd heard as a kid about how the early immigrants went through hardships in getting to this country, but when they arrived, they found opportunity. I equated that to my life. My father got me from infancy to being able to sustain myself. When he rejected me, I accepted that I was on my own. I quit hoping and striving for a reconciliation, and I decided that whatever I wanted in life I would have to create for myself.

"That vision, thinking of myself as a pioneer starting all over again in a new country, gave me strength. I managed to get my life back in order, and a couple of years later, my husband and I got back together. I'm happier than I've ever been.

"I have no ill feelings now. I'm finally at peace with it; it doesn't bother me anymore. I have no expectation of ever seeing him again—it's as if he were dead—I feel completely detached."

When Christy's father rejected her in that moment of extreme need, Christy experienced an epiphany. The cord snapped, and she was free. Buoyed by the release of expectation, she was able to detach from her father and reframe her experience—moving from seeing herself as a victim to imagining she was a pioneer arriving in a new country. The peace of mind that this acceptance gave her infused her with the courage and energy to renew her life and, eventually, even her marriage.

The Divorced Father

Divorce has become the number one family plague of our time. Few couples enter marriage taking for granted that they will always be together. Children either live in a household where divorce has occurred or have friends whose parents have divorced. They inevitably wonder, "Could this happen to me?"

Many divorced fathers continue to involve themselves actively in their children's lives. Too many others, however, drift away. Their own lives intervene, their interests move elsewhere, and the desire to continue a relationship with their children diminishes, sometimes to the point of nonexistence. In effect, this divorced father has divorced his children as well as his spouse.

Studies show that most children have little contact with their fathers after divorce. The 1987–1988 National Survey of Families and Households showed that 30 percent of all children of divorced parents did not see their father at all during the course of a year, and almost 50 percent saw their father less than five times during a year.

The effect on children is predictable. Those who have lived through a divorce, with its attendant emotional turmoil, mutual recriminations, frequent upheaval of school and living arrangements, conflicting loyalties, lowered living standards and fears of abandonment bear scars that, even when superficially healed, often run deep.

"The children are handling it very well" is an often-heard phrase. But this apparent adaptation to new circumstances is usually misleading. Barring situations such as those in which there is spousal abuse, which makes children welcome the safety of separation, youngsters often fantasize that their parents will reunite, and the children will do whatever they think it takes to keep the parent who has left a part of their lives.

Many children sublimate their own needs and become "little adults" because they are aware of the fragile emotional condition of the remaining parent. They attempt to hide their own pain and become caretakers—parenting their parent—in an effort to keep intact what remains of their world.

Psychological fallout can linger for years after the divorce, surfacing as feelings of self-doubt, depression and anger; an inability to commit to a relationship; and fears of making a similar mistake in choosing a partner. This fallout typically does not become apparent until the child of divorce reaches adolescence or is ready to enter a relationship.

This phenomenon is so ubiquitous that Judith S. Wallerstein, author of *Second Chances: Men, Women and Children a Decade After Divorce*, has given it a name: the "sleeper effect." Individuals suffering from the sleeper effect have seemed to cope superbly with their parents' divorce, but suddenly, with their first true love relationship, they fall apart.

"He Pushed Us Out of His Life"

Yolanda entered therapy when she fell genuinely in love for the first time. George seemed to have everything: intelligence, similar values, a fun-loving personality, the same interest in sports, the same taste in music. But despite her attraction to George, she found herself becoming extremely anxious about becoming more deeply involved.

"I've been in control of all my relationships until now," she said. "This is the first time I'm really in love. What if I open my heart and he walks out on me? I would be devastated. He's very understanding, but if I keep holding back I'm afraid I might lose him. It's driving me crazy. I want him, but I'm afraid to go for it.

"I know it has something to do with my parents' divorce. The first year after the divorce, my dad lived in a house pretty close by. My little brother and I would go over and stay for the weekend or just drop by to spend some time with him. He liked having us around and sometimes would cook for us. It wasn't that different, because even when he was married to my mother he was hardly ever home during the week anyway.

"But after he remarried, we had to stick to a formal visitation schedule. We couldn't go over to his house when we wanted anymore, and there were all kinds of rules when we were there. He stopped calling us, and if we wanted to call *him* we had to get permission to call at a specific time. It really made me angry that he pushed us out of his life when he got married again.

"I never had a chance to get close to him after that except when I helped him work in the yard. Eventually, I developed a nervous stomach, because I was always afraid of breaking one of the rules. By the time I got to high school, it got so bad I didn't go over for almost four years. But he never called to find out how I was. Even today, he's never asked, 'What happened?'

"It's made me very distrustful about relationships. I have this deep-down feeling that no matter how good things look, it can all change without warning."

Yolanda's two previous relationships had been with men whose financial and emotional problems made them dependent on her.

Although she didn't realize it, putting herself in the rescuer position and focusing her energies on how she could help them allowed her to feel in control of the situation. Safety lay in fulfilling their needs so that they wouldn't leave her. But those very needs made a mutual, satisfying commitment impossible. When she contemplated a relationship with a man who didn't need her, she was panic-stricken.

Fortunately, Yolanda recognized that she needed help to resolve this problem. In a short time, by bringing her fears out into the open, confronting them, and defusing them, she learned that she had the power to leave them behind. One tool that helped was keeping track of her anxious thoughts with an "Automatic Thought Log." Using this tool, whenever she started to get anxious she could counter her fears with a positive thought. She then transformed the positive thought into an action so that not only her mind but also her body would encode it. Here is an example of how it worked:

AUTOMATIC THOUGHT LOG

1. Automatic negative thought:

"George is going to leave me."

2. Positive thought to replace it:

"George loves me and is committed to making our relationship work."

3. Positive action to encode positive thought:

Read the card George recently sent me and tell myself out loud, "George loves me and is committed to making our relationship work."

You, too, can keep track of your anxious thoughts with an Automatic Thought Log. When you have kept this log for a while, you will probably see that the same two or three anxiety-inducing thoughts keep coming into your mind. Once you come up with positive thoughts to counter these few anxious thoughts, you will always be prepared to deal with them. The most important thing to remember about this exercise is that you *don't* have to believe the positive thought you are telling yourself. In fact, the more outrageously positive you make it, the better. If you find yourself smiling at how far out your statement is, good for you! What you want to do is counter your "inner naysayer" with positive energy so that it gradually diminishes and fades away.

The Abandoner Father

There are two forms of abandonment by fathers. In the emotional form, you are no longer an important part of your father's life. Even if he's in the same house as his children, it's as if he were not there. In the literal form of abandonment, the father simply departs and severs all communication. His children don't know why he left, and they are often faced with the terrible emptiness of not even knowing whether he is dead or alive.

"I Wish He Knew I Got the Bronze Star"

"I wonder what my father would say if he knew his son got the Bronze Star," said Harry, a young marine who was decorated for heroism beyond the call of duty during the Persian Gulf War. "I grew up in a small town in Nevada. My father was a prospector, always looking for the pot of gold at the end of the rainbow. I was about two when he left. From time to time, he drifted back for short visits; then he would leave again. I think the last time I saw him was when I was about ten years old. After that, I told my mother I didn't want to see him anymore. I felt a real strong anger and distrust for him.

"He never sent money or birthday cards. We were so poor, my mother always worked two jobs, sometimes two and a half jobs, to support us. The houses we lived in were always real shacks. We moved around a lot, always looking for a better place to live, so I was continually changing schools. One year, I remember going to five or six different schools. I got so far behind that finally, in the eleventh grade, I dropped out of high school.

"What I do remember about my father is that he was a very stern man with a real John Wayne type of U.S. marshal image. I looked at him and saw what I thought represented the United States: the guy who would make everything right, who would lead his men to victory—which is how I think of myself.

"My father always gave us the message that, even in adversity, you had to just 'suck it up and do it'! I shine the most when things get really bad, like during the war in Iraq. Now that I think about it, he's influenced me a lot. I wish I could tell him that."

Despite the pain and anger Harry felt at his father's abandonment of the family, he admired the mystique his father represented, that of the strong law enforcer who rides into town and makes everything right. The marines gave him a code of conduct that celebrated this stern ethic while also providing a way to express the positive traits that he remembered his father having. Despite the years and distance, Harry treasured the similarity to his father and wished he could acknowledge how much it meant to him. He transformed his dad into an icon, a mythic figure who symbolizes his ideal of masculinity.

Being awarded the Bronze Star was a testament to his courage and his commitment to the values his father stood for. Harry was certain that his father would be proud of him—he just wished his father could know about it.

Harry was able to find comfort when I suggested that he find a photo of his father and talk to the image he saw there. He was to tell his father about his exploits and imagine his father expressing pride and joy at everything he had accomplished. It was a very emotional moment for Harry. For the first time, he was able to weep the tears he had kept inside for so long. It was very cleansing and freeing for Harry. He now feels right with himself and his father.

If you are in a similar situation, you might want to use this technique. Prepare yourself before you actually do it by taking some time to think about the effect your father has had on your life and the kind of person he was. Before you begin, find a quiet place and breathe deeply a few times to quiet your mind and relax your body. Allow your tears and emotions to flow freely, and when you are done, perform a ritual to complete the experience. For example, you might want to burn some herbs to celebrate the release as you say an affirmation, such as "I now release all pain of the past. Love flows now through me and my father, and surrounds us in love and harmony."

You may have a favorite prayer or blessing to use. Do or say whatever seems the most appropriate and healing to you.

Earning Love by Excelling

One of the most common ways that young people try to gain their father's approval is through high academic or extracurricular achievement, such as being a straight-A student, getting elected president of the student council, being chosen captain of the football team, making head cheerleader, becoming editor of the school yearbook, graduating as class valedictorian, or attaining other outstanding honors.

But many children find that no matter how much they accomplish, they can never do enough to really please their father. They become overachievers and have to keep proving themselves again and again. Each achievement becomes diminished by demands for another. If they get four A's and one B+, their father asks, "Why didn't you get all A's?" If they win a supporting role in a school play, they're criticized for not getting a leading part. If they hit one home run, they're told they should have hit two. For these children there is little satisfaction in attaining goals, because no matter how hard they work, it's never sufficient.

As adults, they may choose a profession that their father approves of rather than the field they are really attracted to. An important consideration in picking a marriage partner may be that the potential spouse meets their father's criteria rather than their own. They may even pursue a lifestyle based on his standards instead of asserting a choice of their own.

Love that has to be earned brings little satisfaction. Children who must earn Dad's love know that such approval is only temporary, only as good as the last high grade or success. Failure to achieve the next time might take their father's love away. Because the love is conditional, they are in constant fear of losing it.

What's Wrong with Always Having to Be Perfect?

When love is conditional, there is no emotional security. The pursuit of Dad's approval by attempting to attain impossibly high standards fuels a struggle for success that yields little or no personal satisfaction. This compulsive need to achieve often continues in adult life, creating an inner "no-win monster," a state of mind in which no achievement is ever good enough and satisfaction is always another summit away. The greatest outward accomplishments yield little reward if you end up feeling, "If I'm so successful, how come I'm not happy?"—and you will feel this way if you learned that love demands a price, one that must be paid over and over. To have a satisfying relationship as an adult, you need to jettison this early childhood conditioning and reject the idea that love must be earned by what you achieve. Love is not a commodity—it is a natural emotion that flows freely unless artificial obstructions are put in its path. Real love is unconditional, and you are inherently worthy of giving and receiving it.

When love comes with a price tag, there are hidden costs. Here are some of these consequences:

- Believing that you must constantly prove yourself to keep someone's love.
- Feeling worthless if you don't meet other people's expectations.
- Continually striving to meet unrealistic goals of perfection.
- Never being satisfied with what you've achieved.
- Feeling empty inside despite outer achievements.
- Needing a partner to counteract your feelings of emptiness.
- Needing approval from others to feel worthwhile.
- Being a pleaser who tries to make everybody happy.

One of the most serious consequences of feeling you have to earn love is that you don't believe you deserve it if you haven't "earned" it. The moment your performance slips—whether at work, in your earning capacity, as a lover, in your physical appearance, or in some other external way—you fear that your partner will leave you. It's hard to believe that you can be loved just for yourself, because in the past that was never enough.

External symbols of success alone, however, never lead to internal feelings of satisfaction. If you were indoctrinated with this belief system, you are likely to feel "empty" or "dead" inside. To counteract these feelings, you seek a partner who will bring you the excitement and joy you are lacking—someone through whom you can vicariously enjoy the playfulness and fun you missed out on growing up, when you were too busy striving to achieve to actually enjoy yourself.

This explains many seemingly incongruous couplings: a prominent intellectual and a bubbly, young secretary; a hard-driving businessman and a free-spirited artist, or an obsessively meticulous scientist and an intuitive New Age practitioner.

Many people who encounter such couples wonder what they can possibly have in common. What they don't realize is that these relationships are formed for precisely the reasons that others find them so inexplicable. Those who are success-driven often choose their opposites as partners. Having been deprived of crucial elements of their youth, they seek those whose impulsive spontaneity frees them from their normal focus on work and allows them to play.

Their descriptions of their partners bear testimony to this need: "The only time I feel alive is when I'm with him." "The house looks so dark till she walks in, then everything brightens up." "She makes everything fun." Unable to be playful themselves, they depend on their partners to bring pleasure and lightness into their lives.

Others use addictive behaviors to compensate for feelings of emptiness. Some engage in compulsive work habits, excessive spending, or substance abuse. Others get involved in a series of unsatisfying and volatile relationships whose instability acts as a protective barrier against intimacy, while simultaneously providing the diversion that temporarily relieves inner pain.

Filling the Emptiness and Learning to Play

Daniel, the owner-chef of a highly successful restaurant, was a typical example of someone whose professional achievements were outstanding but whose personal life was marked by conflict and dissatisfaction.

"My girlfriend is driving me crazy," Daniel lamented. "Ever since she moved in with me, she keeps saying that I don't spend enough time with her and that I care more about the restaurant than I do about her. I do work long hours, but I have to be there to take care of things. I bought her a dress shop because I thought if she had something of her own she would be satisfied, but she still complains.

"I don't know anybody who would treat her better. I paid her son's dentist bills, I gave her money for a plastic surgeon to have her nose fixed, I helped her get a Mercedes; but she says I'm not romantic enough. She wants us to hold hands and walk on the beach. I don't have time to walk on the beach; I have a business to run.

"Last month she moved out, and I'm miserable; I have to get her back. Sometimes I ask myself, 'Why am I working so hard?' We went to Europe for three weeks last year and had a wonderful time. It cost me a bundle, but it was worth it. I told her I would take her on a cruise this winter if she comes back; but she says she doesn't love me any more.

"I don't want to lose her. Nothing is any fun anymore. She gets me upset because she's so irresponsible; how can she just leave like that? She's like a kid, but she's the only person who can make me feel happy."

Daniel was like many adults whose emphasis on work and financial achievement never allow them time to enjoy themselves. Despite his intelligence and all the outer attributes of success—money, social status, a home, cars, and expensive vacations—he had not had the opportunity to discover the inner resources that would bring him happiness. Daniel grew up in a strict household where all activities had to be purposeful. So as an adult, Daniel didn't know how to play. He had to find someone else through whom to experience pleasure—a partner whose lighthearted spontaneity and impulsiveness balanced his own work-driven approach to life.

Although his parents lived thousands of miles away, Daniel still heard his father's voice telling him to work harder and achieve more. Without someone else to provide the ideas and the companionship, Daniel didn't know how to have fun.

Daniel needed balance in his life. He achieved this outstandingly in his restaurant by creating an inviting environment and interesting menu. This keen sense of proportion in the career area of his life had to be translated into making his personal life as colorful, harmonious, and enjoyable.

Daniel was being plagued by stress-related headaches, neck pains, and back pains. Like many people who have been trained to keep driving themselves, Daniel found it extremely difficult to slow down without a compelling reason, so his body was giving him the permission he needed to relax.

After learning some simple relaxation techniques that gave him immediate relief, Daniel decided to do something that would take him completely away from his everyday life. He started taking sailing lessons. "When I'm out there on the ocean and I have to concentrate all my attention on the boat, I really feel free," he said. "I know no one can reach me. It's just me and the wind and the water."

Sailing may not be a feasible choice for you as a way to unwind. But the idea is to do something that is totally out of character as a way of breaking out of the singleminded focus that is robbing your life of joy. You want to shake your "mind muscles" loose so that you can develop new perceptions and allow new feelings and ideas to come in.

Bellydancing lessons were the choice of one formerly staid insurance broker. Buying a motorcycle seemed just the way to break out of the mold for a highly intellectual scientist. Art classes allowed an executive to free his creativity and express long-hidden artistic leanings. If you've been wondering what would be the right activity for you, try something you never thought you could do. If your choice is one your friends would have difficulty imagining you doing, that is probably the right choice for you.

The Deceased Father

While adults who grew up with distant fathers often find ways to bridge the gap in later years, a father's death presents an entirely different kind of challenge. Children who lose their fathers through death, particularly if the loss occurs before their birth or during early childhood, have a unique burden to bear because they inherit the mantle of the dead father. The ending of a father's life, coinciding with the beginning of his child's, endows the newborn with all the unfulfilled potential of the husband, son, or brother who was lost. This kind of burden is particularly hard on boys.

Those left grieving are apt to look to the son to take his father's place—especially if the father showed exceptional abilities that were cut off at the very moment of their fulfillment. They might name the son after his father, identify similarities in appearance and personality, or predict that the child will fulfill the father's dreams.

Children accept this identification. Through family myths, old photographs, letters, and anecdotes, they imagine the dad they might have had. Those who are old enough to remember flesh out their recollections with stories from their mother, grandparents, and other relatives. They take bits of anecdote and use them as building blocks to create an image of a dad they might never have known. By endowing that image with heroic qualities that they then strive to emulate, these children make a connection between their birth and their father's death that imparts special significance on their life and places special demands on them.

"I Have to Live My Father's Life"

William, an oncologist at a university medical center whose father had died of cancer several weeks before his birth, spoke of the connection he felt between his birth and his father's death. "I always had a tremendous sense of loss and the feeling that there was much to emulate," William said. "As time went on, I had a conscious desire to do all the things that he had done. I remember, when I was in the third grade, I ran across an article in the encyclopedia about the college he had attended and burst out of my room shouting, 'This is where I want to go to school!' I always had the sense of having to live not only *my* own life but also my father's. Because his life was cut short, I felt it was up to me to fulfill his promise—there was a compelling force drawing me in that direction.

"I calculated to the day how old my father was when he died; then I projected his age at death forward to the corresponding date in my own life. I felt that I had to accomplish everything by the time I was that age. Everything I did after that would be something my father could not have achieved and therefore would have special significance. I had the sense that I had to *do* something with my life, since I was given all this extra time.

"I grew up on anecdotes and odd bits of information and family stories about my father that I pieced together to create the man and gain a sense of what he was like. Now that I'm older and have my own family, those images have lost some of their color and intensity. I've been able to put them aside and move forward with my own goals.

"My six-year-old daughter likes to look at old photos; whenever she sees my father's picture she always asks if I'm still sad. Of course I still feel the loss but not with the immediacy that she associates with that feeling. I'm much older now than my father was when he died. I don't grieve for him as a child grieves for a father anymore; I now grieve for the young man whose life was cut short and for the relationship I never had with him."

When a father dies, the children, family, and friends who loved him tend to create an ideal image to remember and pass on, distilling his best and finest qualities. As William aptly reflected, "One has the example of a 'shining paragon' to strive for."

Acting Out to Get Attention

Some children eventually give up and lose hope that they will ever get the love and attention they crave. At that point, they often adopt the attitude, "If you won't give me your attention because you want to, I'll make sure you pay attention to me because you *have* to."

These are often very bright youngsters with high potential, but despite their abilities, they spurn achievement as a means of gaining their father's approval. Instead, they seem determined to get Dad's notice by engaging in conduct that he finds impossible to ignore. It might be skipping school, getting into fights, stealing, driving recklessly, using drugs and alcohol, or being arrested.

These children use negative behavior to say, "Pay attention to me!" Their rebellion is a way of expressing anger and frustration in a desperate bid for recognition. Getting into trouble may have painful consequences, but it might at least get Dad involved, and many children feel that any attention, even negative, is better than no attention at all.

"I Started Stealing Money"

Bill, an engaging man with a ready smile, recalled how much it hurt not to be able to get his father's affection. A marketing representative in his late twenties, Bill is typical of many men who dealt with his father's rejection by repeatedly getting into trouble as a youngster.

"When I was little, I remember trying to crawl up on my dad's lap or reaching up to him when he came home from work, trying to get him to pick me up—but he always pushed me away. When I was around six or seven, I used to ask him to play ball with me or take me fishing with him, but he never did. I remember how excited I would get when he promised to do something with me on the weekend. But when Saturday came, he always made some excuse. He never kept his promises, and I was always devastated.

"I had a lot of resentment when I was a kid. Around the second grade, I started stealing money from my dad and getting into fights at school. By the time I was in the sixth grade, I was hanging around with kids who were a lot older and getting into much bigger trouble. Things just escalated, and eventually, I wound up at a boarding school for kids with serious problems.

"The strange thing is, although I could never get my dad's attention when I was little and wanted it so much, when I went away to the school, he was there every Sunday to visit me and take me out on pass.

"My anger made me do a lot of things I regret now, but I don't blame him for my problems. I'm responsible for my own actions. But I know how much it hurt to think that he didn't love me."

Negative behavior got Bill's dad to pay attention, but it exacted a high price in the damage it caused to Bill's already troubled self-image. He carried his anger to school with him, where it spilled over into the classroom and earned him a reputation as a troublemaker, further eroding his self-esteem. Expectations of failure and rejection can trigger a downward spiral of self-destructive behavior that does not end until Dad does become actively involved—if not at home, then in court, at a treatment facility, or in a therapist's office.

Like Bill, you may have felt so much pain about never being able to count on Dad being there that you got involved in things you now regret. But when you mature and turn your life around, you can use the knowledge you acquired at so much personal cost to become a better parent—making sure that your kids get the emotional start in life that you missed out on and that you are the father to them that you always wanted for yourself.

Father Surrogates: Grandfathers, Uncles, and Other Father Figures

When fathers are not present or are unable to provide love and guidance, children search for other men who can fill their need for a father. Grandfathers, stepfathers, uncles, older brothers, or other men sometimes step in to fill the void. Surrogate fathers love and nurture the child, offer support and encouragement, are role models for values and skills, act as mentors to help children plan their future, and provide a male perspective to young people making their way through difficult transition points. Grandfathers, especially, occupy a unique niche.

"My Grandpa Took the Time to Explain Things"

"I felt like my grandfather was the only male influence in my life that ever really gave me any kind of love or strength," said Pat. "My mother died when I was very young. After her death we had a succession of housekeepers, and my father didn't have much to do with us kids. My grandfather became my moral rudder—he was the one I went to when I needed answers. He was extremely supportive and told me I could do whatever I wanted. When I was little I always said I wanted to go to college and be a veterinarian. My father would put me down all the time and say, 'Why do you want to do that?' It was my grandpa who always supported me and told me to follow my dreams.

"One of the things I remember most about my grandpa was his garden, and his orchard with the big walnut tree. We used to pick nuts from the tree and bring them back into his workshop and sit and talk for hours while we cracked walnuts.

"I remember one time, I was crying because my father punished me. My grandpa picked me up and put me on his tractor and we spent the whole day working in his garden. He took the emphasis off me being a bad kid and just let me help him prune the trees. He also enjoyed woodworking; so when we went back to his workshop that day he made me a bookshelf. One Christmas, he made me a whole miniature kitchen.

"My grandpa took the time to work with me and explain things to me. He was such an important part of my life—I've never forgotten him and the values he taught me. He was the most wonderful man."

The encouragement, understanding and love she got from her grandfather sustained Pat during the difficult times in her young life. When she had no one else to turn to, her grandfather's support and encouragement provided a solid foundation to grow on. His unconditional love and acceptance was essential to compensate for the absence of her father's affection.

Just one person in a child's life who cares can make the crucial difference. Pat has never stopped cherishing her grandpa's memory, and she credits her most important values to his living example.

"I Found a Father Figure in My Uncle"

Dan found a nurturing male who filled his need for a father's love when he "adopted" his uncle. "My father and I loved each other," Dan stated, "but we did not have a close relationship because he was always criticizing me.

"I remember when I was six years old, my father took me for my first swimming lesson. Afterward, the lifeguard came over and said, 'Great! You did a good job!' I felt really proud; but then my father came over and said, 'No, you didn't. You didn't put your head *completely* under water the way you were supposed to!' He did that every single swimming lesson until it got to the point where I didn't want to go anymore and quit. He was mad at me, but he was the major reason for my quitting.

"What I did then was find a father figure in my uncle. My uncle was very different. He was a nice, easygoing guy who had a son a few years older than me who became like an older brother. I looked up to both of them. I would go over to their house and mess around because I felt really happy there. It eventually got so I spent every weekend and most of the summer with them—I never wanted to go home.

"At this point in my life, I can appreciate how hurt my dad must have been. I know he really thought he was helping me by pointing out everything I did wrong. But I hated him for it, and I just wanted to get away from him."

When the criticisms got too much to bear, Dan sought out a surrogate father in an uncle who gave him the acceptance and warmth he needed. Now that he has children of his own, Dan is making sure to give them the affection they need so that they do not have to look for it in someone else's home. His own experience has taught him well.

Finding Long-Lost Fathers

Children's longing for their dad is deep and persistent—strong enough to span many years and thousands of miles. A compelling urgency to know the man and to find out more about themselves leads some adults to go to enormous lengths to renew contact with a father who has been out of their lives for years.

"I Knew My Father Was a Violinist"

Nancy, a thirty-one-year-old teacher, hadn't seen her father since age four, when her mother immigrated to the United States from Czechoslovakia. "I knew he was a violinist," Nancy said, "and I knew what he looked like from his pictures and my mother's description, but I wanted to get to know him better. So I wrote him and we started exchanging letters. Finally, he came here to attend a meeting, and we met for the first time since my mother and I left Czechoslovakia twenty-five years previously. We didn't have much time together, just an afternoon, but at least I got to meet him.

"The following year, my husband was invited to give a presentation at a conference in Europe, and we took a few extra days to go to Prague. Our meeting was much more emotional than the first time, because we were together longer, and I got to ask him all the questions I had always wondered about.

"He took me to see the house we used to live in, the store where he would take me to get candy, the park where he used to push my carriage—all the landmarks. I found out a lot more about my father. It allowed me to piece things together, and it gave me a sense of who I was. I was able to get answers to questions I'd always wondered about, like why he didn't leave Czechoslovakia with us. It was very emotional for both of us because he had wanted to explain himself to me for a long time. I was amazed that even though I can speak Czech only at a ten-year-old's level we were able to communicate so well with each other. Now that my husband and I have our own family, we've agreed that every two years we'll bring my father over for a visit. I want to make sure our son knows his grandfather.

"Finding my father again has been a very positive experience for me, especially because now that I know him, I can see how much I'm like him. My mother and I are nothing alike, and I had always wondered why I was so different. Now I can see where I got my looks and personality traits."

By finding her father, Nancy gained insight about her emotional makeup and discovered more about her history. It confirmed for her who she was and what her heritage was. She gained a new understanding of herself and an appreciation for a father that she had always been curious about. Despite the intervening years and geographic obstacles, she was able to reestablish the connection with her father and fill in the missing portions of her history. This gave her a stronger sense of her identity and provided an ongoing generational link for her son.

| | | |

Fatherlessness is one of the biggest problems facing families today. Too many children are growing up without the guidance of a loving father; and too many fathers who want to do the best for their children are unable to give the kind of emotional support they need.

What are the solutions? How can men become better fathers and learn to cherish the bond with their children? Perhaps the answers can be found in those fathers who seem to have it all—the Great Dads. They're the kind of father every kid wants. They're your friend's dad who you wished was your own father; the teacher you trusted who was the only man you could confide in; the television dad who always seemed to know exactly how to handle things.

Recommendation

The stories you just read are likely to have brought up a number of issues for you. It is normal to have strong emotional reactions to situations that have deep personal meaning for you. To deal with these feelings, become an advocate for yourself. Write yourself a letter of encouragement, just as a best friend might.

In the letter, acknowledge the difficulties you have experienced, point out the unique personal strengths you developed in response, and applaud your courage in pursuing greater self-knowledge to resolve these concerns. Then place the letter in an envelope and address it to yourself. Mail it a week from the day you write it so that you can read it again with a renewed perspective.

Most people have infinitely more courage than they give themselves credit for. Give yourself the credit you deserve now.

CHAPTER 3

Great Dads:
The Father You Always Wanted

All happy families resemble one another.

—LEO TOLSTOY

Tolstoy was right. Happy families do resemble one another—and so do Great Dads. You've read the stories of men and women who yearned for a close, loving relationship with their father. Now, you'll meet those who actually had that type of relationship, individuals who describe their father as always being there for them, who respected him so much they *wanted* to adhere to the family guidelines, and who portray their father as "the neatest person who ever walked the face of the earth."

Why is it important to know that despite the negative reports we read in the press or hear about on TV, there are countless fathers who are deeply committed to their children? There are two primary reasons. One is because there are many unrecognized Great Dads who give their children a lifelong legacy of competence, self-reliance, self-respect, moral values, commitment to family, and the ability to be a good parent to their own children. Their existence needs to be acknowledged. The other major reason is that if we see these Great Dads in action, we can learn from their example.

What makes these fathers so special? Why do their kids love and admire them so greatly? What can you learn from them? Listen as the children of Great Dads talk about them, and you will gain many insights about fatherhood to help you better understand and deal with your own family.

Characteristics of a Great Dad

My research on women and men who had exceptionally close bonds with their fathers has revealed a number of vital traits shared by these outstanding dads. Each of the stories you will read here demonstrates how these traits were actually expressed. These fathers

- Made a priority of always being there for their children.
- Expressed affection freely.
- Gave their children unconditional love and acceptance.
- Spent time with their children and showed them they *genuinely wanted* to be with them.
- Were physically demonstrative, hugging and patting their children.
- Included children in their activities, including hobbies and work.
- Demonstrated love and respect for their wives.
- Instilled values and self-discipline by example.
- Protected their children.
- Included children in family discussions.

Inner strength, affection, responsibility, humor, and fairness were personal characteristics depicted again and again by people who described their fathers in almost identical terms: "I idolized my dad," "I adored my dad," and "I thought my dad was the greatest man on earth." Above all, children of exceptional dads declared, "I knew I could count on him."

Trust is the one trait that children mentioned more than any other when describing why they admired their fathers so much. They knew that Dad would always be there for them and that they could count on him no matter what. These fathers demonstrated by their actions that their children came first: They would halt an activity in order to attend to their children's needs or willingly inconvenience themselves to attend to their children's welfare. This behavior gave youngsters a certainty about his love that created an indestructible bond.

Dads are role models for a wide range of behaviors that individually may seem minor but that in their sum total constitute respect. Among these are consideration, validation, reliability, courtesy, attentiveness, honoring privacy, and using discipline in a restrained manner. In other words, dads who treat their children the way they themselves want to be treated teach skills that are applicable to every area of life. Above all, Great Dads rarely *talk* about what's right—they *live* the example instead. Their children learn to respect Dad not because of the power he has over them, but because of the admiration they feel for him.

"He Was Always There for Me"

Calvin, a public relations consultant, talked about the deep impression made by his father's dedication to spending time with him despite extremely heavy work demands, and how vividly it demonstrated to him the value his father placed on their relationship.

"The amazing thing is that even though most of the time he worked six or seven days a week at his business, he wasn't an absent father," Calvin said. "Whenever he could, even if he was dog tired, he made time for me. When Sundays came around, which was usually the only day he was home, even though he might have paperwork to catch up on or something my mom wanted him to fix, he and I would always do *something* together.

"As I got older and got into sports in high school, my father would always be in the stands cheering. He was always there for me. If I wanted to talk to him about something, I don't ever remember him saying he didn't have time. Even if my father was in the middle of business, trying to pay bills or figure out who owed him what, he would stop and say, 'What do you need?'"

For Calvin, the fact that his father made time for him was one of the defining characteristics of their relationship. It clearly demonstrated that Calvin's needs were more important to his father than other concerns that also demanded his attention. Every day adults must confront their emotional "in-basket." Whom do they pay attention to? What can wait? How do they prioritize? When fathers take time for their children, they show them that they are valued and that the father-child bond is just as important to the father as it is to the child.

"He Didn't Have to Discipline Me—I Respected Him Too Much"

Adam, a genial man with a warm smile, also enjoyed a great relationship with his dad. In addition to showing affection toward his son, Adam's father was also openly affectionate with his wife. Adam's comments underline the importance of a loving relationship between husband and wife, not only to give children emotional security but also to provide a healthy model for their own relationships later on.

"My dad was a very affectionate man," Adam said. "He'd hug me and kiss me, or just put his hand on my head and tousle my hair. We were a very demonstrative family, and that's something that I've continued with my own children—nobody in our family ever goes out the door without getting a hug."

"As far as my dad disciplining me," Adam continued, "I don't ever remember him raising his voice. He didn't have to—I respected him too much. He just had a way of looking at me or of saying something that I knew meant business. Not that he never punished me; it's just that I admired him so much I *wanted* to please him. During all the time I was growing up, I only remember about three or four spankings.

"The one time I remember most clearly was when I was about fifteen. Like all teenagers, I had moments when I could get pretty obnoxious. I was standing there, pestering my dad about something and violating one of our major family rules: no bringing up problems until after dinner. My dad was reading the paper, but I wouldn't quit. I've forgotten what it was about. All I remember is that he booted me in the butt. Not hard, just sort of a 'cut it out' gesture.

"My feelings were really hurt. I went into the kitchen and started to take my father's inventory, but my mother quickly put a stop to that. She said, 'Just a moment. The man you are talking about is *my* husband. You are talking about *your* father—the man who supports this household. In fact, you are talking about the greatest man you will probably ever know.' That's the one time he disciplined me that I really remember, because I felt so terrible about it."

Like other Great Dads, Adam's father almost never had to discipline him. His relationship with his son was so good it was rarely necessary. Such strong bonds, based on mutual love and respect, help children to internalize their parents' values and behaviors and make them their own. Because behavior is learned, when children consistently experience honesty, consideration, dependability, and other traits that are important to their parents, those are the actions they will express in their own lives.

When Great Dads do need to discipline, children accept it because they know it's fair and it's used to teach, not to punish. When discipline is used to punish, it causes pain, fear, and humiliation and produces only a short-term gain. Children do not learn appropriate behavior from punitive discipline—they learn only to fear being caught. Instead of incorporating the values that the parent is trying to instill, these children learn to use subterfuge.

Consequences appropriate to the child's age and level of understanding help them learn ways of making better choices for themselves. When discipline is used to teach, children integrate their parents' values into their own. Positive discipline teaches children that their actions have effects and that goals can be attained in constructive ways. Good fathers correct children in a way that instructs rather than demeans. They respect their children's dignity by listening to and reasoning with them, setting realistic consequences, being firm but fair, and being consistent—all actions that develop trust and help youngsters grow into self-disciplined adults who respect the rights of others.

"My Dad Never Went Hunting Again"

A prominent member of the judiciary who had trained himself during his days as a prosecutor to hold his emotions in check, Howard was typical of men who were surprised by the tears that welled up in his eyes as he spoke about his dad. He was visibly moved as he described his father's ready willingness to sacrifice his favorite hobby in order to protect him.

"My father was exactly my idea of what a country lawyer should be," Howard said. "He was exceptionally capable; he had loyalty, integrity and warmth; and he cared about people. So, what happened when I was fourteen and we were out hunting with some of his friends is something I'll never forget.

"Now, you have to keep in mind that my dad loved hunting more than anything else in the world, and he waited all year for hunting season. He had just bagged a quail when I got superficially nicked in the leg by some pellets and started yelling, 'I'm shot! I'm shot!' He came running over and saw that I was okay, but my dad never went hunting again!"

His father's on-the-spot renunciation of the sport he loved, because he thought his son might have been hurt, was an act Howard never forgot. It was a profound moment of truth that illuminated his father's love.

"My Father Forced the Intruder Back Out"

Protecting their children and making sure they're safe is another way Great Dads resemble each other. They show their children that they're on their side, either to provide moral support or to defend them physically if necessary. Knowing that Dad is right there and will guard them from harm lets children know how much they are valued. Additionally, it is another way of building children's self-esteem and encouraging them to stand up for themselves later.

One of my most vivid memories of my father stems from being a teenager living in New York City and being followed home from the subway one night. I always thought of my father as a very quiet, gentle man, but that night I was astonished by a ferocity I had never seen as he raced to protect me.

Heading home along the darkened street, I suddenly became aware that a man was following behind me, and I picked up my pace. I hurried to get inside our building, but the building door didn't shut quickly enough, and as I ran down the hall into our apartment I heard him enter the front hallway. My father asked what was wrong, and I told him about being trailed. Springing up from his chair, he ran into the lobby and confronted the man: "What do you want? Get out! Get out!" he shouted, advancing on him. And despite his age and physical slightness, he forced the intruder back out.

It was completely out of character. I had rarely seen my father get angry and never before heard him shout so fiercely. It was an amazing transformation that brought home to me just how much he cared.

Defending his child is one of the most powerful demonstrations of a father's love. It gives children a deep sense of security and safety, and it is an attribute of the Mythic Father that Great Dads naturally express.

"I Was Never Afraid He Would Take Back His Love"

Unconditional love is the cornerstone for the self-esteem and self-confidence that is vital for a child's healthy development. Great Dads may disapprove of their children's actions, but they make a distinction between the child and the behavior. They show that they love and accept the child despite mistakes of judgment or poorly thought-out actions. They correct behavior but do not demand perfection. Instead, they accept their children as the individuals they are, thus bolstering the inner resources necessary to successfully meet the inevitable challenges that arise later on in life.

"My dad was always there for me," Mitch, a commodity broker, stated. "It didn't matter whether I was competing in an athletic event or if I got in trouble. He was there unconditionally! I never felt that if I did anything out of line he would take back his love. He was always a presence—doing things with me, showing up at my Little League games, being there.

"He encouraged me to do whatever I wanted. Even when he must have thought my ideas were crazy and never going to work, he'd say 'Yeah. Go for it!' It was especially remarkable because I came up with so many wild schemes that I did just go for—like setting up a Sunday morning breakfast delivery service to the dorms when I was in college. But my father said, 'Sure. Give it your best shot!'

"Another time, I put a promising career on hold to train for the 'Iron Man' triathlon. My dad just said, 'Okay! Wonderful!' I know there were times when he must have thought, 'I don't know why he's doing this.' As a commodities trader, I've taken my lumps in the market, but then I pick myself up and think 'Yeah. Go for it!' and I know I'll be okay."

Not everyone would take risks like Mitch, but the emotional security fostered by a father's unconditional acceptance of goals—whether Dad believes they are reasonable or not—plays a major role in giving men and women the confidence to try new endeavors without fear of possible failure.

Acceptance also bestows the ability to accept diversity. When children are appreciated for their uniqueness, they are more likely not only to accept their own differences but to value those things that are unique and different in others. In a changing world, where many more racial, religious, and ethnic groups are working and living together in close proximity, the ability to welcome and value variations in oneself and others is a key element in living together harmoniously.

Accepting their children's achievements without demanding that they accomplish at higher levels is another way that Great Dads show their unconditional love.

"My father never pushed me to do anything," Carrie said. "I got B's all through high school, but he never said I should have gotten A's." I was the first one in my family to go to college, even though my father never pushed it. He let me make up my own mind."

This might sound counter to common sense, but instead of being motivated to perform better, children who are forced to excel often rebel by deliberately not achieving to their full potential. By encouraging Carrie but allowing her to come to her own decision, her father enabled her to feel the pride that came with succeeding on her own initiative.

Children often fear that their parents will not love them unless they perform up to expectations. To be valued regardless of external criteria such as scholastic performance, chosen profession, marital status, sexual orientation, or personal beliefs allows a child to feel intrinsically loveable. Individuals feel good about themselves when their efforts are applauded, rather than having the focus exclusively on results. Such approval frees them of the compulsion to measure their personal worth in terms of only outer, material success. Instead, it allows them to experience the fulfillment of inner satisfaction, because they are also able to do things for their inherent value.

To be appreciated as a unique individual with your own thoughts, desires and personality is a precious gift that children of Great Dads cherish. It creates respect for self and others that builds a solid foundation for future positive relationships with family members, friends, colleagues and eventually, their own children.

"My Father Is One of the Most Considerate Men I Know"

Consideration is a vital ingredient in the spectrum of qualities that constitute respect. Dads who are considerate of their children teach them an important skill for fostering harmonious interpersonal relationships in the future. Their thoughtfulness shows in a variety of ways that may appear trivial but that have great impact.

In listening to children and responding to their concerns and questions seriously, Great Dads show consideration. They also do this by giving their children choices whenever possible to give the children a sense of empowerment, as well as the opportunity to learn from their mistakes. Yet another practice by which dads display consideration is by treating their children with the same courtesy that is automatically extended to adults.

"My father is one of the most considerate men I know," Gina said. "If I ever wanted something or needed help, he was right there for me. I remember in the eighth grade, I was falling behind in my math class. I was afraid I wouldn't graduate and go on to high school with all my friends, so my dad said he would help me. He sat with me every night while I did my homework, and helped me figure out the problems. I had a terrible time, but he was patient with me and never made me feel like a dope—the way I did in school. He kept telling me I could do it until I finally got it. I did better in high school, but I don't know what I would have done if he hadn't pulled me through. Remembering that helps me understand how my own daughter feels when she doesn't grasp something."

"My Dad Always Kept His Word"

Keeping their promises is another way dads show respect for their children. "I always knew I could rely on my dad to do what he said" is an often-repeated phrase used by children of Great Dads.

"My dad always kept his word," Marvin stated. "It didn't matter if it was something big, like promising to take me on a camping trip, or something smaller, like remembering to pick me up after my football practice. I always knew I could count on him.

"When he said he would get me a car for my sixteenth birthday if I would save up half the money from my after-school jobs, I never doubted him for a minute. It's not like my parents had a lot of extra money, but he found a car that he could fix up, and when I turned sixteen he handed me the keys. He was always that way. If he said he would do something, you could bank on it. I'm that way too."

Learning that his desires mattered and that his dad's promises would be kept planted the seeds of Marvin's own integrity. Because he experienced that promises made were commitments to be kept, Marvin not only learned trust but also made honoring his word part of his own personal credo of integrity.

In contrast, children who are denied this valuable experience, who learn that Dad's promises don't really mean anything and that he can't be relied on, too often grow up unable to trust either themselves or others. They constantly fear the pain of disappointment. Such children learn to discount other people's assurances, and they often make promises that they too are unable or unwilling to keep.

"My Dad Could Have Left Us Like the Others"

Commitment to providing for his family is one of the most fundamental responsibilities of fatherhood. Of all the characteristics that define the good father, dedication to his family's welfare, which encompasses the attributes previously mentioned, is intrinsic—especially in circumstances where many others have abdicated this trust.

Marie, a physician with an established family practice, regarded her father as a hero in this respect. "I grew up in the urban projects," Marie said, "and when I looked around at the other fathers, mine was a hero. For five children to have a father in that community—to have a father in the house who didn't drink, smoke or beat his wife and children, who wasn't abusive or cruel—to have my father not be like that, was an honor. My father could have walked away, he could have left us like the others, but he *stayed* with his family."

The commitment, courage, and strength that Marie's father demonstrated, his ability to rise above a festering environment and provide love and stability to his family, provided a bedrock sense of security that inoculated Marie against her surroundings and enabled her to surmount them.

"My Dad Told My Brother, 'That's None of Your Business!'"

Validating other people's feelings is another aspect of respect. When Dad pays attention to his children's emotions and treats them with the same regard that he would an adult's, they learn that their feelings are important too.

Shari, who runs a bookkeeping service, keenly remembers how her father saved her from embarrassment. "When I was in the sixth grade, I had a huge crush on one of the boys in my class," Shari said. "I was too shy to talk to him, but I used to write these notes about him to my girlfriend. My brother found one of the notes and started reading it at the dinner table. I was mortified, but my dad just reached over, took it out of his hands and gave it back to me. He told my brother, 'That belongs to Shari, and it's none of your business.' I remember how embarrassed I felt and how grateful I was that my dad got that note away from him. My daughter is also sensitive, the way I was. I'm really careful not to embarrass her, because I know how much it can hurt."

Shari learned what it was like to feel empathy for someone and put a stop to an embarrassing situation. Conversely, some children are ridiculed and made to feel ashamed of normal reactions or behaviors. For a child to be publicly humiliated is a shattering experience that usually causes them to withdraw in an attempt not to call further attention to themselves and risk more embarrassment.

Psychological safety is as important as physical safety. Honoring another person's emotions is as important as respecting their religious beliefs, personal possessions or right to privacy. This respect allows each person to enjoy their own special "safety zone" where they are secure in the knowledge that their thoughts and feelings will not be intruded on.

"My Dad Respected My Privacy"

Showing regard for another person's need for privacy and individual space is another way in which Great Dads show regard for their children. "One of the things that really impressed me about my dad was that he respected my privacy," Allan said. "If my door was closed, he'd always knock before coming in. I've done the same with my own children. None of us would dream of going into a room where the door was closed without knocking first."

The consideration such fathers show for their children helps produce youngsters who not only respect Dad and his values but also respect themselves. The sense of self-worth they get from being treated courteously helps them make good choices that are compatible with the high standards they have developed. In today's social climate, where so many forces are pulling in the opposite direction, development of inner strength is all the more essential.

Consideration also extends to making children a part of planning family activities. As a result of this process, they not only feel they are an important part of the family but also learn valuable skills such as communication, problem solving and negotiation to work out compromises that will satisfy everyone.

Some families hold regular "business meetings," in which children are allowed to voice their opinions on matters ranging from how much allowance is reasonable to where to go on the family vacation.

Children who are not given this opportunity often conclude that they are powerless and that others will make decisions for them. Later in life, they may assume that they can have little influence when important decisions are being made, or they might find it difficult to assert themselves appropriately. They might also react by going to the other extreme: Fearing that their wishes will be ignored, they might use intimidation to ensure that they get their way.

"We All Sat Down and Worked Out a Schedule"

"When I was a kid, all I ever wanted to do on our vacations was go to Disneyland," Mark said. "My parents didn't always see it that way; so we would compromise and go someplace where they could have what they wanted, but there would also be something for me. When we went camping, they'd let me plan some of the menus. It was fun—I usually decided on something weird like spaghetti and peanut butter sandwiches, but as I got older I actually turned into a pretty good cook.

"My wife just started going to school at night, and I knew things would be tight between both of our jobs, her school and my son's after-school activities. We all sat down, including my nine-year-old, and worked out a schedule of who was responsible for what—like he and I do the cooking during the week, and my wife makes out the menus and the shopping list on the weekend. It's worked out well and also gives us some time to do the male bonding thing."

"My Dad Did Something Just for Me"

Cheryl's father is an example of a dad whose actions consistently demonstrated just how important his family was to him and the extent to which he was willing go out of his way for his children when their welfare required it.

"I remember the first time my dad did something that was just for me, instead of for all us kids," Cheryl said. "I was in the eighth grade, I had just made the cheerleading team, and I was elected president of the student council. It was a really big year for me, so when I learned we were moving to another school district and I would have to change schools, I was devastated.

"My father went to see the principal and got special permission for me to stay at the same junior high. I realize now how much he had to go out of his way to drive me back and forth to school every day for a year. It's made me a lot more tolerant of driving my own kids around.

"I always wanted to please him because I respected him so much," she said. "When my friends would say, 'No, I'm not going to do that. My dad would kill me!' I would tell them, 'I don't want to do that because I don't want to disappoint my dad.' I wasn't afraid of him; I just thought so much of him, I didn't want to let my dad down in any way."

Cheryl echoed the words of other children of Great Dads when she stated that respect for her father was the primary influence on her behavior. His willingness to disregard his own inconvenience in order to ensure that Cheryl could continue to participate in school activities she treasured led to deep feelings of respect that were infinitely more powerful in shaping her behavior than fear of punishment could ever have been.

"He Always Taught Me to Respect Myself"

Sometimes it is society, not fathers, that lacks respect for children. For minority fathers, one of the greatest challenges is to instill such a strong sense of self-respect in their children that they are able to withstand the prejudices that will all too often assail them.

Jerrold, a retired African-American civil service administrator who grew up in the segregated South, remembered the pride his father instilled in him during his youth. "He always taught me to respect myself and to respect others," Jerrold said. "I was never taught to feel different from anyone. There was a presumption that you treated people as human beings—the way you wanted to be treated.

"Even when I was little, my father treated me with respect, too. If he asked me to do something that wasn't a normal chore, he would do it as a request, and he would always say, 'Thank you.' For example, if he wanted a glass of water, he would say, 'Son, would you bring me some water?' And then when I brought it to him he would always say, 'Thank you.' I've worked with the public most of my life, and I think my ability to get along with people goes back to my father—he always treated me like a grownup.

"When he played games with me, like checkers and cards, he played for the joy of it. Sometimes I got upset when I lost, and he'd say, 'Oh son, that's okay, you'll win next time.' I wonder if that's helped me deal with some of the disappointments in my life, because I tell myself the same thing: 'If you don't get it this time, you'll get it next time.'

"He had many friends, and he always took me with him when he went to see them. I think I get my outgoing nature and penchant for giving from my father. He rarely disciplined us, but if discipline took place near bedtime, it was important for him to see that we didn't go to bed angry. As I get older, I feel more appreciative than ever of my father. He was the most likeable person I've ever known."

Consistently courteous treatment gave Jerrold a deep sense of respect for himself and others. It enabled Jerrold to grow up with a strong sense of self-esteem despite the racism and segregation he experienced. The dignity with which he was treated became a hallmark of his own self-concept and approach to others.

"My Father Understood Me Even When I Didn't Understand Myself"

Have you ever been faced with circumstances in which you felt completely bewildered or unable to manage? Events, people, conditions—even your own developing needs and awareness—may have caused you to feel unsure and anxious about important decisions that you needed to make.

In these circumstances, a father's understanding or expertise can be of immeasurable help. A Great Dad knows you so well, wants what is best for you, and has the maturity and experience to see things in perspective. His counsel inspires confidence, because you know his judgments are tempered with empathy and love.

Polly, an effervescent sportswoman, adored her father, a man who, despite the demands of a business that frequently took him to other parts of the country, always managed to keep in touch with phone calls and letters.

"I always felt he was there for me, even if he wasn't there physically," Polly said. "When I needed help, he was the person I turned to. I especially needed his advice when I fell in love with someone from another part of the country and had to make a decision about whether I should get married, give up my job and move to a small town hundreds of miles away from my family and friends.

"My dad told me that he didn't want to tell me what to do, but he had observed certain things about Adam and me, and he wanted to share them. Then he went on to describe the qualities he saw in Adam, such as his honesty, his sincerity and the fact that Adam was someone I would always be able to count on. He also said that he knew I loved excitement and the bright lights of a big city, but that in choosing a partner I should look for the things that last instead of the glitter.

"My dad pointed out something that I already knew—I just needed to hear it. I love children, and I always wanted to have some of my own, but I wasn't sure I was ready yet to give up the glamour of the city for a more rural lifestyle.

"My dad said that he realized it was a hard choice, but that for me, marriage and building a family would probably bring more satisfaction. He was right about me. And now, as I look at our children and the life Adam and I have built together, I'm so glad I had my father's advice when I really needed it."

When you are confused and distressed, unable to come to a conclusion that feels right, getting support from someone whose judgment you respect is invaluable. Where you seek that support depends on whom you feel emotionally closest to, who understands you best. In this example, Polly's father had insight into her personality and needs and what would ultimately lead to her greatest happiness. He was aware of her strengths and weaknesses, understood her needs, and knew her well enough to make suggestions that were right for her and communicated in a way she could hear. No wonder Polly idolized her father.

He Inspired Me to Believe in the "Impossible Dream"

Belief in yourself and your dreams is one of the greatest gifts anyone can receive. Whatever your goals are, whether continuing your education, starting a new career, overcoming an illness, or pursuing a seemingly impossible vision, fathers are powerful motivators.

My own father's story of how he came to the United States—his personal myth—is so extraordinary that it's one of the best examples I know of how the "impossible" *is* possible. For me, it is proof that you can achieve anything you want to—if you have the faith and tenacity to do what it takes to accomplish it. His tale of how he managed to overcome incredible obstacles to come to the United States from Japan at the beginning of this century taught me that if you take the steps that lead you to your goal—however insurmountable they might seem—you will get there. It is the philosophy I live by.

My father was born in 1884, only fifty years after Commodore Perry sailed into Tokyo Bay and opened Japan to the Western world after 350 years of isolation. It was another age, as removed from today as a rickshaw from the space shuttle—especially in the semi-feudal farming village, deep in the mountains, where my father's family lived. The seventh son in a family of thirteen children, my father was a mischievous and fun-loving boy who engaged in frequent pranks such as placing snowballs in his teacher's bed or threatening to wipe his nose on his sisters' best kimonos so they would give him candy.

However, when he was thirteen years old his entire life changed. He read a book about democracy that had such a profound effect on him that he vowed to himself that he would find some way to go to the United States. It was a decision as improbable as Tom Sawyer deciding that he would go to Japan—and as seemingly unachievable.

My father started to take English lessons from a local missionary, but he became dissatisfied with his rate of progress. Deciding that he needed more practice, he walked six miles to the nearest railroad station every Sunday to wait for the train, hoping that an

American would get off so that he could practice his English. He did this for almost two years. Occasionally a German or Frenchman would appear, sometimes an Englishman, rarely an American.

One Sunday as he waited on the platform his persistence was rewarded. The train stopped and an entire American family—father, mother, and children—came tumbling out. They were making a grand tour around the world and had decided to visit the local shrines.

My father approached one of the sons who appeared to be his age and struck up a conversation, telling him about his dream of coming to the United States. The boy's father, a banker from Vermont, became interested and told my dad to contact him if he ever did make it to the United States.

It was all the encouragement my father needed. Despite his family's objections, he left home and walked about 150 miles to Yokohama, where he was determined to find a job on a boat that would take him to America.

Because he could speak English, he quickly found work on the docks and made friends with the officers of various ships. After a year of searching for a berth to the United States, he was hired as a cabin boy on a British sailing ship—the bark *Brilliant*—and with great excitement, he wrote his American friend that he was coming to the United States.

The journey from Yokohama to Boston was a difficult and hazardous one. The ship sailed from Yokohama to Australia and New Zealand, then across the Pacific to Chile, around Cape Horn, and up the coast of South America before finally landing in Boston. But at age nineteen, one year after leaving Japan, my father landed in Boston harbor, where his American friend met him and took him to live with his family in New England.

I grew up hearing that story over and over again. It became part of my belief system: "Nothing is impossible—you can do anything you want!"

Great Dads go beyond the daily responsibilities of parenting to inspire their children by their own dreams and personal achievements. Their example of daring to reach for long-cherished goals, pursuing every avenue that might take them closer and being willing to persist despite seemingly insurmountable odds is the fuel that inspires their children in pursuit of their own goals or dreams.

How Can There Be More Great Dads?

Reading the accounts of Great Dads, it all seems so simple. Give your children a lot of love and affection; show them that you care by being there for them; use example rather than words to shape their behavior; apply discipline sparingly, but be firm and fair; have a deeply loving and respectful relationship with your spouse, so your children will feel secure; respect their individuality and privacy; and give them unconditional love. This is the ideal.

For some fathers, these principles are ingrained. They require little thought because their expression is natural. For others, it is much more difficult to carry out precepts of being involved, affectionate and supportive.

It's much easier to be a Great Dad if you've experienced having a Great Dad yourself. If that's the example you grew up with, treating your children the same way that you were treated is as natural as breathing. You're not consciously aware of trying to be a good father. You just *are* one, because you don't know how to be anything else. It's a lot harder if you didn't have a dad you admired and looked up to as you were growing up.

If you're a man who longed for a father who was dependable, treated you with respect, protected you and provided you with belief in yourself, you almost have to invent yourself as a dad. You probably promised yourself, "My kids will have the kind of dad I always wanted for myself." And when you became a father you probably succeeded in giving your children some of the things you had missed out on. Others times, you may have worried, "Am I repeating the same things that happened to me? "

In the following chapters, you will discover how other men have successfully resolved these questions. You will be inspired by stories of men who have created new models of being a loving husband and father, and women who have overcome troubled relationships with their fathers and developed more satisfying bonds with the men in their lives. You will see how both men and women have worked through old issues to create the deeply fulfilling lives they always desired.

Recommendation

Every father has qualities that can be admired. Make a list of the qualities you value in your father. Depending on the nature of your relationship, your list might be lengthy, or it may be very short. Whether you can discover only a few qualities that you value, or whether there are many, what is important is to recognize what those qualities are and the effect they have had on your life.

This will be very easy to do if you admired your father. It will be much more difficult if your relationship was troubled or there was abuse. However, every human has admirable qualities, regardless of how overshadowed they are by the negative or destructive ones.

Did your father have a love of music that he passed on to you? Was he a great sports fan who kindled a lifelong interest in fitness? Was he able to defuse anger with just the right word or touch of humor? Was he a risk taker who imbued you with the confidence to pursue new endeavors?

When you have made your list, next to each trait you valued, write down how that has affected your life. What is it about that quality that you are grateful for? How different would your life be without it?

If Your Father Has Not Been a Part of Your Life

Even if you know very little about your father, you probably have some clues. Look for the areas where there are marked differences between you and your mother. These are the gaps where your father's characteristics may be showing up. Are you a quiet one-to-one person, whereas your mother thrives in large groups? Do you prefer a rational, well-thought-out approach, while your mother tends to be more intuitive? Do you enjoy being at the cutting edge of new ideas and movements, in contrast to your mother, who opts for a more conservative approach? Do you have an artist's eye for bold color combinations, whereas your mother chooses a more conventional palette?

All these are clues about abilities and interests that you may have inherited from your father. Adopted children are often amazed when they find a birth parent to discover how similar they are to that parent. Take a closer look at what you value in yourself. If you didn't get it from your mother, there's a good chance you inherited it from your father.

Make a List of the Qualities You Wish Your Father Had

Now that you've read about what Great Dads are like, you have some ideas about what kind of father you wish you'd had. List the characteristics of your ideal father. How would your life have been different if your father had possessed them? Even if he didn't have them, you can acquire these attributes for yourself. Everybody carries the seed for every potential. Give some consideration to how you could develop these qualities in yourself at this time.

SECTION II

My Father,
My Self

CHAPTER 4

Self-Esteem:

How Your Relationship with Your Father Affected Who You Are

No one can be comfortable without their own approval.
—MARK TWAIN

Self-esteem is the immune system of the psyche. It is one of the most essential components of a satisfying life. It is a critical wellspring of success or failure in all areas of existence: relationships, family, career and even emotional and physical resiliency. Therefore, a healthy sense of self-esteem is one of the most valuable gifts a father can give his children—fundamentally influencing whether they become adults who achieve to their potential and experience life to its fullest or whether they will continually struggle against the burden of self-doubt.

This chapter will focus on a father's role in promoting self-esteem. For those whose fathers did not boost their self-esteem, this chapter provides examples of people who also faced that problem and shows how they were able to remedy the situation as adults.

The fundamental truth is that children who grow up secure in the knowledge that they are valued and accepted become adults who are comfortable with who they are. They acquire the inner strength and optimism that helps them pursue their dreams and bounce back from disappointment. In contrast, those who are afflicted by feelings of self-doubt and never feel "good enough" must learn to believe in themselves and resurrect their birthright of self-esteem from the ashes of indifference, criticism or abuse.

Self-esteem is a natural condition—all children are born with the potential for it. What happens after birth however, determines whether they are able to develop and maintain it. Some grow up in environments where self-esteem is nurtured. Others must consciously acquire it in maturity.

When a father spends time with his children, gives them affection and encourages their efforts, he gives them a head start in the world. Because they feel secure in his love, they gain the confidence necessary to seize opportunities and overcome obstacles. Having acquired beneficial core beliefs about themselves early in life, such children develop an emotional foundation deep enough and strong enough to enable them to withstand hardships and allow them to reach as high as their aspirations direct them.

This foundation is constructed from the elements of a father's daily interactions with his children. This ongoing day-to-day relationship creates self-esteem and paves the way for its outward manifestation—self-confidence.

Eight Essential Building Blocks for Self-Esteem

These are the eight essential building blocks that a father must provide to instill self-esteem in his children.

- Provide unconditional love and acceptance.
- Give time and affection.
- Protect from harm.
- Instill values.
- Encourage competence.
- Teach responsibility.
- Foster empowerment.
- Demonstrate a belief system.

In the stories that follow you will see how different dads applied these building blocks into their children's lives. You might recognize how one or more of these critical factors has affected you or a loved one. If your father was not able to provide you with these elements, this chapter will help you find ways to provide them for yourself. You will read stories about others who had experiences similar to yours. The affirmations following each story and the guided imagery script at the end of this chapter will help you remove any negative messages you currently carry around with you and help you develop a new sense of self-worth.

"This Is My Son"

One of the ways a child's self-esteem is formed is from continuous, cumulative interactions that say, "You're okay," "I love you," or "You can do it!" and convey approval and encouragement. When experienced repeatedly over time, these messages gradually form an important foundation for self-esteem.

Dads also help develop self-confidence by serving as role models for what a self-assured individual looks and sounds like. When you watch your dad interact with others, it gives you a pattern to emulate until your own poise is fully developed.

Stanley, a well-known speaker and corporate trainer, talked about his father's influence on his career. "I never gave much thought to how important my father was in building my self-confidence," Stanley noted, "but when I look back at the times we spent together, I can see how much he helped me without my even realizing it. Whenever he took me somewhere, he'd always introduce me to his friends by putting his arm around me and saying, 'This is my son.' It really made me feel important. I never had the feeling he was thinking, 'Go away kid; you're bothering me.'

"I would watch how he acted with his associates and try to be like him. He seemed to be the leader in every group—he always looked so self-confident. When I was first starting out in the speaking business, I consciously tried to project that same aplomb. He was a good role model for me."

Being included in his father's activities and absorbing his self-assurance was a great help to Stanley when he first started his career. By emulating his father's confident manner, Stan was able to slowly build his own confidence until he developed sufficient assurance to feel poised in front of any group. It was an extremely effective way for him to acquire the professional image he desired.

AFFIRMATION

"I can be confident and self-assured at every occasion."

"You Can Do It!"

The words you hear also play a role in developing your self-concept. What you hear is an extremely powerful force for fostering the beliefs you have about yourself. Words of encouragement heard in childhood linger long after they are uttered, and they serve as constant reminders that success is possible.

Janine, who operates a small financial services business, had an exuberant, enthusiastic dad who kept reinforcing the idea that she could succeed in whatever she attempted. "My dad told me I was pretty, smart, and could do anything in the world that I wanted. One of the things he always said to me was, 'Kid, you're all right! No matter what they say about you—you're okay!' After I left home, there were many times when remembering his words helped me keep me going.

"He had a great sense of humor. He was a teaser and a kidder, an elbow-in-the-ribs kind of guy. When I look through the old family photo albums, we always had our arms around each other, goofing off. Those good times and positive messages had a big effect on who I am and how I deal with things today. It's easier for me to take risks, like starting my own business, because I have a positive approach to life."

Her father's supportive words—"You're okay! You can do it!"—continue to echo in Janine's ears, giving her the confidence so that she *can* succeed in anything she attempts.

AFFIRMATION

"I can accomplish anything I set my sights on."

"He Always Said, 'Be Your Own Person!'"

Kirsten was also encouraged to stretch her capacities as far as possible by a father who believed in encouraging her to try her wings and strive for independence. "My father gave me education and travel," Kirsten said. "He had an auto parts business where I helped out in the summer and during school holidays. When I went to college he told me, 'If you stick to your studies and get good grades in your courses next year, I'll send you to Europe for the summer.' I would have tried to do well anyway, but his offer really motivated me.

"After I earned the trip, he gave me some advice. 'Don't go as a tourist,' he said. 'You've been a history major—get into the spirit of the country. Meet people from all walks of life and see what makes them tick. Everything you've studied will come alive when you go abroad.' The following year, he said if I got good grades he would pay for a trip to Asia. I spent the summer traveling through Asia and developed tremendous confidence traveling alone. I felt I could do anything.

"More recently, when I got bored working for a big corporation, he encouraged me to go into business for myself. He said, 'The best thing to do is be your own boss and don't work for anyone else. The postal service business seems real interesting. Find an existing operation and see if you can buy it.' I did, and even though I work much harder than when I had a job in the corporate world, I enjoy it a lot more."

Kirsten's father had faith in her ability to travel through Europe and Asia as a single woman on her own. His belief that she could handle any situation that arose and benefit from the experience of meeting a wide variety of people was a major factor in building her self-confidence.

AFFIRMATION

"I am an independent, self-assured person wherever I go."

"Never Let the Door Open that You Don't Go Through It!"

Even seemingly insurmountable obstacles such as racial barriers have been overcome by dedicated fathers who fueled their youngsters with an irresistible drive to succeed.

Marie's father, despite his quick intelligence, wealth of knowledge and dedication to learning, was prevented from achieving his potential because of his race. African-Americans of his day were banned by segregation laws from most education and career opportunities. In addition, they suffered the daily indignities of Jim Crow laws, which prohibited blacks from using certain restaurants, theaters, beaches, golf courses, and other public facilities.

"I knew what my father could have done if he had the opportunity," Marie said. "He's a good example of what a genius will do if you take away everything that would enable him to move up. He took all his creative energy and gave it to his children. When the laws were changed, I realized that there was no limit to what I could do because I had his genes and I had the opportunity. It would have been a crime for me to do anything less.

"He always told me, 'Never let the door open that you don't go through it. Even if there's just a crack—that's all you need!' His principle was 'If there's something you want to do, consider what it would be like if you *don't* do it and what it would feel like to say, 'I could have had this, if only I'd gone and done that. Then imagine that you do perform the work that's needed, and compare the results. You know what it would be like without the effort; what would it be like if you just went ahead and did it?'

"When I was interviewed for medical school, they asked me why I wanted to attend. I said, 'Why not? If there is a reason for me *not* to attend, I'll examine it—but otherwise, why not? *And*, I've got all the requirements.' I'm like a mountain climber—I wanted to climb that particular mountain because it was there."

The energy and creativity that Marie's father lavished on her imbued her with the conviction that she could master any challenge that presented itself. His support went far beyond expressing faith in her. He gave her a powerful tool with which to examine any major decision that would ever confront her. His ingenious suggestion that she imagine the difference in her life if she accomplished her goal, as opposed to not pursuing it, provided immediate clarity. It was a potent spur to dispel the fear, inertia and indecision that so often prevent accomplishment.

Too many times, people do not go after their dreams because they fear possible failure, only to berate themselves years later with regrets. Marie never had to experience the disappointment of missed opportunities—her father's wise counsel prevented that.

AFFIRMATION

"I will seize every opportunity that presents itself."

"I Always Knew I Was His Favorite"

Some children feel they have a special bond with their father and sense that they are his favorite, even if there is no outward evidence of such preference. For the favored child, this is another tremendous boost to self-confidence.

If you held a unique position in the family because you were the oldest child, the only boy or girl among your siblings, the baby of the family, the smartest, or the child who most closely resembled Dad, you may have been his favorite. Perhaps you just sensed you were his favorite without knowing why. Most fathers try not to show favoritism, but sometimes the signs are unmistakable. A favorite child is likely to get more attention than the other children, receive more leeway for transgressions or be allowed extra privileges. And being dad's favorite can pay off in an additional measure of self-confidence and the expectation that other people will also react favorably to you.

Norman, a recent college graduate who was about to start a sales career, acknowledged the benefits he received from knowing he was his father's favorite. "I don't know why I felt special," Norman said. "I know my dad tried to treat all of us alike, but somehow, I always knew I was his favorite. Maybe it was just that he was a little more patient with me, cut me a little more slack, was more willing to give me the benefit of the doubt—there was just something that made me feel that he preferred me. I knew I could get away with more than my brothers and sisters, even though I didn't take advantage of it—although if you ask my brother, he'll say I got away with murder.

"I think that having been the favorite gives me more confidence to approach people and pursue the things I want. If there's an opportunity, I go after it because I think I've got just as good a chance as anybody."

Expecting favorable reactions from people is a common feature among those who grew up feeling preferred. When Dad has always given you that extra pat on the back, you anticipate that others will also respond positively. This gives you an added boost in pursuing your goals. You go into situations expecting to succeed, and more often than not, you do.

Most fathers try to avoid showing favoritism because it usually creates a sense of competition among siblings. Frequently, brothers and sisters of favored children will find their own special niche to excel in. Some develop winning personalities that make them extremely popular with their peers, others cultivate a special talent, such as playing an instrument, yet others excel academically as a way of calling attention to themselves. Sometimes, these competitive struggles persist into adulthood. Usually, they diminish and fade away as those who jockeyed for position within the family reach maturity and become friends.

AFFIRMATION

"I have unique talents and gifts that I share freely with others."

"My Dad Held Me More Than the Other Kids"

Sally is an entrepreneur who started her first business at age sixteen. Her confidence was strengthened not only because she had a Great Dad who tried to make each child feel special but also because he encouraged her to acquire skills that were usually denied to girls at the time.

"My dad was affectionate with all of us. He tried to make each of us feel special. But I liked to think he held me more and talked to me more than any of the other kids. When I was little, I was always around my dad—sitting on his lap and keeping close to him. I wasn't treated any differently, but I still felt that I was the special one. I could just see it in his eyes.

"In the second grade, I remember taking a big piece of plywood home and splashing it with paint in all kinds of weird colors and shapes. When I showed it to him, he didn't say, 'What's that?' He praised it and said he loved the different colors. Thinking back, I realize how vulnerable I was back then and how easily he could have crushed me if he had made fun of it.

"He also treated me just like my older brothers in a lot of ways. When he was digging a ditch or putting in a fence, I worked right alongside him with a shovel in my hand. He encouraged me to do things girls never did back then, like deliver a paper route with my brothers. It gave me a lot of confidence that I could take care of things, and that I knew how to get things done."

Both Sally and Marie were fortunate in having fathers who were far ahead of their time. Their progressive views liberated them from traditional restrictions of race and sex and encouraged them to pursue whatever goals they desired.

AFFIRMATION

"I have the power to be anything my heart wishes."

"No One Will Ever Harm You"

Some dads give special treatment subtly, not wanting any of their children to feel that they are getting any more or less than the others. For Marie, whose father taught her to pursue every opportunity, there was never any doubt. She always knew that as the youngest of eight brothers and sisters, she was "the baby"—and her father's favorite.

"He was right up front with it," Marie said. When he came home, I was the one he came to first. All kids think their fathers are perfect—I thought *my* father was the *most* perfect. 'Don't bother my baby,' he would say 'Nobody bothers my baby.' Later on, if I needed a strong hand to defend me, my father was right there. He always said, 'No one will ever harm you.' It was such a powerful statement of support. I knew he would shake the earth for me; he would give up his right hand for me.

"My earliest memory is when I was about two years old. I was sitting in a high chair at the table, and I heard my father's old car come down the street. He got out, his hands all loaded down with tools, and he looked so exhausted coming up the walkway that I yelled out, 'Somebody get up and open the door for *my* daddy!'

"I learned so much from my father—he was a walking encyclopedia. And he could explain things so they made sense. It made his opinion more important to me than anyone else's. When I found out what my father thought about things, it shaped my own views. I could form an opinion and go to him and test my judgment against his, because that was my standard. My father was my mentor—the more I became like him, the more confident I became. But he was never domineering; he never tried to impose his opinions.

"One of the most valuable things he taught me was to never get yourself into a situation where you can't be the one who makes the decisions about your life. Whether it's about getting up in the morning, going to work or what you're going to do that day—never let someone else control the things that are important to you. I have acted on that all my life. My father gave me the room to grow. He gave me the foundation and then let me go."

Marie's father gave her a bedrock foundation of fortitude that incorporated his values, knowledge and love and gave Marie the strength of character and confidence she needed to break through daunting barriers of race and poverty to realize her potential—a heritage of dignity and faith she proudly affirms to this day.

AFFIRMATION

"At every moment I am in control of my experience."

"My Dad Never Put Me Down Because of My Weight"

Today, ideas about ideal body image and other superficial standards of what "should be" also create barriers against acceptance and opportunity. They place an onerous burden—especially on young women. Children who deviate from the norm are often mercilessly teased. But a father's reassurance—"You're special; only you can be you; no one else can take your place!"—can help young people acquire positive attitudes toward themselves despite being different.

Teresa, a student teacher, went through a difficult period of being tormented by other children at school because of her large size. She knows firsthand how important a father's encouragement is.

"I can remember as a kid, always being teased a lot because I had a weight problem," Teresa said. "So from the time I was about six years old, my father took me to Weight Watchers every week. I have vivid memories of him taking me there and to support groups to help me understand about diet and nutrition. He also enrolled me in Weight Watchers summer camp every summer.

"I'll always appreciate my dad because he never put me down because of my weight—especially because I was so vulnerable at the time. He was very supportive. He helped me understand that I had things that made me special even if I didn't look like everyone else, and that I'm beautiful even if I'm different. It's given me a really good attitude about myself."

Even though her body size did not conform to the cultural norm, Teresa's dad made sure she got what she needed. Through educational and support groups, special summer camps, and encouragement, Teresa's dad helped her appreciate herself so that despite other children's teasing, she grew up feeling confident and attractive.

Despite variation from society's strictures, each person has unique qualities, or "treasures," that often lie so deeply buried within that the person is unaware of their presence. One of the primary outcomes of fathers building their children's self-esteem is instilling the belief that they are in possession of such gifts. Whatever is unique and valuable about the child need not be specifically identified—they simply have to know that they are accepted for themselves so that these gifts can develop.

An important component of building self-esteem for those who did not receive it in childhood is to identify these treasures. Think about the gifts you have that you don't usually give recognition to. If you have difficulty identifying what is special about you, imagine that you are your best friend. How does he or she see you? What do they think is special about you? How would they answer someone who wanted to know about your good qualities? Are you a loyal friend? Do you offer an empathetic ear? Do you have a quick sense of humor? Decide now that you will validate these and other qualities so that your self-esteem can grow.

AFFIRMATION

"I am a perfect, whole, complete human being exactly as I am."

"My Father Taught Me What I Needed to Survive"

The most destructive forces cannot extinguish the unquenchable light of self-esteem and self-confidence instilled early in childhood. They fuse together to form an indomitable spirit that can withstand anything. Most people will never have this strength fully tested. But during periods of great crisis, the inner fortitude and resilience gained through a father's love can literally make the difference between life and death.

Hannah is a pediatrician and Holocaust survivor whose elegant designer clothes and beautifully decorated home present a vivid contrast to the horrors she describes in the concentration camps. In recounting her years in Auschwitz, Hannah emphasizes how critical her father's teachings were to her survival—teachings instilled during the early-morning walks she shared with her father during childhood. During those quiet moments together, Hannah's father often talked about his experiences as a Russian prisoner of war during World War I. He focused on the tenets that had sustained him, not knowing that one day they would save Hannah's life too.

"My daddy inspired me with the tremendous concept of finding hope in the middle of hopelessness," Hannah said. "I was enormously impressed by his telling me that he didn't allow *anything* to make him bitter. He taught me what I needed to know to survive the Nazi death camps—how not to allow any external forces to murder my spirit. He used to quote Henry David Thoreau, the American schoolmaster who was jailed for his beliefs, who said, 'Even though I am surrounded by mortar and stone, I am freer than my captors!'

"My daddy also taught me about the immense strength to be found in friendship and unity," Hannah continued. "I knew that the only way to survive the camps was through cooperation. So a few of us joined together to form a tightly knit group where each of us watched out for the other. We discovered that one of the secrets of survival was to care for someone other than yourself.

"My daddy had a passion for living—he was a true bon vivant. Every moment of freedom was precious to him after losing it as a young man. He was an immensely charming, handsome, elegant man who always took great pains with his appearance. When I wear designer clothes now, it's my way of saying, 'I miss you, Daddy. I love you.'"

Hannah's father gave her a gift that saved her life. His teachings about the strength of the human spirit and the power of cooperation enabled her to survive the concentration camps. By holding fast to them and remembering the words 'Never let anyone murder your spirit!' she preserved the courage to survive one of the worst examples of inhumanity.

AFFIRMATION

> **"My inner resources are indestructible—I am in charge
> of my world."**

Overcoming the Scars of Put-Downs

Like Hannah and Marie, those who succeed against tremendous odds usually have been strengthened by the love and self-confidence that was instilled in them in childhood. However, some children are denied this birthright. When they succeed, it is despite experiences that seem designed to cripple their souls. Such adults seem to have been born with a sense of purpose that impels them to achieve in spite of their handicaps.

There is a painful contrast between the inborn courage and determination found among those who received Dad's love and support and the hard-won struggles for fulfillment of those who grew up with negative messages. Adults whose fathers cast doubt on their aspirations or informed them that they were incapable of reaching their goals often accept this judgment and allowed their dreams to die. Others fight for what they want, and their drive toward accomplishment is fueled by their need to prove their fathers wrong.

If any of the following stories relate to your own experiences, don't despair. There are ways to overcome the effects of negative messages received in childhood. Read on to the end of the chapter, where you will find suggestions for resolving these issues as well as a guided imagery script designed to boost your self-esteem, with directions for its most effective use.

"You'll Never Amount to Anything!"

Sarah, a graphic designer who owns her own printing company, rebelled vigorously when her father belittled her vision of a career in commercial art. "I was thirteen years old when I decided that I wanted to be an artist," Sarah said. "When I told my father I wanted to go to art school, he became enraged and shouted, 'No! No! No! You'll just get married, make babies, and never amount to anything!'

"It triggered something in me that wanted revenge. I wanted to show my dad, 'Oh, yes, I will! I'll prove to you that I can do it!' So I went into overachievement mode and excelled in *everything*. School, sports, you name it—I had to be the best to prove myself to him. When I got bored with girls' sports, I got on the men's swimming team; I was the first woman in the county to compete on a men's athletic team. I was a competitive swimmer for five years in the American Athletic Union.

"Then I tried out for the boys' water polo team because they didn't have one for girls. I made Junior Varsity and earned my letter, but it was hell being the only girl on the team. I could outswim most of the boys, but the ridicule from my fellow teammates was worse than that from the teams I competed against. And even though I did get to play, I also got kicked under water a lot. My dad said I could play as long as I didn't get hurt but that if anything happened, I'd have to leave the team. So I couldn't tell him or anybody in my family what I was going through.

"I went on to create a women's swimming team. After going through the hell I did with water polo, I had to make a difference for the women who followed me. The following year, there were three girls on the water polo team, and they didn't get nearly as much harassment. So I broke the sex barrier.

"I held a number of marketing jobs after graduation, and I did some freelance graphics design before establishing my own print-ing company. Even though I had trouble getting financing and selling my services to new customers, nothing that I've done since then has been as tough as breaking into the men's swimming and water polo teams. After that, I told myself I could do anything."

Sarah's determination to prove her father wrong was so fierce that despite physical pain, discouragement from her father, and relentless harassment from her teammates, she still emerged a win-ner. Overcoming such brutal obstacles proved to Sarah that she could accomplish anything she wanted to. Blessed with extraordinary mental and physical abilities that steeled her convictions, Sarah over-came the discouragement of her father's disparaging remarks.

AFFIRMATION

"I am worthy of success in all my desires."

The Hidden Scars of Criticism

Other children are more vulnerable. They too may achieve success later in life despite the corrosive effects of early criticism, but their outward success often hides scars that continue to ache and that deny them the satisfaction they have earned. The disapproving words they heard continuously have robbed them of the ability to acknowledge or enjoy their achievements. Feelings of emptiness often lead them to a focus on external symbols that represent ful-fillment, because inner happiness eludes them.

The contrast is glaring between the self-esteem and emotional stability that result from receiving love and approval and the pain and lack of self-esteem that result from growing up with unremitting rejection and criticism. In the former you receive a self-regenerating source of inner well-being. In the latter, you are subject to an erosion of self-worth that can sometimes take years of therapy to erase.

Brainwashing is a mind-control technique that inundates a vic-tim with a message over and over under stressful conditions until eventually the person's ego breaks down and they believe the message. Like a victim of brainwashing, if you continually receive negative messages that attack your self-esteem, you gradually begin to believe the damaging words, eventually becoming your own worst critic.

If you are one of these people, no matter how excellent your performance, you have difficulty accepting praise. No matter how good your track record, you feel a continual need to seek reassurance. Despite outward success, your achievements feel hollow. There is always the fear that everything will be taken away from you or that someone will discover you're a fake.

"My Father Was Always Putting Me Down"

Douglas, an architect specializing in nightclub design, is typical of people who spend a significant portion of their adult lives hampered by badly damaged self-esteem.

"My father was always putting me down," Douglas revealed. "Nothing ever satisfied him. He was extremely volatile, always screaming and yelling, and quick to blow up if things weren't done exactly his way. He was very hard on me and very demanding about doing things the right way. I always envied the other kids and would tell them, 'I wish I had your parents.'

"The way it's affected me is that I cannot take compliments; I don't ever think I deserve them. I'm very critical of myself, and even if people say I've done something perfectly, I tell myself I could have done it better. I also have a bad temper, so I have a hard time getting along with people. My partner and I get into fights all the time because I'm very critical of him and want things done my way."

Nagging self-deprecation and volatile anger are severe liabilities. They interfered with Douglas's personal and professional lives to the point where he was unwilling to be burdened by them any longer. He vowed to discard the worn-out mental habits that kept sabotaging an otherwise successful life and decided to acquire new beliefs that would allow him to experience happiness and fulfillment. "I'm almost forty years old now," he declared, "and I'm not going to live my life for the next forty years the same as the first forty."

Deciding that he needed help to change, Douglas started therapy. It was a courageous decision that allowed him to get his father's voice out of his mind and take back control of his thoughts. Once he started to process his experiences and practice with the self-affirming tools he acquired, Douglas was able to make his thoughts work *for* him rather than against him.

AFFIRMATION

> **"I welcome happiness into my life."**

"How Come They Have Confidence and I Don't?"

Hilary, an exceptionally able and dedicated computer technician, also endured relentless criticism as a child, with similarly damaging results. "All my life, I was constantly being put down by my father. Even though I always got A's in school, all I ever heard was: 'You think you're so smart? You're a dummy! You don't know anything! Just because you talk so fancy doesn't mean you're any smarter. What do *you* know?'

"Now I'm doing it to myself. I don't know why, but I'm always putting myself down. My boss keeps telling me what a great job I'm doing. She wants me to apply for a supervisor opening, but I'm afraid to even though I know I could handle it. I don't know what's holding me back. I'm very supportive of other people, but when it comes to me, I'm my own worst enemy."

Neither Hilary nor her supervisor could understand what was keeping her from going after a promotion that she was eminently qualified for. But there was a hidden reason holding her back. Just below the conscious surface of Hilary's mind lurked the thought, "You're going to fail and make a fool of yourself. Then everybody will know how dumb you really are!"

When she thought of the new job, she could hear her father's voice saying, "You're not so smart. Who do you think *you* are?" She knew he was wrong, but the emotional impact of his statements had left her devastated. Fortunately, her boss kept pushing, and Hilary finally decided to get help.

"I'm tired of always putting myself down—it's driving my

husband crazy too," she said. "I know I'm as good as anybody else. I ask myself, 'How come they have the confidence and I don't?' Whatever it takes, I know I have to change."

Hilary recognized that the memory of her father's critical voice was undermining almost every area of her life. She was no longer willing to live with the results. Like Douglas, she reached a point in her life where she knew she had to take a stand. By getting help to change her thinking patterns she took the first step on the road to healthy self-confidence.

Psychological self-recovery is a journey that varies for each individual. Hilary's work focused on identifying destructive old thought patterns and learning how to replace them with positive new ones, which would allow her to perceive herself in a more realistic and beneficial way.

Like most people, Hilary found that changing her thinking was difficult at first. Regarding yourself in a more positive light when you have previously thought of yourself in only negative terms is like trying to use only your left hand when you are right-handed— it feels awkward and artificial. But six months after Hilary started erasing her old, self-sabotaging "tapes," she successfully applied for the managerial position she had long coveted.

Hilary's newfound confidence was a priceless gift to herself— a gift that those who are more fortunate receive naturally in childhood. But at any age, it is never too late to work on your self-esteem and gain the advantages of believing in yourself. You can achieve an immediate effect from something as simple as saying "Stop!" when you have a self-critical thought, then taking a deep breath and repeating to yourself an opposite phrase, *even if you don't believe it.*

How we see ourselves now is usually how we saw ourselves as children—through the mirror held up by those closest to us. For Hilary, as for Douglas, Marie, Hannah, and so many others, the image of ourselves that we received from Dad is a potent influence on the image we now hold as our own.

AFFIRMATION
"The more I change my thoughts, the better I feel."

The Legacy of Self-Esteem

The effects of early conditioning are so powerful and far-reaching that the greatest legacy a father can give his children is the good opinion they have about themselves and their place in the world.

If you look back at yourself and your childhood, you may notice that the foundation that was laid down in those early years colored almost everything that followed after: how you view yourself, the quality of your relationships with others, the decisions you make, the goals you strive for, and the possibilities you envision for your life.

If you received approval and respect as a child, you probably view yourself as a good and worthwhile person, and you expect that others will regard you that way too. If you could rely on your Dad—if he kept his promises to you and was responsible in his actions—you are likely to take pride in being trustworthy. If you knew you were loved and accepted, your adult relationships reflect your ability to love others and accept love in return.

But if you grew up in an environment where you felt of little consequence, if discipline was harsh or unjust, if your opinions or desires were usually ignored, or if you were constantly put down, then it is likely that your self-esteem and self-confidence have been stunted. You probably find it hard to believe that others could love or admire you, and you discount yourself despite others' positive comments.

Clients sometimes remark, "If you really knew me you wouldn't like me." Incredibly, the people who say this are in reality intelligent, talented, personable individuals who to all outward appearances have everything. So how can they make such a statement? Financial achievement, social status, physical attractiveness, or even a loving mate do not erase feelings of self-doubt for adults whose childhood was scarred by constant criticism or abuse. Without conscious effort, they find it hard to believe that others are genuinely attracted to them or that their achievements are legitimate.

Fortunately, there are remedies. Pain from the lack of Dad's approval and its resulting burden of self-criticism can be removed through a variety of means. It need not continue to interfere with your enjoyment of the rich and satisfying life you deserve. No matter how long you have struggled, it's never too late to give yourself a needed boost in self-respect and self-confidence.

Self-help books such as David D. Burns's *Feeling Good Handbook*, Nathaniel Branden's *Six Pillars of Self-Esteem*, and Patrick Fanning's *Visualization for Change* provide many exercises that allow you to work on these issues in the privacy of your home. Numerous support groups address this issue and offer valuable guidelines for change. For those who want a more individualized approach, psychotherapy takes you on a path of discovery that can dramatically change your life for the better.

Years of experience and training have proven to me that the most rapid and effective way to reverse negative brainwashing is to defuse the hostile inner messages by substituting life-affirming new ones. Two of the most powerful techniques are affirmations and guided imagery meditations. I have created hundreds of both to use with clients over the years and have witnessed their gratification when the desired changes took place.

These potent tools create beneficial beliefs, feelings, mental images, and self-talk that work *for* you instead of against you. Here is a guided imagery meditation I would like to share with you.

Recommendation

Do the following meditation every day until you start to feel a difference. This usually takes from two to four weeks. Then follow up periodically to reinforce the positive message. I usually suggest the following reinforcement schedule to clients: three times a week for two weeks, then once a week for two weeks, then every other week for three months, then as needed. To get the maximum benefit, make a tape of the script so that you can be totally relaxed when you do it.

Remember, you are always in charge. You can stop at any time. If there is anything that you need to stop and attend to, you will quickly become alert and be able to do so. Extraneous thoughts that come into your mind are natural. People often think you have to actually "see" pictures during guided imagery meditations. That is unnecessary—simply let yourself imagine or sense what you might see if you could. Some people see nothing; they imagine what *might* be there. Others see only colors or receive impressions of vague shapes. Whatever you imagine or sense is right for you.

You may find other thoughts intruding: "This is silly." "I should be doing the laundry." "I have to remember to call the plumber tomorrow morning." "Where did I put those files on the Jones account?" Your mind is getting rid of clutter. Just notice these thoughts and let them float away again.

To begin, allow yourself to relax comfortably in a favorite chair, or lie down if you're sure you won't fall asleep. Rest your hands in your lap. Uncross your legs and let your feet rest flat on the floor. Then read or listen to the following meditation.

"Ideal Self" Guided Imagery Meditation

Take a few deep breaths, and as you exhale, let your eyes close and your body relax even more. Imagine all your worries and concerns flowing outward with each breath . . .

Now imagine that you are in a beautiful, peaceful environment. It can be a real place or imaginary—any area where you would feel safe and tranquil. A colorful garden, a sunny meadow, a secluded beach, or a quiet, shady forest . . . wherever your favorite environment is. Let yourself feel the peace and tranquillity of this special place. Take a few moments now and enjoy it.

(*Short pause here if you're taping.*)

Now look ahead of you. In the distance, there is someone who looks very much like you. This person is your height, has your coloring and resembles you very much. But there is something different about this person. This is the person you would *like* to be—your ideal model. This person has all the attributes and characteristics you would like to possess—your Ideal Self.

This person is radiant, glowing, full of love and energy. He or she is smiling and beckoning to you. Start walking toward this person, and as you do, take all those old thoughts that are troubling your mind and throw them away.

Imagine that the old thoughts you want to discard are like the pages in an old, tattered book. Rip each page out, crumple it up and throw it away. These thoughts might be "I'm not good enough," "Nobody could love me," "I'll never amount to anything," "Nothing I do ever works out," "I can't do anything right." When all the pages are gone, throw the book away.

Now you are standing in front of your Ideal Self. This person has everything you want that you currently feel is missing: intelligence, attractiveness, talent and a bright inner light that represents their indestructible belief in themselves. Step forward and embrace this Ideal You, absorb these qualities and feel the strength, vitality, self-confidence and sureness you have always craved. Draw all of these qualities deeply into you. They are filling every cell of your being. Your body and mind are becoming saturated with the wonderful feelings of self-worth, love and faith in yourself that you are absorbing.

New thoughts are flooding into your awareness: "I am a worthwhile person," "I am loveable," "I can succeed at anything I choose to do," "I deserve to have the things I want" and other thoughts that you want to believe and make your own.

Stay within this luminous embrace as long as you like. Then move back and thank your Ideal Self. Turn around and start walking away. Your Ideal Self will come part of the way with you. Say good-bye and thank your Ideal Self again, then continue to walk away alone. As you turn around for one last look, you will see your Ideal Self waving good-bye to you. You are now the person you always wanted to be. The Ideal Self will always be there for you if you feel the need to renew this connection.

Take your time returning to full waking consciousness. Move your head, move your hands, feel your back against your chair.

Then, when you open your eyes, be aware of the new possibilities you now see before you.

Allow yourself some time to review this experience. Then, note in your journal what happened and how you felt.

Remember, it's never too late. Self-esteem is your birthright. You have the right and the power to reclaim it!

CHAPTER 5

The Father-Son Relationship:
Masculinity, Sexuality, and Fathers

*I am that father whom your boyhood lacked and suffered
pain for the lack of.*

—HOMER

Masculinity, sexuality, and the role of fathers are inextricably
entwined in a complex pattern of interaction among nature, family teachings and society's expectations. This volatile compound of
social pressures and developing sexuality gives fathers a major role
in exemplifying maleness and setting standards of behavior. How
dads view themselves as men, how they interact with wives or significant others and the information about sexuality and being a man
that they convey to their sons are all major determinants of how
those sons will view their own masculinity.

In psychoanalytic terms, a child's first "object"—the first person
he or she identifies with—is his or her mother. For girls, identification with the mother is part of a natural progression from infancy
to womanhood. From playing with dolls to having her first menstrual period, which in many cultures officially announces that she
is now a woman, to legal coming of age, a woman rarely questions
her femininity to the extent that boys do their masculinity.

Boys have a much more difficult task. They must give up their
identification with their mother in order to learn to become men.
In order to do this, boys must have a male figure that they can
begin to identify with. If Dad is in the home, and he is a loving parent with a close bond to his son, this will occur naturally, and the

identification will bind him more and more closely to his father. He will echo Dad's characteristic expressions, copy his actions and start to separate himself from the world of girls.

During these years of masculine identity formation in childhood and adolescence, a male role model is essential. Once a boy's masculine identity is firmly established, he can recognize qualities in himself like empathy and nurturance, qualities he formerly saw as relegated exclusively to females. But without a strong sense of maleness, achieving such balance is almost impossible.

Boys need to go through an educational process to reinforce their sense of competence as a man. This need is so great that almost all earlier societies throughout the world had arduous and lengthy initiation rites for young males to induct them into manhood.

The need to differentiate himself as a male is so strong that, even today, when teenage sons of divorced mothers enter puberty, they often decide to live with their fathers. This serves as a modern-day equivalent of ritual separation from women, a rite of passage to enter the company of men. Jungian analyst Guy Corneau has written extensively on this issue and points out in his book, *Absent Fathers, Lost Sons*, that in order to become a man, a son must recognize himself in his father first. For this to happen, however, the father or a father figure must be present.

Formation of Sexual Identity

Sexual identity—how you view yourself as male or female—is the strongest component of your personal identity. The consequence of complex processes that start at birth and reflect the interplay between your inborn tendencies and the environment around you, it results in a well-formed gender identity by the time you are age five.

As soon as parents become aware of a baby's sex, gender-based expectations and patterns of interaction are set into motion. From the tiny baseball shirt for a baby boy to a pink hair band for a baby girl, the socialization process that shapes sex-role behavior starts early.

By age three, most children have developed a clear impression of their sexual identity and insist on being treated in the "right" manner for their gender. Although there is controversy regarding the degree to which female and male behavior is learned versus how much is genetically programmed, the fact is that most children engage in play activities divided along sex lines. Boys most often choosing trucks and other action-oriented toys, while girls usually choose dolls and other female playthings or gender-neutral toys (such as crayons, board games, puzzles and coloring books).

Our society is revising its notions of what is "normal" masculine or feminine behavior and personality qualities. Assertiveness, sociability and adventurousness were once identified as positive male characteristics, but they are now acknowledged and encouraged in women also. Nurturance, patience and emotional sensitivity, which were historically classified as female traits and carried negative connotations, are now recognized by many not only as inherent in men as well as women but as desirable characteristics for both sexes.

Today, we recognize that men and women are much more alike than they are different, and that differences exist along a continuum and are complementary to each other. Sex role definitions now focus on the positive qualities of each gender and recognize that they are not mutually exclusive traits but exist to a greater or lesser degree in each person.

This more egalitarian climate places a critical responsibility on fathers for fostering attitudes that allow their children to explore and develop the full range of their sexual and personal identities. Ideally, fathers provide a healthy representation of masculinity so that sons and daughters can feel secure in their own sexual identity. For sons, fathers furnish a direct role model of what being male is all about. For daughters, they provide validation of femininity.

The parents' relationship, peer influences, other role models and the media also affect sexual identity. However, the nature of a son's relationship with his father, or other father figure, plays a major role in shaping his self-image and adult relationships.

Between Father and Son: The Male Bond

In the past, fathers trained their sons for manhood. They took boys hunting, taught them to fish, worked with them in the fields, or engaged in the multiple tasks that bound families together. Fathers were the primary arbiters of what being a man looked like, sounded like, felt like, and even smelled like.

Last names like "John's son" or "Johnson," "William's son" or "Williamson," show how closely sons were once identified with their fathers. A boy's name was a clear generational link that joined him to his father and to his own sons in a long line of patrilineal descent. Hereditary occupations also bound them. "Baker," Miller," "Smith," "Shepherd," and "Gardener" tracked the occupations that passed from generation to generation. Bonds were further strengthened by traditions of community and place that allowed families to trace their roots back for generations.

But how does a father explain his job if his child has never visited his place of employment? How can he use shared work to form a bond? Today, most fathers' work is an abstract concept known only through dinner table conversation and television depictions of men in similar occupations.

Fathers no longer automatically initiate their sons into maleness through working together at shared tasks. Instead, masculinity remains primarily defined by physical characteristics and such personality traits as independence, willingness to take risks, aggressiveness and outgoing social behavior—traits that are also expressed symbolically through competitive sports, powerful vehicles, winning over competitors in business and risk taking.

In the place of shared work, the quality of a son's relationship with his father is the critical factor that enables a boy to develop a secure masculine identity. A good relationship is crucial, because boys must see masculine traits as being desirable in order to want to emulate them. The general rule is that the more a son admires his father, the more he will want to be like him.

Paradoxically, a boy who has experienced verbal or physical abuse from his father will sometimes adopt these same behaviors in order to be strong enough to resist a father he dislikes and fears. As a small, weak child, he saw his father as all-powerful—able to impose his will without hindrance. To avoid being a victim, the only alternative he may see is to become like his oppressor. This is the situation with many young men who become part of gangs and other anti-social groups. In the absence of healthier options, they join to gain strength and a sense of belonging.

Fathers who want to encourage their sons to develop healthy male traits can do so most successfully by themselves demonstrating responsibility, competence, assertiveness and independence—as well as consideration, courtesy and strong family ties. Such positive role modeling is the single most effective way to give sons the self-confidence and social competence they need to function successfully as adults.

"You Could Always Count on My Dad"

Rock-solid reliability was Gerald's father's hallmark and gave Gerald an example he was determined to follow. "My father was a small-town lawyer and one of the people I admire most in the world," Gerald said. "The feeling I had about my dad was that you could always count on him. He was always a friend to me as well as a father. He would help me with my school projects or drive me to soccer practice—whatever I needed. To get his approval, I did what I thought he wanted me to do, like doing the chores and being a good student. He didn't say much—he would just look at me and smile. But I always knew that he was happy I was his son. He was proud of me.

"He was dependable, fair, and strong, and very well respected by everyone in town. I would go down to his office and see how people treated him, and I wanted that kind of respect when I got older. That's the reason I went into law. I wanted to be like him, and in a lot of ways I think I am. Now that I'm the same age he was when I was a kid, I can see how much we're alike."

Gerald's father serves as a perfect example of how a boy's identification with his father takes place. He had a father he admired enormously; demonstrations of strength of character, dependability, and the respect of others; and a warm, trusting bond with his dad. Emulating his father as closely as possible, even to the point of following the same career, was a natural, progressive part of his development.

"I Was Convinced that Nothing Could Go Wrong"

Mechanical skill and expertise is another widely recognized masculine trait. Ben, whose father was a long-distance bus driver, admired the masterful deftness with which his dad could maneuver vehicles, whether driving a giant Greyhound bus with dozens of passengers or the family car.

"Even though my dad was gone most of the week, I still felt close to him," Ben said. "When he came home from his week on the road, he would tell us all about the different adventures and colorful people he encountered. I used to imagine him at the wheel of the bus overcoming potential hazards and getting everyone safely to their destination.

"Every Sunday when he drove the family to church I would sit in the backseat with a feeling of complete confidence because my father was driving. As I listened to the changing of the gears, I was absolutely convinced that nothing could go wrong. I think that's why I've always been comfortable in a car, whether I'm a passenger or a driver."

Ben was deeply impressed by his father's ability to handle a huge bus and all its passengers safely. It made supporting the family seem adventurous and admirable—and even included a powerful metaphor for masculine strength and competence in the massive vehicle that his father so expertly controlled.

"He Taught Me to Make Arrowheads"

Mark, whose Air Force father and Japanese mother provided him with "a lot of relatives to visit in some of my favorite places," grew up in a small Western town, where he too learned to equate maleness with competence. A specialist in artificial intelligence, Mark spoke of how his father's ingenuity and knowledge of survival skills impressed him as a youngster.

"What especially fascinated me about my dad was how much he knew," Mark said. "He was raised on a farm and could *do* a lot of things; he had a lot of skills. For example, he taught me how to make arrowheads and carve fishing floats. When I was six, we lived in an area with a lot of rattlesnakes. My friends and I used to go out looking for snakes, so my dad got me some real arrows and taught me to shoot them.

"One of my most vivid memories of my dad is of one winter when I was about fourteen years old. The ground was completely covered from a snowfall the night before. A bunch of us were hanging out when my dad said, 'You can catch a rabbit with your bare hands in the winter.' None of us believed him, and we started kidding him about it until he got mad and insisted we all go into the woods with him so he could prove it was possible.

"We hiked through the woods for a while and then he stopped us and pointed to where he said he could see steam coming out of a rabbit's nostrils. We couldn't see any steam, but he crept forward and suddenly reached down and grabbed this rabbit by its hind legs and held it up in the air to show us. We admitted that it was true that he could catch a rabbit with his bare hands, and he let the rabbit go.

"I've never forgotten the times I spent in the woods with my father—hunting, fishing, and learning all the woodsman's skills he taught me. I've decided that when I have children I'm going to leave my career, even though it will mean a financial sacrifice, and move to a rural area so I can give my kids the same experiences I had."

Not every father can bond with his son by teaching him traditional outdoor skills. There are many other expressions of masculinity. Perhaps your dad led your Boy Scout troop, coached your Little League team, helped you bake cupcakes for the team picnic or advised you on science projects. What counts most is not the specific activity but the enjoyable time you had together that helped you develop a secure sense of your own masculinity as you matured into manhood.

When the Father-Son Bond Is Broken

A father who has been wounded by the physical or emotional unavailability of his own father might find it difficult to be a dependable, nurturing role model for his children. Even if that is what he aspires to, being a good father requires knowing how.

Men who have had the good fortune to have close relationships with their fathers emulate the characteristics of the good father they personally experienced. Those who did not have this advantage must consciously decide to acquire these skills in order to carry out their good intentions.

Additionally, the wound carried by men who did not have a close emotional connection with their fathers often leads to an inability to form a deep emotional attachment to their own sons. They become distant strangers in the same way that their fathers were to them.

If such a father's marriage ends in divorce and couples cannot agree to put their children's needs first, physical separation or conflict with a former partner can distance these fathers from their children even further.

"When I Needed a Father Figure, He Wasn't There"

Wes, a jazz pianist, had a good relationship with his father until his parents' divorce. "Things between me and my dad were great until age eight, when my parents got a divorce," Wes said. "My dad moved to another state and remarried and basically just forgot about me. I didn't see him at all for the next three years, and then only a couple of times during my teens. He knew I didn't want him to move away, so I've had a lot of resentment. Right when I needed a father figure the most, to show me how to be a man, he wasn't there.

"I visited him once when I was nineteen. It was the legal drinking age back where he lived, so we went out and had a beer. That was kind of fun—finally a father-son thing after all those years. I just wish I could have had it sooner."

When fathers are absent, sons may become anxious about their mastery of masculine behavior. Unless other male role models are available, acquiring self-confidence in oneself as a man is difficult. Countless young men have expressed feelings of anger, sadness and insecurity because they have been deprived of a father. Their resentment and lack of male guidance frequently lead to lower academic achievement, poor social adjustment, or difficulty relating to male authority figures. This is especially true if poverty, lack of social support and a starkly deprived environment intensify the loss.

"I Was the Only Boy in a Family of Four Women"

Bob's father "just took off" a few months after he was born. A husky carpenter, Bob has a muscular appearance that fits the stereotypical image of the macho construction worker. Inside, however, he feels exactly the opposite of that image, and he is pained by the difficulties he faced developing a positive male identity as he was growing up.

"I was the only boy in a family of four women," Bob said. "I had two sisters, my mom, and my grandmother, so I felt like I was the little 'guy' in the house—I was there to take care of all the manly things. I helped my mom and grandma and got a lot of approval for that, which made me feel good.

"But I was embarrassed in school because I didn't have a father. My buddies always did things with their dads, but I never had one to teach me things like how to ride a bike, or throw a ball, or any of the guy things. I learned to ride a bike by watching other kids, but it frustrated me that there was no one there to show me.

"My mom tried to get me into sports like tag football in junior high, but I only lasted a couple of weeks because I didn't want to get hurt. I heard a lot of negative comments from the rest of the team about that. Maybe the other kids had fathers to encourage them and tell them how to prevent getting bruises or a black eye by blocking. But a mother sits you down and wants to fix it.

"I've never had anyone to roughhouse with, so I was afraid of getting beat up. It still bothers me that I don't know how to defend myself. If a fight started today, I'd have to pick something up and coldcock the guy, or I'd have to talk my way out of it. That's given me an image of being wimpy.

"When I was a kid and somebody picked on me, my mother used to say, 'Stand up to him.' But how can you stand up to somebody when you don't know how? That's what hurt the most. You don't want to be outrageously violent, but at least a kid should be able to defend himself or take a punch. At this age, I'm not too worried about fighting, but it still bugs me.

"I had a woman raise me up. She did her best, but it still doesn't replace a man. You don't have that power image to back you up when you need it. I guess that's what I miss the most—having a father figure to bring me up as a man."

Bob grew up surrounded by women who loved him but couldn't give him what he desperately wanted—a masculine role model to identify with. In a household of four women, it was inevitable that feminine values would dominate and that Bob would often feel lost in a woman's world. To feel sure of himself as a male, he needed to balance his exposure to women's demeanor and behavior with masculine attitudes and actions. In that way, he could acquire the outlook and skills that would give him confidence in himself as a male. He could have learned to be comfortable with male horseplay and roughness so that he could defend himself and not fear being seen as weak by other men.

"I needed a father figure to show me how to be a man" are words that echoed over and over in the course of my interviews. Boys desperately want to acquire qualities of manliness, and they hunger for a father's physical presence to provide them with an example of these qualities. They are eager to assimilate the actions, words, intonations, attitudes and body language that differentiate men from women so that they can gain the confidence to feel at ease with both other men and with women.

"I Was Surrounded by a Community of Fatherless Children"

John, an African-American social worker, had contact with his father fewer than a half dozen times in his life. He bitterly recalled how difficult it was growing up as a young man without male guidance.

"The relationship between me and my father was basically nonexistent," John said. "I remember all his broken promises and all his lies to me when I was a young boy. It was a very painful time.

"As a child, I was surrounded by a community of fatherless children. I thought it was normal for kids not to have fathers. It didn't bother me till high school. At that point, I realized I had a biological father but not a father as defined by most Americans. A male child who doesn't have a father figure, a man in the house, doesn't learn how to be a man in terms of responsibility, being competitive and knowing how to treat women. He misses out on things that a father would teach his son. There's no one to imitate if he's not there.

"I'm most affected by not knowing how to be competitive—not knowing how to compete against peers in athletics, school and my career. In high school, I wanted to be more aggressive in sports. I wanted to be in the limelight; but I didn't know how to go up against others. I didn't experience male bonding with other men. There was no male to instruct or guide me. No one to teach me about sports, family, girls, dating—*all* aspects of finding out how to be a man.

"My mom taught me to treat others well. She could tell me, 'Be nice, be kind, be sweet, open the door for a lady.' But she couldn't *show* me. It's much more meaningful when a father *shows* you.

"Because I didn't know how to be forceful, I wasn't the leader in my relationships. I was equal or lower because I wasn't taught how to take the initiative or stand up for myself.

"I have my own ideas, and I'm beginning to believe in myself and respect myself more. I force myself to stand my ground with people and say, 'I don't like this,' 'This is how I see the situation' or 'I was hurt by what you said.' I do a lot of self-reflection— analyzing my thoughts and myself. I've come to the realization that I have to be my own person. But so far as values and goals go, I've had to internalize everything myself."

John is painfully aware of what was missing as he was growing up and how it affected him. Father deprivation has left John struggling to fill the gaps he feels in his personality with behaviors and attitudes he has been forced to acquire on his own. What comes naturally to those whose father taught them by example, John has had to discover for himself. His dedication and insight, however, are invaluable allies as he focuses his energies on developing the relationship skills and personal attitudes that will bring him the fulfillment he desires.

Adolescent boys often believe that there is a secret male "mystique" they must acquire to be accepted as men. They feel they can acquire this identity only from an older, experienced man who possesses the secret knowledge. When they admire their fathers, they want to develop the same masculine traits in themselves. But when fathers are absent from their sons' lives, young men feel unprepared to assume male roles. When they feel as if they have been cut adrift and forced to create their own model—from the media, or other sources—they become keenly aware that they lack a father to initiate them into the ways of manhood.

Men's groups exist in towns all across the country. They have arisen to fill men's needs to heal the scars of emotional and physical abandonment by their fathers. In these groups, men can safely mourn the loss of male presence in their lives and start the process of healing. In his book, *At My Father's Wedding: Reclaiming Our True Masculinity*, psychologist John Lee, a leader in the growing men's movement, states, "The old tyranny was the injunction 'Don't feel. Don't talk. Don't grieve. Don't trust other men.'" In reclaiming their masculinity, men have been freed from these soul-destroying rules to embark on a journey of self-discovery and wholeness that allows them to become complete individuals, husbands and fathers.

If you are a father who missed growing up with a trusted masculine role model, you can still ensure that *your* son receives the type of close-knit fathering you always wanted for yourself.

Parenting classes are extremely effective and have proven invaluable for those who do not have a prototype for effective parenting. A class not only provides much-needed support—it's also a relief for parents to find that others struggle with the same problems. Individual parents can share their solutions to common situations, to everyone's benefit.

Companies that take an active interest in maintaining high employee morale often offer free parenting classes. Others are sponsored by churches, the YMCA, and other community organizations. In addition, there are numerous books with helpful, practical tips on how to handle every problem that occurs in the course of raising a child from infancy to maturity. Some of these will be found in the Bibliography at the end of this book.

No one should feel that they must know everything. Learning from others is not an admission of failure—it is a demonstration of dedication, self-confidence and maturity.

AFFIRMATIONS

"I am a good and caring parent."

"I am comfortable with myself as a man."

"I gain strength by allowing myself to be true to my feelings."

"As I continue to grow, I can learn from other men
who know how to grow."

Fathers, Sons, and Sexuality

Fathers, or father surrogates, who are secure in their own sexuality play a critical role in helping sons develop their own secure male identity and healthy sexuality. Young men with strong attachments to their fathers develop feelings of pride in their maleness that allow them to be more effective in many areas of life, especially in their relationships.

Despite negative influences from peers and the media, studies have shown that boys who have positive paternal role models not only have more self-confidence and better social skills but also are more resistant to destructive group pressures. Unlike those who feel uncertain about their masculinity, they do not feel the need to prove themselves through exaggerated boasting, bravado, thrill seeking, and other stereotypical behavior.

In addition, the healthy expression of sexuality is more commonly found among men whose close relationship with their father leads them to adopt the standards and values for relationships that guide their own ideals of sexual expression.

"I Saw My Parents Making Love"

Sex seemed natural to Vincent when he entered adolescence because of the openly affectionate behavior he observed between his mother and father. Although Vincent's father did not talk to him directly about reproduction, he emphasized the need to be responsible when engaging in sex.

"My dad was a commercial fisherman of the old school," Vincent said. "We never had a man-to-man talk, but there was a subtle understanding. I would go to dances and know I had to observe a certain standard that he always taught me: respect for the girl; respect for the parents.

"I remember one time, when I was in the sixth grade, walking in the house and seeing my parents making love in their bedroom. I turned right around and walked to the park and thought to myself, 'That's okay. I know I didn't get here by accident.' It was a shock but not scary or anything, because I always saw my parents kissing and things like that.

"My dad didn't talk to me about birth control. He thought I would find out at school or down on the docks or something. That's one way I'm different from him. I've talked to my son and told him I want him to respect himself *and* the girl, like my dad taught me. But I've also told him that part of respect is being responsible about preventing pregnancy."

Sex and sexual attitudes are interrelated. Ideally, children learn about the facts of sex from their parents in a way that is appropriate to their age and that presents sex as both natural and something to be treated with respect. Sexual attitudes are taught by the actions and attitudes children observe between their parents. Sex is on the continuum of love and intimacy. When affection is freely and openly expressed and children are allowed to ask questions about sex and are given answers, sex can be placed in its proper context as an expression of love.

A child's reaction when he interrupts parents in the act of making love depends a great deal on his age. If he is young, he has no way to interpret it and wonders what is going on. A simple, matter-of-fact explanation appropriate to the child's level of understanding will usually suffice. An older child may simply acknowledge that his parents are human beings.

The most important factor in whether the child experiences anxiety or not is the parents' response. If parents shows extreme discomfort, the child will interpret what was witnessed as something shameful. If parents maintain equanimity, the child will also take it in stride.

Sometimes, parents' reactions lead to confusion and doubt. If your parents' reactions have left you with any residue of unease in your current life, a few sessions with a trained therapist should eliminate any lingering effects.

"There Was No Pressure to Date"

Respect for others also means respecting yourself. A young man who has a strong sense of his masculinity will not feel the need to prove it by engaging in sexual activity. Instead, he may decide to hold off, especially if he decides that sexual involvement would interfere with more important goals such as education and a career.

Mark, a very grounded man whose parents' marriage was notable for affection and laughter, enjoyed having many women friends. But his career priorities led him to defer dating until after college. "I didn't date in high school or college," Mark said. "I put most of my time into studying, because I wanted to go to medical school.

"I had a lot of girl *friends* that I did things with, like play sports, go to Shakespeare festivals, go to the movies, things like that. I enjoyed going over to their houses just to socialize—they were very intelligent, mature girls.

"None of my high school friends dated either. Back in the little town I grew up in, none of us had a car, there was only one movie theater in town, and no one had a job, so it wasn't that easy to date, anyway. We spent a lot of time with girls, but there just wasn't much to do dating-wise. I was going camping and taking advanced training in Boy Scouts till I was seventeen. There was no pressure to date—or even any means. College was very much the same. I lived in a coed dorm. We were all friends, we all went to dinner and the movies, we just buddied around together.

"I'm getting married now, at a much later age than most of my friends; but for me, it was the right decision. I've been able to do a lot that I couldn't have done if I was worried about somebody else. Now, I'm ready to settle down and make my family my number-one priority."

Seeing so much love and respect between his parents gave Mark a lot of confidence about his own masculinity. He didn't feel the need to prove himself with sexual encounters that might have distracted him from his goals. Instead, he enjoyed the freedom that bearing no responsibilities afforded him. He was able to try new experiences and establish himself first, so that eventually he too could create the same kind of close-knit family he grew up in.

"My Father Always Stressed that Sex Was Sacred "

Still other men find a happy medium between deferring their sexual impulses and losing themselves in relationships. Theodore, the son of an ex-priest, was raised with extremely high ideals in all areas, especially that of sexual behavior. But as a young man, Theodore's own personality and sexual desires differed markedly from what was expected of him.

"My relationship with my father has been very close," Theodore said. "He has always been comfortable with a lot of physical affection, and all five of us children got a lot of hugging, loving and roughhousing. I look the most like him, and my sensibilities are the most like his, but he never played favorites. All of the children were treated equally.

"The only problem was that my father had such high ideals that when I measured myself against him I always felt so unworthy, whether it was my moral nature, my tendency to procrastinate, or whatever. It made me feel inadequate. I felt less than I thought I was supposed to be. In the last couple of years, however, I've been able to merge the expectations of what was expected of me with what I actually am.

"A lot of it had to do with my sexuality. I had my first orgasm at age eleven. I was terrified, but finally I figured out it was okay. My dad always stressed that sex was sacred. It was not to be used in a frivolous way but only in the context of marriage or in a committed relationship. He was very open, but I never went to him with questions. If he found a *Playboy* in my room, he'd give me a big lecture about masturbation—it was turning inward, being selfish—but I never felt guilty about it.

"My father ingrained moral behavior in us so strongly, I was good about not lying, cheating or stealing. But in terms of sexuality, I lived the life of a normal young man growing up in the Southern California culture. I was very much influenced by that culture—my parents couldn't shield me from it. I lost my virginity at eighteen and then had a series of girlfriends. Some of my relationships were serious; some were trivial. That was the one area in my life where I really diverged from what I was taught.

"I didn't reject anything my father told me; but I didn't want to live by his rules. I said, 'For now, I want to live the way *I* want to live.' I thought of St. Augustine saying, 'Lord, give me chastity, but not yet.' Now that I'm married, I'm totally committed to it. We're willing to work on our marriage, because we know it doesn't come easily."

Theodore was fortunate. His father did not seek to impose his own extremely high ideals on his son. By wisely allowing Theodore the opportunity to work out his own values, he made it more likely that his son would eventually come back full circle to the moral precepts he was raised by.

"I Always Felt that Sex Was Dirty and Wrong"

The opposite effect is found in rigid, punitive households where sex is regarded in a harshly negative manner. Boys raised to fear sexuality tend to be extremely anxious about their masculinity and develop highly distorted views of women.

Jim was raised in a small Southern town by his Pentecostal preacher father, a rigid disciplinarian who condemned most forms of social activity between men and women and taught Jim that his body and all expressions of sensuality were sinful.

"In spite of my father's teachings, I had my first sexual experience at age seventeen," Jim said. "It was with a local girl who was slightly older than I was, in the back of her father's tool shed. It was a very hurried experience, and I didn't have the faintest idea what to do. I didn't understand why everybody said it was so great. I had a few more sexual encounters after that, but I got into the "sin" syndrome and really came down on myself with guilt.

"My first year in college I got married, because I figured it was the only way I could have sex legitimately. But my wife got pregnant, and I had to go to work to support us. For the entire fourteen years of our marriage I always felt that sex was "dirty" and "wrong." Our marriage should never have been. We had nothing in common, and I never had anyone to talk to. But the Fundamentalist belief is that divorce is second only to murder. I have a woman friend now, and we have a good relationship. But it's taken me years to get over my upbringing."

Teaching children to fear sex does not dissuade them from irresponsible behavior. Instead, ignorance and fear leave young people unprepared to deal with the concerns their emerging sexuality raises. It precludes any rational discussion of sexually transmitted disease, pregnancy prevention and the need for maturity and responsibility. Fear instills feelings of guilt about normal psychological and physiological stages of growth, and it makes healthy sexual relationships almost impossible. In fact, such rigidity and emphasis on the "evils" of sex often lead to a compulsive obsession with it that is highly destructive to the individual and those around him.

Sexuality is such a powerful force in young people's lives that fathers as well as mothers need to learn how to talk to their children about it and give them accurate information that also conveys their values. Pediatricians, health clinics, school nurses, libraries, Planned Parenthood, adolescent programs run by religious institutions, youth groups and health and psychology sections of book stores are all excellent sources for information on how parents can talk to children of all ages about sex.

Lack of information about sexuality is a potential disaster in the making. If you find that you have trouble expressing yourself in this area, talk to your physician, nurse, counselor or someone who works with young people to get rid of your own discomfort first. Usually, this is just a matter of learning to be comfortable with the vocabulary. Once you have mastered that, you will be able to convey your attitudes in the manner that best reflects the principles you wish to uphold.

"I'm an Incest Survivor"

Jed, a neatly dressed, soft-spoken man in his mid-thirties, grew up in a family plagued by generations of sexual abuse.

"I'm an incest survivor," Jed stated. "My father, who molested me, was an incest survivor; my grandfather was a bigamist and an incest perpetrator; and my great-grandfather's family sent him to the United States because he got in trouble with a woman. It went on generation after generation. My kids may be the first in God knows how many generations not to be incest victims.

"Why? I can spot some real critical differences. I've done a lot of work on core issues. I've done Twelve-Step work, Adult Children of Alcoholics, and I spent three years in therapy. From time to time, as issues come up, I go back and work on them.

"What kept my kids from being molested by my father is that I became aware of my own incest, and I made sure he never had access to them. I've done some conscious disassociation from my father and his way of doing things. My father was highly respected in the community. I know he had trouble reconciling his image with the incest and felt a lot of guilt over that. But he never got the help to stop it."

"The incest was an abuse of his power. My father was the undisputed master in the house. "He was treated like God, and we were all in awe of him. He was a pillar of the church and held in high esteem by everyone. To the neighbors, we were the model family. But inside, we all lived in fear of him."

Jed chose to break the generational pattern of sexual abuse. He protected his children by making sure that they were never left alone with his father. He also found the enormous courage required to examine what had happened to him and get help to make sure that it would never be repeated again.

Jed rejected the repressive authoritarianism that created an environment in which his father was able to abuse his children. Instead, he is committed to an equal partnership in which he shares responsibilities and roles with his wife. Jed is especially proud that he is providing the affection and safety for his own children that were denied him as he was growing up.

Each father deals with his and his children's sexuality in a way that reflects his own comfort and security in this area of his life. Some have family backgrounds in which the emphasis on the evils of sex is extremely destructive. For others, sexuality falls within the larger framework of human experience and is viewed in the context of love and commitment.

If you too are an incest survivor, you are not alone. It is estimated that 25 percent of women and approximately 12 percent of men have suffered some type of sexual abuse. Programs such as Parents United work with husbands and wives in families where sexual abuse has occurred to prevent its reoccurrence. There are also programs for adults who were molested as children. Many of these are free programs that are professionally led and are sponsored by civic organizations. They can be found through your yellow pages or local psychological or mental health organizations. As with other recovery groups, everyone remains anonymous, and everything that takes place in the group is held confidential.

If you have experienced sexual abuse, remember that *you are not to blame*. Get some type of therapy, whether through a self-help book, support group or individual psychotherapy. Therapy is essential to help you deal with the many issues that can cloud your life and prevent you from experiencing the happiness you deserve. You will find that the others in the group are ordinary people just like yourself. No one will pass any judgments on you. If you have not gotten help already, I urge you in the strongest possible terms to get it now. It will make an enormous difference in your life.

Many books are now available to help survivors of childhood sexual abuse. *Male Survivors: 12-Step Recovery Program for Survivors of Childhood Sexual Abuse*, by Timothy L. Sanders, specifically deals with the issues faced by men who have experienced sexual abuse. He explains the issues involved in abuse and then breaks recovery into twelve stages with exercises, affirmations and inventories for each. This book would be an excellent adjunct to any treatment you are now participating in. If you're not quite ready for a group, it will get you started in the right direction. I do, however, encourage a professionally led group or individual therapy. When you are delving into this area, so many issues come out that it's crucial to get the help of an experienced professional who can provide a safe container for the emotions that arise.

AWARENESS EXERCISE

Here is an awareness exercise adapted from *Male Survivors* to help you focus on your strengths. It will help you to see the positive survival strategies you have developed, which you may not recognize as strengths. Focus on these strengths and nurture them.

To begin this exercise, make a list of your positive mental and emotional attributes. This list could include attributes such as courage, thoughtfulness, kindness, analytical thinking and intuitive thinking.

Make a list of your positive spiritual attributes, such as commitment, faith, sincerity, devotion.

Make a list of your positive attributes in the sexual area, such as empathy, sensitivity, tenderness, passion.

Make a list of your positive physical attributes, such as vision, hearing, strength, endurance, neatness.

Add to these lists as you become aware of additional strengths in any area.

Review these lists. Notice how these strengths enrich various areas of you life. They may have been born in adversity, but you can now use them to enhance your relationships, reach cherished goals or motivate yourself during difficult times. As you look over your lists, you can honor them further by reading them out loud and affirming them. For example, if one of your strengths is thoughtfulness toward others, after reading aloud, "I am thoughtful toward my friends and loved ones," you can validate this by adding, "Yes, that's true about me and I honor it."

AFFIRMATIONS

"I deserve the gift of healing."

"I have the right to choose my friends."

"I deserve to be surrounded by loving people."

"I Told My Father I Was Gay"

Adolescent struggles with sexuality are almost always difficult. For a young person who comes to the realization that he or she is gay, those struggles are magnified many times over. A father's strength and conviction at that time can provide the support that enables a young person to come to terms with his or her sexuality.

"Coming out" to parents may be one of the most difficult things a young man or woman must face. Until recently, severe societal sanctions led most homosexuals to keep their sexual orientation secret. But in recent years, especially since the advent of the AIDS epidemic, gays and lesbians have become more visible and society is slowing becoming more accepting of them. Many gay men have begun to acknowledge their status to their families—especially if they tested HIV positive and were in need of support.

But not all families extended that assurance. Some turned their backs and refused further contact with their children. Many other parents, however, faced with the illness and possible death of their child, overcame fears and prejudices and rallied to their aid. Some fathers do not need the impetus of death to accept their children. Their love is great enough to embrace all facets of their child.

Allan had that kind of father—a genial, easygoing man you could always count on. One who rarely lost his temper, except on one memorable occasion. "I think my parents knew I was gay," Allan said, "but they never said anything about it. I had my first romance when I was twenty-one. It was with a friend of my college room-mate who looked like Jack Armstrong—a real all-American guy. His mother found out about it and called me up at the dorm about 6:00 A.M. and said, 'I want to talk to your father this morning, or I'll call the police.'

"I drove home just terrified. I thought my life was over. I woke my father up and asked him to come into my room and talk to me. He said, 'What in the world is wrong?' I said, 'You know Bob?' But I was so scared I burst into tears before I could even speak. He just said, 'Son, is it what I think it is?' I said 'We've had an affair.' My father just looked at me and said, 'So? What's the problem?' I told him all about Bob's mom and that she had threatened me with the police. My dad asked me if Bob had admitted to all this, and when I said 'Yes,' he said he'd call his mother.

"That's when I saw the formidable side of my father," Allan stated. "He picked up the phone and called Bob's mom and said, 'I understand that there's been a problem. I assume that you're a very intelligent woman who can run her household, as I can run mine—and I'm assuming you will. Good-bye.' Then he advised me not to see Bob anymore.

"To show you what kind of a man my father was, he gave the guy I had a thirteen-year relationship with money to go to beauty school. He told him, 'I know you want to go, and this will be good if you and Allan ever want to go into business."

Fathers often blame themselves if their sons are gay. However, homosexuality is not anyone's "fault." Research confirms that homosexuality is a genetic trait that is found in approximately 10 percent of the population. Almost all homosexuals describe knowing they were "different" even as children but not being able to pinpoint that difference until they were attracted to a member of the same sex, usually during adolescence. Many have struggled with their sexual identity for years before admitting they were gay to themselves or to others.

As society becomes more aware, the tide of acceptance is slowly turning. However, the openness with which Allan's father accepted Allan's homosexuality is all too rare. Many adult children are fearful of revealing their sexual orientation because of anxiety about being rejected. Many fathers secretly suspect the truth but are afraid to openly acknowledge it. Homosexuality is one more trait among many in a child's emotional and physical makeup. Fathers hope that their child will possess whatever characteristics they deem desirable, but every child is unique. The ability to appreciate each child's special gifts is a true measure of a father's love.

Homosexuality has only recently become more acceptable. Formerly, it was classified as a mental illness, and gay men lived in fear that they would be found out. Repressive social strictures forced many men to deny their homosexuality and attempt to suppress it by marrying and raising families. When social restrictions loosened and it became safe to "come out," many of these marriages ended in divorce, often with devastating effects on the unwitting spouse.

Like straight fathers, homosexual fathers have a variety of parenting styles. Some are closely bonded to their children; others are workaholics who are often immersed in their own concerns. Children of homosexual fathers who have come out usually continue in the relationship; many even find that the relationship improves because the underlying tension of living with a secret is removed.

Contrary to common beliefs, none of the men I interviewed felt that their sexuality had been affected by their father's orientation, although they said they had wondered about their sexuality at first because they were aware of the possible genetic component.

"Once He Came Out of the Closet, He Was More Fun to Be Around"

Sheldon described his career navy father as a "work-driven, fairly distant, 'functional' father." "He gave us all the fundamentals, but we never had any fun as a family," Sheldon explained. "My father was extremely successful, but he didn't know how to enjoy himself. There wasn't much allowance for normal kids' mischief. During high school, I couldn't just sit around the house on weekends. I had to keep busy pulling weeds, washing the car, doing chores. When I went to college I didn't have any interest in going home—I could have more fun elsewhere.

"During my senior year at college, my father came out to us. It was a shock to me, but my real concern was for my mother—she was completely devastated. I didn't see him for a while. Not because I blamed him for being gay but because I wanted to keep my life simple. My difficulties with my father are not because he's gay—he has no choice about that. It's because I saw people with great relationships with their families, who'd be excited about going home for Christmas, and I resented not having that.

"Once he came out of the closet he was more fun to be around. We have a much better relationship than when I was growing up. At this point, we get along just fine. I just wish him happiness.

"As far as my own sexuality, I've always had good relationships with women. All my relationships have been really good. I've also been very open about my father with close friends. I'm not ashamed of it, and I've never gotten a bad reaction.

"My father said before he came out he was a 'stranger in his own soul.' I would advise anyone in this situation to work through it, be open-minded, endure the pain and reconcile yourself to what is. If your father is homosexual, that's irrelevant. Be open-minded and accepting, take care of your own emotions, and appreciate the diversity."

Living a lie imposes a terrible penalty on all those involved, both on those who are forced by society to hide who they are and on those who are unknowingly caught in the deception. As the rules change, families such as Sheldon's suddenly find that a major part of what they believed to be true was a mirage, and each individual must adjust to a new reality. The real issue when a father comes out is not sexuality but family relationships. A new configuration has been born that requires a complete reversal in perception.

Recommendation

Many difficult issues can arise when you learn your father is gay. Some kind of support can be of great assistance in dealing with those issues. Parents, Families and Friends of Lesbians and Gays is a nationwide self-help group that offers free information and meetings. If you are going through an experience such as Sheldon's or know someone who is, this group would be an excellent source of advice. And remember that whatever a man's sexual orientation is, once he has reared a child, he never ceases being a father.

| | | |

Boys need their fathers. They need the role modeling and male guidance a father can give them. Without a father in the home, boys might have no way to learn healthy male behavior in order to feel secure in their masculinity. They find it difficult to gain the necessary confidence in themselves as men and experience hardship in asserting themselves appropriately. Often, they struggle with the insecurity of feeling they do not really know how to be a man, with all that implies in their behavior, relationships and sexuality. To help meet these needs, male relatives, teachers, coaches, and other father surrogates, men's groups, mentors and male therapists can all play an invaluable role.

Ideally, all young men would be able to receive the guidance and approval they need from loving, dedicated fathers. They would know from their father's example just what it means to be a man in every aspect of personal, family and community life. Under such beneficial conditions, sons would gain an invaluable sense of confidence in themselves as men and a blueprint to follow in their own lives.

CHAPTER 6

The Father-Daughter Relationship:

Femininity, Sexuality, and Fathers

A woman's sexuality is powerfully influenced by her father . . .
he is the first man to whom she gives her heart, and how
he reacts strongly influences her future with men.

—WILLIAM S. APPLETON, M.D.

A daughter's interactions with her father, the quality of the relationship she sees between her parents and her self-image as a woman are all inextricably entwined. It's universally accepted that fathers play a major role in reinforcing culturally approved concepts of masculinity for boys. Less widely recognized is the fact that a father's approval is also a significant factor in bolstering social competence, intellectual achievement and self-confidence in girls. His example of healthy masculine characteristics such as assertiveness, goal orientation and independence can be emulated by daughters as they integrate those characteristics with their feminine traits in order to attain their highest potential.

"Mirror, Mirror . . .": Feminine Identity and Fathers

Dad is also the mirror through which a daughter first views herself as a woman, reflecting her first awakening to her emerging femininity. As young men need fathers to learn how to *be* male, young women need fathers to learn how to *relate* to males.

Women's roles are taught not only by mothers, who demonstrate them, but also by fathers, who respond to them. If Dad held your mother in high esteem because of her keen intelligence, valuable insights when important family decisions needed to be made and contributions to an enjoyable family life, then you are also likely to express those traits. If he was openly affectionate toward your mother, praised her unique talents and appreciated her femininity, then you no doubt concluded that it was desirable to be female and sought to emulate your mother's example.

But when fathers denigrate women and express negative views of female traits, then daughters come to the conclusion that women have little value and develop unflattering views of themselves. In order to find meaning in their lives, such women often seek a man who will become the pivot around which their life revolves. Having never learned that men and women provide balance to and complement each other, they seek to alleviate their feeling of emptiness by focusing on filling the needs of another.

There is more than one family environment in which a girl can develop a healthy regard for feminine characteristics. One is the egalitarian family, in which both parents play equally important but complementary roles, and leadership shifts according to need. Another is the more traditional family, in which the father is slightly more dominant and the mother plays a strong and respected supporting role. In either case, for a girl to gain greatest confidence in her femininity, it is vital that her father be confident in his own masculinity and demonstrate that he values his daughter's feminine traits.

Femininity is the emotional awareness of oneself as a woman. There is no particular way of behaving that defines "feminine." It's not about anything outside; it's about what's inside, and it can be expressed in many diverse forms. Despite the obvious physical differences, men and women are much more alike than different. Both possess such attributes as imagination, creativity, empathy, insight, intuition, reasoning skills, logic and analytical abilities, language skills, assertiveness and aggressiveness.

However, traditional divisions of labor, in which women assumed primary responsibility for child-rearing tasks, required that women develop greater sensitivity and interpersonal skills. This, combined with women's historic dependence on men to provide for them and their children, encouraged women to develop attributes that would foster the creation of permanent bonds.

Today, many of these conditions have changed. Women have achieved much greater independence and are freer to express all the various facets of their personality. But which personality traits women develop, how they are expressed and whether or not women value them is still very much influenced by their relationship with their father.

As definitions of femininity expand beyond traditional stereotypes, they are no longer viewed as the opposite of male traits but instead are regarded as valuable complements. As women achieve higher positions in the business world, their greater proficiency in interpersonal skills such as communication, empathy, adaptability and sensitivity to the needs of others are becoming increasingly valued. Fathers who encourage development of these abilities provide daughters with invaluable resources.

I will always be grateful to my father for teaching me that femininity could take many forms and that desirability did not depend merely on physical attractiveness. My father had a multitude of friends, both men and women of all ages and circumstances, and he found something to prize in each.

I have vivid memories of how admiringly he spoke of the various talents possessed by his women friends. Some he described as excellent businesswomen, others as wonderful mothers. Some had a great sense of style, others were described as extremely witty. Some were magnificent cooks, some were highly intelligent. Others were lauded as talented artists or musicians. Yet others were praised for being hard workers, for being exceptionally attractive or for any number of other qualities that he found admirable. His enthusiasm instilled in me the comforting thought that a man could find you desirable for whatever you happened to be good at. I never felt that I had to measure up to some external criteria of beauty or desirability. It was reassuring to know that any unique quality I possessed would be sufficient.

I learned that though beauty might be one way to appeal to a man, it was by no means the only way to attract male attention. In fact, since one of the traits that appealed to my father most highly was wit, I became adept at employing humor to lighten difficult situations and to keep from taking anything—especially myself—too seriously.

Men do not *create* women's desirability, but their reaction to a woman leads her to evaluate her own desirability. The qualities a father praises are the qualities daughters will usually seek to possess. Sometimes they are external attributes, sometimes they are internal—in either case, daughters view them as valuable and are likely to develop them. In the best of all worlds, fathers validate all their daughter's positive attributes and provide a climate in which they can continue to grow.

"I Was a Tomboy"

Tina, a young woman who is constantly on the go as she tends to her thriving catering business, received positive messages from her father despite her unconventional behavior. Tina's high energy, blonde hair and even tan endow her with the prototypical California look. Despite her feminine appearance, however, during her childhood Tina had no interest in traditional girls' activities.

"I was a tomboy," said Tina, "and that's how my dad treated me. I was very active, and I liked the outdoors, so I was the one who'd go fishing with my dad and do other outdoor activities that my other sisters didn't want to do.

"I did the same things with my father that a son would have done. I liked the outdoors and sports, but I also could do things at home like cooking and cleaning. My father was just as happy to see me in jeans going hiking as to see me in a dress going to church.

"I'm glad I got that validation when I was younger. My dad never put any restrictions on me as to what I could do. It's given me a lot of confidence."

"My Father Liked Smart Women"

Lynn, a banking attorney, described how her father's approval of her intelligence helped her feel comfortable with her colleagues and succeed in a predominantly male profession. "My father liked smart women, and we have a lot of fun bantering," Lynn said. "So I never felt I had to play dumb to be attractive.

"Probably because of my relationship with my dad, I've been able to survive in what is still a male-dominated profession. I enjoy working with men. I'm not necessarily being 'one of the boys,' but I'm able to relate to them, and my friendships with men are very strong."

Tina and Lynn's fathers gave them full scope to develop. They encouraged their daughters' nontraditional interests and gave them the confidence to succeed in all arenas. Engaging in easy companionship and outdoor activities usually reserved for boys built their confidence about being women and relating to men—an enormous advantage to them in the business world.

Old habits of thinking die hard, however. In some families boys are still considered more valuable than girls. If a father who was disappointed to have a daughter does not overcome his disappointment, her experience of rejection can have long-lasting and painful consequences. The pain of feeling unwanted, unaccepted or "defective" in some fundamental way can create pervasive feelings of self-doubt that severely diminish a woman's potential. In some cases, it gives a woman the fierce determination to overthrow her father's negative view of girls and to prove him wrong.

"It Was Just Not Okay to Be a Girl"

Sarah, a hard-driven woman who owns her own advertising agency, will never forget feeling rejected by her father because she was a girl. "I was just a toddler, about two years old. My crib was in my parent's room, and I remember being there and hearing them arguing. My mom was saying, 'She's going to need her own room.' My dad said, 'We can't afford a bigger place. It was *your* idea to have a girl, and now we have one and she's costing us all this money.' That's when I realized I wasn't like my brothers.

"When I got a little older I could see it was just not okay to be a girl, because Daddy didn't play with little girls. I remember being about five and begging him to bounce me on his knee. He turned me away, saying, 'No, you're too big.'

"Later, when I got into my teens, I was convinced that being a girl was not cool, so I became a tomboy. I wore T-shirts, jeans, short hair and no makeup. I fought my feminine identity every way I could. I rebelled against dresses; I fought against wearing a bra. My father's reaction to my changing body was to deny it. He didn't want me to grow up and become a woman.

"All during high school, I wasn't interested in boys. I dated a gay boy for five years because it satisfied both of our needs to fit in. I wasn't even interested in boys until after college. I had crushes here and there, but I didn't know what to do about them.

"Up until four years ago, I still didn't like being a woman. I hated my body, I hated my breasts, I hated having a period—I hated everything that made me a woman. I discounted women. I wasn't interested in them except for a couple of close friends. I had predominantly masculine energy.

"Then, all of a sudden, in one of my therapy sessions, I 'got it' and started crying so loudly, I lost control. My whole body went into a dramatic rebirthing. That was when I really accepted being a woman. Now, I'm not ashamed of my body anymore. I took some sexuality courses, started enjoying men, and found out I'm a passionate woman.

"I don't look at men as competition any longer. I don't feel I have to compete with my brothers. And I'm working off the residue of needing approval from my Dad."

Sarah hated being a girl because she blamed being a female for robbing her of her father's love. So she became a "superachiever" to prove that she was as good as any son. But none of her achievements brought her satisfaction: she could never deny the fact that she was a woman and, therefore, could never gain her father's acceptance. In an attempt to disown her femininity, she even denied herself the right to be in a relationship.

When she got help, Sarah was able to rid herself of her debilitating self-hatred. Self-acceptance enabled her to form satisfying relationships, and now she is with a man who appreciates all parts of her—just as she does.

If you experienced a situation similar to Sarah's, the following affirmations to heal your "inner child" will help resolve those issues.

They are inspired by John Bradshaw's book *Homecoming: Reclaiming and Championing Your Inner Child.*

"INNER CHILD" AFFIRMATIONS

For greatest effectiveness, tape these affirmations first and then listen to them while you are in a relaxed state. Sit in a comfortable chair with your feet on the floor and your hands in your lap. Start by taking a few deep breaths to relax your body. When you are taping, pause between each affirmation so that you can repeat the affirmation after hearing it. Do this every day for one month.

"Welcome, _____ (your name) _____ ,
I'm so glad you're here."
(*Repeat*)

"I'm so happy that you're who you are."
(*Repeat*)

"I've been waiting for you."
(*Repeat*)

"I'm so glad you're a girl."
(*Repeat*)

"I've been wanting you so much."
(*Repeat*)

"You're very special to me."
(*Repeat*)

"I love you just the way you are."
(*Repeat*)

"I'm going to take care of you. You're safe here."
(*Repeat*)

"God loves you."
(*Repeat*)

Allow yourself to feel the emotions that arise. They have been with you a long time, but they will now flow away and leave you feeling lighter. Later, write down your feelings in your journal. You may want to add your own special validating affirmations to this list.

Fathers, Sexuality, and Coming of Age

A major part of you is your sexuality. As the physical expression of your feminine identity, it is an integral part of your personality and dictates how comfortable you are in relationships. If your femininity was validated and you received healthy messages about sexuality, then you are also likely to enjoy sensual expression.

In healthy families, your father helps build your poise for future interactions with boyfriends. You gain confidence about your sexuality from Dad's positive reactions as you mature physically and emotionally. When problems arise in relationships, you are able to count on him for advice or support: Nonverbal messages also shape your perceptions, especially the powerful messages you pick up about the value of women from watching how your father and mother interact.

"My Dad Taught Me to Respect Myself"

Wendy, whose parents operated a dress shop together, remembered the positive messages she got from her father about men and relationships. "My dad was a warm, 'I love life' kind of person, who used to come bouncing in and announce, 'Honey, I'm a tiger!' Wendy said. "He loved life, he loved people, and he loved to sing. He was very dramatic. I remember him coming into the shop carrying flowers and singing to my mom.

"Every Valentine's Day I'd get a card from him. One Valentine's Day he came in and recited a poem to my mom: 'How do I love thee? Let me count the ways.' He just loved to love, and he taught me that it's okay to show love and affection.

"My father never actually spoke to me about sex," Wendy continued, "but he taught me to respect myself. The unspoken message I got from him was that he trusted me to be responsible. He believed in giving suggestions or advice and then letting me choose my own way. Sometimes I was right and sometimes I wasn't, but my dad was always very supportive. He'd say, 'You learn from it, and you go on.'"

Wendy was fortunate to have a father who actively nurtured her appreciation of herself as a woman. His unspoken message of trust, responsibility and self-respect gave her the moral stamina to resist the pressures for early sexual involvement that can be so detrimental. Additionally, he gave Wendy a powerful message: Romance continues throughout life. You're never too old to make the dramatic gesture, create the little touches that makes those closest to you feel special and continue to celebrate love in your life.

Many parents refrain from discussing sexual matters with their children because they fear that they will put ideas into their children's heads. This has the opposite effect of what is intended. When adult sexuality is expressed in a loving and healthy environment, children learn to treat it with respect. According to the National Longitudinal Study on Adolescent Health, which began in 1995, young people who have observed positive relationships between their parents are *less* likely to participate in early sexual experimentation. In contrast, those who do not have such beneficial examples often use sex as a way of gaining the affection and acceptance that is lacking at home.

One major milestone in girls' coming of age is their first menstrual period. Some are aware of its significance and proudly announce their new status. Others are uncertain what changes this will cause in their lives and are unsure how to react. Still other girls, who have no idea what is happening and in some cases even believe they are injured, avoid telling anyone because they are embarrassed.

How a father responds sets the stage for a girl's view of her normal bodily functions. If he validates her new status, she takes pride in her developing womanhood. But if he reacts negatively or tells her such things are "not discussed," she believes that something shameful is happening to her.

"I'm Very Healthy Sexually "

Lynn, the attorney whose easy bantering with her father allowed her to enjoy an equally natural camaraderie with her male co-workers, credited her open enjoyment of a robust sexuality to her dad's approval. "I feel that I'm very healthy sexually," Lynn said. "I enjoy sex. I'm not afraid, and I'm very expressive and free. I'm probably more like a man that way than a woman.

"When I was in my teens, my dad always told me I was attractive, and that was a neat thing to hear. He was very open about sex. I had my first period the day we moved to our new house. My mom announced it at the breakfast table. She said, 'Lynn is a woman now.' My father said, 'That's nice.' My mom said, 'No, you don't understand, Lynn is a *woman* now.' My dad sat up and said, 'Oh, that's great! That's great!' He has been tremendously accepting and supportive all my life."

For a young girl to hear her father, the most important man in her life, voice appreciation of her sexuality and repeatedly avow that she is attractive is an extraordinary confidence builder. Wherever she goes, whatever setting she's in, Lynn will feel that she is an attractive woman who is valued by men. That conviction was established throughout her childhood by her father's validation. The confidence it breeds has given Lynn a tremendous boost in achieving success in all areas of her life.

"My Period Was a Badge of Womanhood"

Confidence as a woman is heavily influenced by the spoken and unspoken messages daughters get from their dad about their sexuality, the maturing of their bodies and his reaction to their coming of age, including the onset of menstruation. Cheryl's father gave her positive messages in all these areas. "I adored my dad," Cheryl said. "He always treated my mom with respect; they always worked together. It was never, 'Wait and ask your father,' or 'Ask your mother.' You asked permission of whomever was there, and the other would back them up.

"They were very affectionate with each other. I remember walking in their room one time when they were making love. They both just looked at me and said, 'What do you want, Hon?' It made me feel like there was something very natural about sex, and that you didn't have to hide it or be ashamed of it.

"I couldn't wait to start my period. For me, it was a badge of womanhood. I remember one time, my mom, sister and I—we all had our periods—and my father went to the store to buy us some Kotex. He wasn't embarrassed at all, and I thought that was neat."

Cheryl is comfortable with her sexuality and proud to be a woman. Seeing lovemaking as a natural activity, her father's lack of embarrassment about normal bodily functions and the affirming reactions from her father when she "became a woman" all helped her take pride in herself as a woman.

"My Dad Talked to Me About Boundaries"

Teresa's father was also very open about acknowledging and validating her developing maturity. Additionally, he deferred to Teresa's changing body awareness by allowing her to decide how much physical contact she wanted and what expressions of affection she was comfortable with.

"My father was very aware of my becoming sexualized when I got into my teens, and he was very careful about touching me. I can remember him saying to me, 'Teresa, you're growing up now; you can't walk around in T-shirts and underwear anymore.

"When I got my first period, he said, 'Wow! You're becoming a woman, that's what that means!' And he got excited about it with me. He and my mother talked about sex and gave me books to read. They said that I should ask them about anything I wanted to know. At age seventeen when I had my first boyfriend and started to become sexually active, my father never made me feel bad about my sexual behavior.

"When I got older, my dad talked to me about boundaries—but I never felt any rejection. He always wanted me to know that we would never do anything that could be interpreted in a sexual way. But he also didn't inhibit me from becoming womanly or sexualized. I knew his man-woman type love was for my mom. It was very clear that my mom was the person he was sexual with. I'm grateful to him, because his attitude gave me a great base for feeling confident about myself, which I think has helped a lot in my career and marriage."

Unfortunately, not all women receive such healthy messages about their bodies. Some fathers have difficulty showing affection even when their daughters are younger. When these girls enter puberty, these fathers often become so uncomfortable with their daughters' burgeoning physical maturity that they become even more distant. If you were rejected in this way, you probably felt that there was something wrong with you. Your father's discomfort with your maturing body might have led to feelings of embarrassment or shame that diminished your view of yourself as a sexual being. If this is the case, you can affirm your pride in yourself as a woman now by repeating the following affirmations to yourself.

AFFIRMATIONS

"I'm glad that I'm a woman."

"I enjoy my body."

"I'm happy and proud of myself as a woman."

"He Pushed Me Off and Said, 'You're Too Heavy!'"

Eileen, whose slender figure is the result of steadfast dieting and exercise, spent much of her childhood seeking a closer relationship with her father, only to lose all hope for achieving it as she neared adolescence. "My father grew up poor, and he worked hard to give us the things he'd never had, but he didn't give us any attention. I was constantly trying to do things to please him so he would notice me. I was a good kid, always getting good grades and never getting into any trouble.

"When I was little, I remember crawling up on the chair and trying to get on his lap. He didn't respond, but he would let me sit there. When I was around eleven, though, he wouldn't let me get on his lap anymore. He pushed me off and said, 'No, no. You're too heavy!' I always felt self-conscious about my weight after that, like I was this big, heavy thing, even though I knew I wasn't.

"The only really wonderful thing that I remember from when I was a kid is that he let me stand on his feet while he danced with me. But about the same time that he stopped letting me sit on his lap, he stopped letting me dance on his feet anymore."

A father's negative reaction to his daughter's changing body has a major effect on a girl's self-image. Fathers who become uncomfortable when daughters enter puberty give their daughters damaging messages about the undesirability of becoming a woman just at the time that girls need support for the social, emotional and physiological transformations they are undergoing.

Young women are sometimes uncertain about how to cope with their changing bodies and emotions and look to parents for clues about how to react. They need confirmation that the changes are natural and desirable. If a father becomes uncomfortable with his daughter's emerging sexuality and unsure about the appropriate response, he may invent reasons for pushing her away. Reasons such as "You're getting too heavy" ring false. They do not address the real issues, and they confuse girls even more. The most desirable approach, one that will keep a young woman from feeling rejected, is the one Teresa's father took—talking honestly about boundaries.

A woman's sexual identity is also adversely affected when her father leaves his family and does not maintain contact with his daughter. Unless there is another father figure to provide positive male affirmation, a girl in this situation may later have difficulty establishing satisfying relationships. Having been rejected by the first man in her life, she might feel reluctant to take a chance with another.

Conversely, as a way of gaining the male affection and attention she yearns for, a young woman may engage in sexual activity before she has matured enough emotionally to handle it. Psychologist Mavis Hetherington, who studied the effects of father absence on adolescent daughters, stated that girls who had lost fathers to divorce were more likely to seek attention from and be flirtatious with men than girls who lived in two-parent families or whose fathers had died.

Other women feel such a deep longing for connection and reassurance that their intense need drives potential partners away. Relationships buckle under the demands for unconditional love that were lacking in their childhood. Only by coming to grips with the underlying loss and becoming whole first can such women learn to be interdependent rather than dependent and attain the fulfilling love they hunger for.

Girls who have grown up without a significant male figure and have not had the example of a man and woman who care deeply about each other, have no model for how to act with boys and may feel painfully shy in their presence. If they have not had a male presence in their home to converse, joke and interact with, to them men become mysterious creatures who are viewed with bewilderment, suspicion or awe. Finding safe male friends such as surrogate brothers or father figures can help develop the desired ease. This will allow you to practice being with men and to become comfortable in their presence in a casual, natural setting without the stress of dating situations.

AFFIRMATION

"I am grateful for my growth toward wholeness and the new awareness of love that comes into my life today."

"I Never Talked to Boys"

Emmy, whose parents divorced when she was one year old, feels she has lost out on relationship skills because she did not have a father in the home. "I was always very shy, especially when I was little," Emmy explained. "I always wanted people to like me and be my friend, but I didn't know how to approach them.

"When I got into high school, I never talked to boys—I didn't know how. I started to date a little when I got into college, but I'm just now beginning to feel more comfortable with men. My best friend has a great family. I love her dad and brothers, and being around them has helped me understand men better. They're not such a mystery anymore; I can relax around them now."

In order to establish a healthy love relationship as an adult, it is essential that a girl have a good relationship with her father, or a father figure, during childhood and adolescence. Without such a father-daughter bond, women often fall into a pattern of becoming involved with emotionally unavailable men, in an unconscious attempt to rectify the past and gain the love from the current man that was denied earlier.

Dad is the first man and usually the most important male influence in a daughter's life. His influence will affect all other relationships with men. He is the first man a daughter receives affection from, the first man to show her approval, the first man to make her feel special. His acceptance and positive regard have a lifelong effect, not only on her self-confidence as a woman but also on her future relationships with men.

Incest: The Ultimate Betrayal

When this powerful need for Dad's love is taken advantage of and betrayed, as in the case of incest, the results are devastating. Incest has been so well hidden, its consequences are so far-reaching, and the pain it inflicts is so devastating that only a small portion of its effects can be examined in this book.

Incest is the most basic betrayal of a child's need for love and safety. It is physical and psychological violation at the most profound level. Yet it is so widespread—cutting across all boundaries of class, financial status, race, religion and geographic location—and so damaging that it can be regarded as an epidemic.

Incest scars its victims for life, leaving in its wake a multitude of destructive symptoms: depression; suicide; sexual promiscuity; teenage pregnancy; prostitution; runaways; school failure; alcohol, drug and food addictions; inability to trust or form stable relationships; and other self-negating or self-injuring behaviors.

Part of the problem is that, until recently, most incest victims were shamed or frightened into silence. They were told that no one would believe them, that they would be responsible for their father being put in jail, that they would be taken away from their family and put into an institution, that they had to keep the abuse a secret because it would hurt their mother if she knew, that no one else could love them the way their father did. These and other statements are designed to manipulate the child into believing that *she* was responsible for the abuse and that any negative consequences would be her fault.

In a total reversal of responsibility, the child's reality is distorted and manipulated so that she (or he) assumes the guilt for the adult's act and feels too overwhelmed by shame to report it.

Incest survivors show enormous personal courage and determination when they go back and face what happened to them in order to come to terms with it and make themselves whole again.

"I Just Wanted Him to Admit What He Did"

Clara, who has spent most of her career working as a publicist for various political candidates, exemplifies the kind of difficulties incest victims must overcome. To all outward appearances, Clara is a vivacious, bright, successful woman with many friends and a reputation for getting things done. Yet she constantly struggles against paralyzing mood changes and bouts of self-doubt. Only her closest friends know that several years ago, after another failed love affair, Clara admitted herself into a hospital to seek help with feelings of hopelessness so overwhelming that suicide seemed the only solution.

For most of her life, Clara struggled against deep-seated feelings of shame. Her relationships continually repeated the same pattern: finding a partner who needed her, hoping that this relationship would be "it"—the one that would finally give her emotional security, and then awakening to the realization that her partner was unable to meet her needs. Occasionally, Clara dated men who were stable and seemed able to commit to her, but she dismissed them as "boring" and soon ended the relationship.

Like many incest survivors, Clara couldn't remember much from her early years. "I hear other people talking about their first-grade teacher, or the house they lived in when they were eight years old, but my life before junior high is almost a total blank." One of the few memories she did have was of lying in her bed at night and pretending to be asleep when her father came into her room. She remembered hoping that he would leave her alone and holding her breath while telling herself she didn't feel anything. "I found a place in my mind where I could hide," she said. "It wasn't me it was happening to; it was somebody else.

"My dad always told me that if I told anyone I would destroy the family and bring shame on myself. When I was thirteen, I tried to tell my mother about it, but she told me I had a filthy mind to make up something like that. When I was fifteen, I moved in with a boyfriend's family, and I've had almost no contact with my father since because I can't stand pretending everything's okay when it's not. I'd like to confront him. I just want him to admit what he did."

Clara struggled for years to overcome the feeling that she was fundamentally damaged. After her last failed relationship, she finally decided to reach out for the help she needed. Since then, she has grown much clearer about who she really is. Having successfully put the past behind her, she is determined to pursue the life she knows is possible.

"I've come a long way," Clara said. "I know I've still got some work to do. But the difference between how good I feel now and how miserable I felt then is night and day. Now when I get up in the morning, I look forward to the day. For the first time, I feel really good about myself."

Fathers who break the incest taboo wreak psychological devastation on a girl. They ravage her self-esteem, create deep-rooted sexuality problems that last for years, destroy her trust in men and sabotage her future relationships. The self-loathing that results often leads to long-lasting depression, problems with addiction and even thoughts of suicide.

What's important to know is that incest survivors can be healed. Despite the past, it is possible for an incest survivor to feel like a worthwhile human being instead of harboring shame. Although a lot of hard work must be done to overcome the damage, survivors can change their perceptions of themselves and achieve wholeness. As thousands of courageous women have proven, it *is* realistic to hope for a better life and succeed in achieving it!

Recommendation

Open your journal and take a few deep breaths to center yourself. Place a glass of water and some tissues by your side for when the emotions arise. After a few deep breaths, feel your body centering itself. Let your eyes unfocus and allow your hand to start writing about what you lost and what you need to grieve for. Just let your hand write. It may scribble away, then pause for a moment, and then start again, furiously writing without pausing. Don't worry about spelling, punctuation, grammar or anything else that would stop the flow. Later on, you can read what you wrote. For now, let your hand go.

Fathers and Sexuality: Living with Difference

Unquestioned obedience to ingrained habits of thinking can wreak havoc when new situations arise. Ideas that have never been examined and automatic reactions that are unthinkingly applied to normal human conditions cause enormous amounts of unnecessary pain. They sever relationships that could have provided years of satisfaction and deprive people of the opportunity to care for one another. This situation can arise when a daughter comes out to her father as a lesbian.

"I Never Thought a Daughter of Mine Would Become One of Them"

"My father was in the navy for the first seven years of my life, so I hardly ever saw him," May revealed. "It was always a joyous reunion when he came home, but I felt abandoned and angry when he left again. Finally, he retired and came home permanently, but my life changed. He became the master of the house, and his word was law. Not even my mother was allowed to have an opinion.

"I was angry before because he kept leaving us, so when he came home for good and tyrannized us all I really started to hate him and did everything I could to flout his authority. I didn't brush my teeth, I got poor grades at school, I wouldn't wear the orthopedic shoes that had been prescribed for me. Outwardly, I conformed to all his rules, because I was so afraid of him, but inwardly I was in complete rebellion. The only place I got love in those years was from the pastor and his wife.

"My first strong attraction to a girl came when I was in junior high. We were friends until high school, when she got more interested in boys. I started dating boys too, because that was the thing to do, but I still had crushes on girls. I didn't know why I felt that way—it didn't feel sexual—I just would be so strongly attracted.

"After high school I got married and had a baby—again because all my friends were doing it, and that was the thing to do. Our marriage didn't last, and I found myself a single mother with a daughter to support. Then I fell in love with a co-worker, and for the first time, somebody returned my feelings. That was when I discovered the sexual aspect of my feelings.

"It was a very confusing time. I grew up hiding all my true feelings inside and portraying this perfect conventionality outside. I didn't know how to deal with all the chaos going on inside me. I finally went to see a therapist who helped me straighten out my emotions and accept myself for who I am.

"A few years later, my partner was discussing politics with my father when the subject turned to homosexuality. He was so disparaging that she asked, 'Are you telling me that if your daughter was gay you wouldn't have anything to do with her?' My father said, 'Absolutely not!,' and the truth finally came out. When I called he told me, 'I never thought a daughter of mine would become one of *them*. I don't want you in my house.' I didn't see him or any of the relatives for eight years after that. So effectively, I was cut off from my entire family.

"Searching for answers, I took a personal development class. The instructor said, 'You would rather be right than in relationship with your father.' That remark hit me. I wrote my father a letter for Father's Day telling him everything I appreciated about him: his willingness to take care of his family when so many men didn't, his lifelong interest in learning, his love of the environment, which he passed on to me, and despite his authoritarian attitude, his deep love for my mother. We started to build our relationship, but he blew up again, and once more he cut off all ties with me.

"A few years ago, my mother went into a nursing home, and my father soon followed. My brother invited me to go see him, and when we walked in, my father said, 'Well, look who's here!' He was genuinely glad to see me, and I was glad to see him too. I knew he couldn't help who he was, and I felt I had made peace with him.

"Now, I feel great. I'm glad I wrote the letter, because the truth is there were parts of my father I was grateful for. I would rather have the relationship than be right. I feel good and I'm glad. I want fathers to know that your daughter came into this life the way she is—it has nothing to do with you. So many fathers think people will blame them for having a gay child, so they distance themselves. No one with any true knowledge will blame you. We're all doing the best we can.

"I spent years during my childhood praying each night that I would wake up in the morning with a penis because it would make me okay; it would enable me to do the things men could do and have the privileges that were extended only to men in the culture I grew up in. Now, I'm happy with who I am—but it's taken a long time and a lot of work to get here."

Children are who they are. They are of our flesh and blood, but they possess their own spirit. They come into the world with a particular eye color, hair color, right- or left-handedness and body type. These are all inborn genetic characteristics over which children have no control. The same is true for homosexuality. Being gay is not a choice. It is a physical fact.

Sexuality is a vital factor that can color an entire life, but although of overriding importance, it is one of many components that comprise an individual's total being. If inborn sexual orientation is accepted, then the child is free to develop *every* aspect of herself. If it is denied, then the attempt to repress the undeniable results in agonizing distortions that the individual must eventually heal. Estrangement from one's family is especially painful, and reconnection must usually be preceded by much personal growth.

Fatherhood is about unconditional love and acceptance. In the end, your relationship with your children is the only thing that really counts. If you are a father who grew up in an environment that denounced homosexuality, acceptance may be difficult. Seek support and meet other mothers and fathers who have come to terms with this issue. The longest, loudest applause at the yearly Gay Pride parade is for PFFLAG—Parents, Families and Friends of Lesbians and Gays. If you are a woman who is still struggling with your sexuality, almost every metropolitan area has support groups, therapists specializing in sexuality issues and other resources.

"The Divorce Was a Much Bigger Deal than My Father Being Gay"

"My parents divorced when I was twelve because my father came out to my mother about being gay," Vivian, a college student, related. "My parents never argued, my father always was interested in our activities, we were very affectionate—we were the perfect, happy nuclear family. So it came as a huge shock when they told us they were getting a divorce. It was a much bigger deal that they were getting a divorce than that he was gay.

"My dad moved into an apartment nearby, and we had regular visits with him. He took us to the zoo, Sea World and whale watching, or we would just hang out and do puzzles the way we had done when he was at home. My dad was really good about staying involved in our lives after he left. He would drive way out of his way to take us to religious school and soccer practice or to attend our school events. He was much more involved in our lives than a lot of my friends' fathers. It's never made me question my sexuality. I've always been attracted to guys. My friends know, and it's just not a big deal—the divorce was what had the biggest effect.

"What I value about my father is his sense of humor and how he listens to me. I like to be with him and talk to him. He's very open, and when I was going through hard times I knew I could go to him and let him know about what was going on in my life without being lectured or yelled at.

"The whole experience has been very positive for me because it has exposed me to a whole new group of people. I come from a racially mixed background and I don't think very many people are as unprejudiced as I am. People are just people; and everybody's different."

The most important thing about her father, as Vivian pointed out, was not his sexuality but the type of man and father he was: committed to his children, willing to do whatever it took to remain as involved in their lives after the divorce as he had been before, and providing the acceptance and support that allowed his daughter to reveal her concerns openly. His commitment to remaining an important part of her life was what mattered.

Fathers and the Masculine-Feminine: Bringing Balance to Identity

As old notions of sex roles rapidly change, archaic distinctions based on brawn and womb no longer apply. Female pilots were shot down during the Iraq war; women hold high public office in the Senate, Congress and state government. They exercise leadership and executive abilities as heads of Fortune 500 companies and are now heralded for possessing relationship skills such as communication, team building and leadership.

It is therefore more important than ever for fathers to instill girls with feelings of competence that are not restricted by gender. Dad's example of his equality with Mom is vital, as is his encouragement of his daughters' interests, without regard to traditional gender role. In this new vision of personal identity and sexual wholeness, a father's own personal growth contributes to the development of his daughter's. It is a continuing process that has brought numerous changes in the way families work—and in daughters' expectations for their own future relationships.

"My Dad Was Forced to Take Care of Us Kids"

Teresa's parents' marriage evolved from one that had operated along traditional, gender-restrictive lines to one that was a partnership of shared interests and responsibilities. "My parents married really young," Teresa said. "But some time in the mid-sixties, after the four kids were born, my mom got very depressed. She had a full-time job *and* she had to take care of all of us and my father. She did everything for him; he was like another one of the kids. Finally she got tired of it and told my dad, 'I've had it. You either have to work on the relationship or I'll leave.'

"My dad fought her. He said, 'What's wrong with you? Why aren't you happy? You knew this was our arrangement from the beginning.' So my mom went into therapy and was angry with my father for a long time. Finally, my dad tried to change; but he wasn't sure what to change. It took him years to modify his actions; but they both worked very hard on the relationship.

"Then my mom went back to school and started to get her stuff together. My dad was forced to take care of us kids while she was in her classes. My mom said, 'These are your kids. You learn to take care of them or they're not going to have a father. That's when he developed a close relationship with us. I'm the youngest, so from as early as I can remember, he was affectionate and tried to be a good father.

"He was just as interested in my activities as in my brothers'.

He taught me to play softball—he never made a distinction between male and female roles. He encouraged me in whatever I wanted to be.

"My parents are very happy now," Teresa continued. "They're so caring with each other. I've seen a complete transformation. My dad says, 'Yeah, I was a real jerk to your mom for the first years of our marriage, and she finally made me realize it.' They always talk about deciding to stick together at the point where most people choose to divorce—they decided to work things through and they have. It's given me the most incredible role model for my own marriage."

Teresa's father spent his youth learning the expectations and role behaviors of one era. As his family evolved, he was forced to enlarge his capabilities to take on the responsibilities of a new age. It was an effort that demanded a complete turnabout—a whole new way of thinking and acting on his part. The rewards are spectacular, however, and the entire family takes pride in making such a major transition successfully.

| | | |

Fathers have much more influence on all aspects of a daughter's development into a woman than is generally realized. From images of femininity to feelings about her sexuality to eventually choosing a mate, girls are heavily influenced by their fathers. Those who receive appreciation from their fathers develop a healthy self-regard. A father is the first man in a girl's life, and her relationship with him predicts the type of relationship she will go on to have with every other man who is important to her.

If she had a loving relationship with a father who instilled confidence in her femininity, she will be comfortable around men generally—an important factor not only in her relationships but also in her professional success. She will be balanced in her expression of male and female traits and will be able to get along equally well with both men and women.

If you missed out on being validated by your father, it is still possible to take steps as an adult that will help you heal the wounds and detach from the past. The first step to healing is to make the decision to detach from the past and reclaim your sexuality. This requires changing how you think about yourself. There are many ways to do this, but regardless of which approach you use, the underlying aim of all therapeutic tools is to help you let go of old emotional burdens and create a new reality that serves you better.

Some methods that have worked well for people are affirmations; using your journal to record positive thoughts and accomplishments that occur during the day (even the smallest and seemingly insignificant is worth of notice here); stopping yourself when you have negative thoughts and replacing them with positive ones; using the techniques of the Automatic Thought Log in chapter 2; employing visualizations such as the Ideal Self Guided Imagery Meditation in chapter 4 to create a belief in a new image of yourself; and learning more about your inner process from books such as those in the Bibliography at the end of this book. If early deprivation of positive messages was severe, you might want to look for a support group or individual counseling to initiate the process and get you started in the right direction.

Taking charge of your life and discovering more about yourself is one of the most exciting adventures you can embark on. Wherever you are at this moment, it is possible to reclaim your sexuality and experience fulfillment of yourself as a woman. Remember that you are doing this for yourself and that you are the one who is in charge of your choices.

CHAPTER 7

"A Marriage Like My Parents Had":
Fathers as Trainers for Relationships

A good marriage is that in which each appoints the other guardian of his solitude.

—RAINER MARIA RILKE

Remember the plans you made as you were growing up about your future marriage? The idealized image you had of your future husband or wife? The beautiful home you would live in? The great children you would have? Perhaps you planned to wait until your career was established before finding a mate. Or maybe you met your future partner while still completing your education and spent long hours constructing a vision of your future together.

Perhaps your plans worked out as you intended. You met the perfect mate, got married, created a home together, and started a family. On the way, you encountered the usual ups and downs, but you worked them out, and today, your marriage bond is stronger than ever, its solidity unquestioned.

Ideally, that's how it's supposed to work out. But with approximately 50 percent of all marriages ending in divorce and an even higher proportion of second and third marriages failing, we must ask ourselves *why* marriages are so difficult to maintain.

Are expectations too high? Is there simply an unrealistically romantic view of what a long-term committed relationship is all about? Or is some other factor at work that subtly undermines our best intentions?

Few people realize that marriage is the one of the most challenging commitments anyone will ever make. When two people unite, they also bring together at least two families, two sets of complex social and psychological needs and habits, children, the legal system and money. Possible complications abound. Yet, few people have acquired the skills necessary to translate initial romantic love into a successful, lasting marriage—one in which the partners work together to surmount the inevitable problems that arise and grow in ever-deepening commitment and love.

Whether you are happily married or miserably joined is often a reflection of the type of marriage your parents had. There is no school for marriage. The mental "marriage manual" you are using may be filled with remembered images of loving actions and affectionate words that you duplicate in your own successful marriage. Or it may contain destructive approaches for meeting needs that you automatically slip into when under pressure.

Replaying what you saw your parents do is almost inevitable unless you consciously decide to do otherwise. Without thinking, you might expect your partner to behave in a certain manner, react angrily when his or her habits conflict with yours, perceive situations in ways that cause you anxiety or unthinkingly use gestures, words, or tones of voice that you later regret.

People who have lived together contently for years often wonder why they start having problems after they get married, even if they have already shared their lives for many years. Although they are still the same people, and nothing has altered except their marital status, couples often remark, "I don't see how a piece of paper, like a marriage license, could have had such an effect on the way we act toward each other."

What couples who have lived together don't realize is that a marriage comes with a set of unwritten expectations and "rules" based on each partner's previous experience and upbringing. In contrast, there are no rules for living together. People who live together without being married are inventing their relationship based on ideas that come from previous experience, friends and romantic examples shown on television and in the movies; they are free of the expectations that color "married" behavior.

When they get married, most couples tend to fall into the patterns of behavior they observed between their parents. Society exerts some influence, adding to the couple's expectations of what married behavior should be, but the primary influence remains the example they got from their family of origin. From who takes out the garbage to who has primary responsibility for child care to whose job it is to maintain the family's vehicles, roles learned in childhood suddenly become the basis for the couple's own marriage.

These presumptions can work for or against you. If your parents had a good marriage, you grew up witnessing mutual love, respect, affection, humor and tolerance for each other's foibles. You have a model of how a satisfying relationship looks, sounds and feels that has given you a head start on creating the same in your own life. But if your parents' marriage lacked these elements, you must struggle to unlearn old habits and acquire new ones that make your relationships more satisfying.

Daddy: The First Man in Your Life

"My Father Was Really Fun!"

Daddy is the first man a woman knows intimately. His appearance, the manner of his speech and timbre of his voice, the feel of his body as he hugs you, his gestures and mannerisms, ways of interacting with you and your mother, what he does around the house—these innumerable bits of sensory information that create the mosaic of "Daddy" are imprinted in your consciousness as the template of "man" and "husband." Good or bad, he is the man who provides the first standard against which all other men will be measured.

If you're a woman, he is the first admirer who tells you you're pretty, the first male who praises your intelligence and talents, the first man to show you affection, the one who protects you and teaches you his hobbies and skills. If the relationship is good, Dad becomes your hero, and you look for his qualities in other men. If the relationship is not so good, you may still be drawn to men with your father's qualities because of your unconscious desire to resolve deeply buried needs that still exist.

Creativity and a sense of humor are what Heather, a professor of art history, remembered most vividly about her father. "My father was really fun," Heather said. "He was very spontaneous, creative and imaginative. For example, he would hold us upside-down and let us walk on the ceiling. When you came to our house, you saw these footprints and handprints all over the ceiling. Whenever we did something special, it was always his idea.

"We had an old horse, Blackie, that we would load up with blankets and a lunch, and then we'd find walking sticks and go for a hike in the hills. My father would tell stories along the way that would make it an adventure. We'd pretend to be pioneers or Indians, and make up names for ourselves. Sometimes he would tell us there were wild horses in the mountains and that if we saw one and caught it we could keep it. Other times he'd help us name our walking sticks, and we'd pretend they were horses. I think that's why I've always been attracted to men in the arts. I love that creativity—the sense that you can let go of reality and pretend like a kid again."

Visitors to Heather's house may have wondered what kind of household would have footprints and handprints on the ceiling, but her dad's freewheeling creativity extended Heather's horizons and ignited her imagination. Learning that anything was possible, she could launch into the exuberant flights of imaginative freedom that continue to stimulate her.

"All My Girlfriends Loved Him"

Catherine also had very positive memories of her father—especially of the unique way he would relieve her mom after a long day of caring for the children. "My mom sometimes got overwhelmed taking care of three little kids," Catherine remembered. "My brother was five, my sister was three, and I was two. We were a handful, so on days when she needed a break, my dad would take over when he came home.

"My dad loved music and loved to dance, and my mom played the piano. When things got too hectic, he would take us into the living room and put us on his toes and dance us around the room while Mom played the piano.

"All my girlfriends loved him and wished he could be their father because he had such a great sense of humor. He was the one who would come through for us and take us to concerts and things. He was a wonderful dad."

Catherine, like Heather, was blessed with a lighthearted dad. He could quickly change her mother's mood after a long and tiring day by whisking everyone out of the kitchen and into the living room for some musical frolic. When she got older and wanted to go to events with her teenage friends, they all knew they could count on her dad to drive them there.

Women like Catherine, whose fun-loving father was actively involved with his children and was emotionally supportive of her mother, look for the same traits in the men they form relationships with. They have seen the positive effects of this type of man on their mother. They remember the good feelings and happy times, and they want to reexperience the same joy as adults.

Women who have not been as close to their fathers often seek a partner who is Dad's opposite in order to get the love and affection they crave. Years of observation have shown them what they *don't* want. In considering a possible mate, they look for someone who possesses the qualities that were lacking in their childhood relationship with their father. Whatever they missed most strongly —acceptance, communication, outward displays of affection, easygoing tolerance, humor, a more reliable presence—is what they will seek in order make up for the earlier loss. Some succeed in creating relationships that are very different from those of their parents. Others discover that the men they are drawn to possess disconcerting similarities to Dad.

"My Dad Has a Good Heart, and He Tries"

Lynn never had the closeness with her father that she craved, so she vowed that when she got married, it would be to someone warm and affectionate. It took work and maturing to find the right man, but Lynn's experience shows it is possible to overcome the effects of rejection and create a loving relationship of your own.

"My dad has a good heart, and he tries," Lynn said. "It's just that my generation is much more aware than my father's. He has a lot of issues and problems, but he just doesn't have the tools to see what's causing his anger, so he struggles through and does his best.

"Depression babies, like my father, learned that 'how you feel is not important.' They were told, 'If you're hurting, I don't want to hear about it.' Everything is always supposed to be fine! When I was growing up, my father couldn't give me what I needed because he didn't know how. He did what he did because that was what he learned from his own parents.

"Where it hurt me most was in my relationships with men. It took me many years of therapy to realize that it's okay to have feelings. You don't always have to be 'fine,' because if you're always 'fine,' then you never deal with what's making you feel bad.

"I got in a pattern with men throughout college and business school, where I had what I'd call 'pseudo-relationships.' I'd choose men who were already taken or unavailable to me for some reason. We'd be friends, and I'd sleep with them, but I never fell in love. I believe that relationships involve your heart, your mind and your body, but I never had a relationship where all three of those were engaged. But despite that, I always wanted to get married and have kids. I just had no idea how I was going to do that.

"Last year, I met a wonderful man who comes from a great family, and I fell in love for the first time. We got married a few months ago. I feel like a pioneer because I never saw a healthy relationship at home, and until I met Tod and his family I had no idea what that looked like. I can remember my dad saying, 'Marriage is a lot of work—like having another job.' So when I got married, the conclusion I came to was 'If you run into any rough spots, you put your head down and keep going.'

"I know my parents love each other. They just don't have the information to figure out what they're doing wrong and how to fix it. They just muddle through. Tod and I are lucky—we have the tools to create a good relationship, and we're committed to hanging in there and making our marriage work. Half of our friends who've gotten married in the last five years are getting divorced. But no matter what, our marriage is going to last!"

Finding a partner who is from a warm and loving family is a big plus if you want your marriage to work, because your partner will already know something about what makes a marriage a success. Another plus is having insight about the problems in your parents' marriage and using the tools you have available to you such as the self-help books listed in the Bibliography, support groups, relationship workshops and individual or couples counseling. Lynn had the awareness to resolve most of the issues from her childhood and therefore set a good foundation for the kind of marriage she had long envisioned.

Looking for Daddy: Women and Father Figures

Most women who have had absent or distant dads seek a partner who will make up for that loss. Some search for a man who hails from a loving family that they can become part of. Others look for an older man who they hope will make up for the nurturing that they missed out on. Men who have not had a strong father presence in their lives may search for a mentor; women who missed this presence may be attracted to older men as partners.

"I Saw How Devoted He Was"

When Bonnie was eight years old, her mother divorced her father after discovering he was having an affair. Although Bonnie had fond memories of her father from before the divorce, he subsequently moved far away. Apart from infrequent birthday and Christmas cards, Bonnie had almost no contact with the father she deeply missed.

When she was twenty, Bonnie met a widower named Robert. Robert was fourteen years older than she and was struggling to raise his three daughters after the death of his wife the previous year. "I was impressed with what a good man Robert was," Bonnie stated. "I saw how devoted he was to those three little girls and how hard he tried to make a home for them. My heart just went out to him, and to them. He hadn't been able to keep a housekeeper—none of them could handle the responsibility of three kids under five who had just lost their mother. The house was a mess, there was laundry all over, the children ate whatever they wanted; it was total chaos.

"We dated for two months, and then he asked me to marry him. Everybody thought I was crazy to consider it. But when I saw how much Robert loved the girls, I couldn't say 'No.' We had some rocky times at first, but it's worked out very well. Robert is very stable and completely committed to our home and family. I was never comfortable in high school with guys my own age, maybe because I didn't grow up with a father and didn't know how to act around them. Robert is mature; I know he loves me and he'll always be there."

Like Bonnie's, some marriages between younger women and older men work out extremely well. When older men have learned through experience, they know what's important and they can give the devoted love their wives crave. Not only did Robert love Bonnie as a woman and his wife, but his love for his daughters enabled her to experience a father's affection vicariously. His commitment and his steadfast dedication to their family gave her the emotional security she longed for.

"Even Though He's Much Older, I Felt Very Comfortable"

Sometimes, the quest for a father figure backfires. Rather than achieving the loving relationship with an older man that she desires, a woman in this situation might find that a husband's conflicting loyalties lead to the same feelings of rejection she experienced with her father.

A navy career kept Sherry's father away from his family most of the time. But even when he was home, he never paid much attention to her. "I was always trying to find ways to please him, so he would notice me," Sherry said. "I wrote him long letters when he was at sea, hoping he would write back to me, but the most I ever got was a postcard. As an adult, I realize he loves me in his own way, it's just hard to tell from his actions. When I was a kid that hurt a lot.

"I didn't date much when I was younger. I've had lots of male friends, but never anything serious. When I met Paul last year, even though he was forty-two years old and I was twenty-five, I felt very comfortable with him because we had so much in common. We're both interested in sports and the outdoors; and he knew so much about things, it really impressed me. Paul has traveled extensively in Europe and the Far East, is knowledgeable about politics, and is so well-read it was like getting a college education just being with him.

"I was thrilled when he asked me to marry him, even though I was a little concerned about his desire not to have any more children. I had always wanted a family of my own. The real problem began soon after we got married. Paul's oldest daughter, who is just a few years younger than I am, got a divorce and started coming over to our house constantly.

"Everything has changed since she entered our lives. I almost never have Paul to myself, because whenever he's home, she's there too—talking about her problems, wanting him to drive her someplace, asking him to fix something at her house. I hate to admit that I'm jealous, but he spends more time with her than he does with me. Paul says she's going through a rough time and he has to support her. But I want my husband back."

The idea of an older man who will give you the love and attention you have always desired is very appealing. However, most older men have been in previous relationships. Children, ex-wives, former in-laws and established friendships can interfere with a younger woman's desire to be "the only one." If you look to your mate for the unstinting love that was denied to you during your childhood, you may be disappointed. His prior obligations may interfere, and he will have to find ways to accommodate all the demands on him.

Some couples work things out by agreeing that a current emergency must be given top priority for a limited time period; others find outside sources of support or arrange counseling for the person in crisis. Some women decide that they will take on greater responsibility for their own happiness and let go of the demand that their partner fill all their emotional needs.

Fathers, Sons and Husbands

Fathers teach sons many important things, both tangible and intangible. Some have to do with the lengthy process of building a son's masculine identity. Participation in a range of activities from Boy Scouts and Little League to hiking, camping and fishing help fathers bond with sons and foster their confidence as future men.

Other ways of teaching sons are more indirect, especially in the areas of relationships and communication. The relationship you saw between your father and your mother—and the love or conflict that existed between them—formed the basis of your own attitudes about relationships. How disagreements were resolved, whether Mom and Dad had a union based on equality or on dominance and how affection was expressed between them all exert a powerful influence over your own later relationships.

"My Father and Mother Were a Great Pair"

Rick, a garment manufacturer who has achieved notable success in the competitive world of the fashion industry, deeply admired his father. He was especially impressed by the warmly loving relationship between his parents and the way in which decisions and authority within the family were equally shared. "My father and mother were a great pair. They worked together in my dad's business and gave each other a lot of support, pitching in anytime the other needed help.

"After my wife and I got married, she told me that the reason she decided to marry me was because when we were dating, she saw my father sneak up behind my mother and kiss the back of her neck. She said that's when she decided I was the one, because she said to herself, 'If that's the kind of background he comes from, he'll make a good husband.'

"My father always gave me the impression that he and my mother were equals in the relationship. I never felt that either of them was more important. When a hit-and-run driver injured my father, my mother ran the business and I stayed home from school and took care of my dad. I took over making the meals, setting the table, cleaning the house and changing the dressing on my father's leg. I've tried to do the same things in my own marriage. My wife and I are very affectionate with each other; and we help each other out and treat each other like partners."

His mom and dad's example of love and respect was an enormous benefit to Rick. Shared responsibility and decision making came naturally to him, so in his own marriage he was able to recreate the warmth and sense of partnership that he admired so much in his parents.

"Fifty Years with the Best Man that Ever Lived"

"A wonderful man who devoted his life to his family" is the way Tim described his father. "My mom and dad had a perfect marriage," said Tim. "They were married almost fifty years and got along just great. One time we were sitting around, talking about the lottery or something like that, and my mother said, 'When it comes to good fortune or riches, I can't expect anything more—I had fifty years with the best man that ever lived.'

"I can see why my mom said that. He was always there for his children; and if he was that dependable with the kids, imagine how he must have treated her all those years. The last time I saw my dad was in the hospital just before he died. He reached over and took my mom's hand and said, 'We raised good kids, didn't we, Anna!'

"The most important thing I learned from my father is that the family always comes first. There was never any doubt where he stood. He was a solid presence that you always knew you could count on. I've turned down several promotions because I didn't want to take the time away from my family. I want my wife and kids to know they can count on me, the same way we could rely on my dad."

Tim sees his own twenty-eight years of married happiness as a direct result of the example shown to him by his father, and he has honored that legacy by continuing the tradition with his own children.

As Rick's and Tim's stories show, observing positive models is an extremely powerful method of acquiring the attitudes that make for deeply satisfying relationships. Years of exposure to their father's love and commitment to his family left indelible impressions that are continuing in their own marriages. Even if you didn't have the bene-fit of this kind of example, however, you can still create the loving marriage you desire.

"I Would Watch My Friends' Dads"

In contrast to these loving examples, many sons had poor relation-ships with their fathers and observed conflict-ridden marriages as they were growing up. If they are aware of the potential pitfalls, such men try to avoid lapsing into similar patterns. They find positive role models to emulate so that they can create a more loving environment in their own marriages—both as husbands and as fathers.

Nelson, a carpenter who prides himself on his craftsmanship, is an example of a man who has made a conscious decision to act dif-ferently than his father did. "My dad was an alcoholic and extremely volatile," Nelson said. "We never knew what was going to happen when he got home. Sometimes, he'd be all right for a little while, but as the night wore on and the level in the bottle got lower, he get meaner and meaner. His word had to be law, even if he was wrong. I can remember night after night, hearing him yelling, and I swore I'd never have anything like that in my own life. For some reason, he was a lot tougher on my two older brothers than he was on me, so I escaped the brunt of his abuse. I just tried to stay out of his way as much as possible.

"I spent as much time as I could out of the house with my friends. I used to watch their parents be all loving with each other and wish I could have a family like that. From an early age, I decided I would do things differently. I actually set out to create my own model of a father. When I was at my friends' houses I would observe what their dads did. I used to watch *Father Knows Best* all the time. It was like an escape for me. I put together the pieces from my friends' dads and TV fathers to get my ideas of what a loving hus-band and father would be like."

Nelson knew he didn't want to repeat in his own life what he saw between his parents. He yearned for the kind of happy home life he saw his friends enjoying. But he was acutely aware that he didn't have the faintest idea how to make that possible. So he became a self-taught student of successful marriage, culling ideas from every source he encountered.

Nelson's awareness enabled him to make good on his vow that his life would be different, and he and his family are reaping the benefits. His experience is a testament to the fact that it is possible to break the cycle of unhappiness experienced in early years and create an entirely different environment for your own children.

"I Decided I Never Wanted to Be Like Him"

Other men solve the problem of creating a good marriage by deciding that the risks of strife are so great that they would rather forsake altogether the goal of having a family. There is no happiness in the memories they associate with childhood and family—it is an era in their life that they want to leave behind and forget.

Tony decided that the only way he could be sure of not repeating the violence he experienced in his youth was not to have any children at all.

"I don't want to have any children. No way!" Tony asserted. "My father had a drinking problem. He was mean, with a chip on his shoulder. If a situation came up he dealt with it by getting drunk and breaking things—some of that has rubbed off on me.

"Sometimes he would take me someplace, and then stop for a drink on the way home. I can remember in the winter, sitting in the car waiting for him, and freezing for two or three hours while he was in the bar. If you tried to get him out, he'd have another drink just to spite you. It was terrifying when we drove home. He'd be driving in the wrong lane, heading toward a car, and I'd have to yank on the steering wheel at the last minute. I made a decision never, ever, to be like him; although it scares me now to realize how much I am. I'd never put a kid of mine through that hell."

Tony felt he was too much like his father to risk having children. Rather than taking a chance on repeating the violence with his own offspring, Tony choose the certain safety of not having any children at all. It was a decision made from awareness.

There are many reasons for having children: your image of a

family is not complete without children, you want to bring a new life into the world that symbolizes the joy of your union with your mate, you feel you have a lot of love to give and could provide a good home to a child, you had a happy childhood and want to share and relive the pleasurable experiences you had with a child of your own, your spouse insists on it, all your friends are having children.

If you had a brutal childhood, it may be hard to conceive of yourself providing a happy childhood to children of your own. And often, none of the other reasons is sufficiently compelling to induce you to risk inflicting harm. If you feel temperamentally incapable, the hazards might just seem too great.

But if you want to give a child the love and nurturing you didn't have, or become a parent by marrying someone who already has a child, you can make it possible by recognizing that you need to acquire the skills to deal with children on a daily basis. There are many fine parents who have dedicated themselves to overcoming the handicap of abusive early years. They are aware of what was missing as they were growing up and are determined for provide it to their children. They train themselves for parenthood and are extremely conscious of the effects of their words and actions. For them, healthy parenting is truly a mission.

Humans have an endless capacity for change and growth. Given the will and the intention, there are almost no obstacles that a person cannot overcome. Parenting, like so many other skills, is simply a matter of having the desire and acquiring the means. Anyone who wants to be a good parent and is willing to obtain the tools can learn to implement them.

There are many parenting programs through work, church, community organizations and other groups that can help you acquire the competence you desire. Books and audiotapes can give you practical ideas. Videotapes give demonstrations of how to utilize effective parenting concepts. Neighbors with happy families can serve as role models. Even informal gatherings of friends can be a good place to exchange ideas and learn from each other. Whatever your relationship with your father, whatever kind of marriage your parents had, you can create a harmonious family environment that fulfills your need for love and happiness.

AFFIRMATIONS FOR PARENTS

Affirmations for yourself:

"I can trust my inner wisdom."

"I can be the parent I want to be."

"I'm so glad to be a parent."

"I can learn new ways of doing things."

"My confidence as a parent grows daily."

Affirmations for your children:

"I love you just the way you are."

"I will always love you."

"I'm so glad you're my son / daughter."

"I like to watch you learn and grow."

"I'm so proud of you."

Acquiring Communication and Relationship Skills

Communication is one of the most vital relationship skills. The primary complaint when couples enter marriage counseling is that they are unable to communicate with each other. But whether your relationships are well honed or need improvement, the quality of them depends to a great extent on the communication style that prevailed between your father and mother.

If your parents were open and discussed concerns honestly without recrimination, you learned that it's okay to bring up problems. You saw that people can disagree, get angry or argue with each other and still remain on loving terms. If disagreements quickly evaporated and heated arguments rapidly gave way to laughter and joking, you absorbed some valuable lessons: it's okay to express your opinions and feelings, you don't have to be afraid of quarrels, and if you quickly dissipate minor grievances you will prevent them from building up into major confrontations.

But if your parents never argued in front of you and their disagreements took place behind closed doors, you may not know how to voice your needs or respond to your partner's concerns. Fear that arguments will escalate may lead you to avoid confrontation alto-gether—possibly allowing resentments to build or your partner's concerns to go unanswered.

Covert antagonism, in the form of days of silence, oblique mes-sages that never come to the point or sarcasm, is also extremely debilitating. Innuendoes are like toxins: They lead to angry reac-tions, and problems never get solved. Even if you know how destructive these methods are to a relationship, you may find that, to your dismay, you sometimes fall into them.

Having been an unwilling spectator of arguments that turned frighteningly loud and violent might have caused you to avoid con-frontation at all costs. You pretend that everything is okay when it's not, apologize when your partner becomes angry even if it's not your fault and never bring up issues that you fear will provoke an argument.

Avoiding communication on potentially touchy issues under-mines relationships, because it destroys trust and intimacy. What you can't talk about becomes an area of your life that you close off. As more and more concerns are relegated to the "Can't Discuss" zone, you begin to feel emotionally separated from your partner, and the relationship declines. It's at this point that many couples enter coun-seling in order to break the impasse and rebuild their relationship.

Communication and relationships are indivisible. Without good communication a relationship cannot survive. It is such a funda-mental skill that many helpful books have been written on the subject. Some of these are listed in the Bibliography at the end of this book. You will also get extremely useful ideas from listening to how other couples use communication skills to build happy marriages.

"There Was a Lot of Affection Between Them"

Affection is not generally thought of as a form of communication, but it's one of the most powerful ways to let your partner know how you feel about them.

Mark, a computer scientist who recently got married after living with his fiancée for several years, talked about how his parents' idyllic marriage affected him. "My mom and dad really enjoyed their time together. They both had a great sense of humor, and they were always laughing and joking. They were also very social—going over to other couples' houses where I would play with their kids, or having people over to visit us.

"I saw my mom and dad not only as parents but as regular people who liked to do things and have fun. There was a lot of affection between them. They weren't at all bashful about holding hands and kissing in front of the kids. They argued, but it was never a big deal. What I learned from that was 'Gee, sometimes people have disagreements, but it's okay.'

"My parent's relationship has been a major influence on me. I'm openly affectionate, and I like people. My wife's father was a pretty distant man, so she loves to spend time with my family because of how free we are about hugging and kissing. One thing we've decided to do that I learned from my parents is if we have a fight, we'll always make up before we go to bed."

Mark is keenly aware of how unusually good his mom and dad's relationship is. Their example of good humor and quick resolution of momentary blowups showed him how to openly express his feelings instead of stifling them or weighing what he says, and it has served as an inspiration for his own marriage. Mark and his wife are extremely fortunate. Their good communication skills mean that as they encounter problems they will deal with them directly—and their marriage will grow stronger each time they do so.

One of the main barriers to communication is that many women and men have no idea how to deal constructively with the inevitable problems that arise. When emotions become aroused, they don't know how to release them effectively. This is especially true for those whose parents were distant from or hostile to each other, because these people grew up without a model for how to communicate anxiety or anger appropriately.

If you were frightened by angry quarrels as a youngster, you might hesitate to express yourself for fear that you will provoke an angry reaction. If you didn't see how open discussions could settle differences, then you might have problems expressing your concerns. Or you might not know how to be assertive rather than aggressive. All of these factors could lead you to avoid confrontation entirely.

Some families go to the other extreme. Instead of shouting, they keep everything in. But the pretense that nothing is wrong does not solve the problems that unavoidably arise—it merely pushes them under the rug so that everyone has to tiptoe around. Even if the intention is to protect children from quarrels, it will usually back-fire, because children tend to sense that something is wrong anyway, and the increased tension simply adds to their fears.

If you have learned from your family to always suppress your emotions, you are likely to experience a completely disproportion-ate reaction later on—usually triggered by a trivial incident that is unrelated to the original event but becomes the "last straw." If you fear your anger, you need to learn how to calm yourself enough to express your feelings appropriately so that you can resolve them while they are still manageable.

A calming technique that many have found effective is to count from one to ten very slowly, taking a deep breath in between each number. At about five, you start to feel the difference; at eight, you will be noticeably less stressed; and at ten, most of your anger will be gone. If you need to, simply repeat the process again to clear your head and enable you to feel more in control.

Some anger is deep-seated and stems from an accumulation of happenings that often have roots in the past; it continues to affect the present because it is triggered by events that rekindle old emo-tions. On the other hand, some anger is a momentary response to an immediate situation and quickly dies down. In both cases, this breathing technique does work and will help you to either get rid of situational anger more quickly or else calm yourself down enough to deal with the situation appropriately.

Anger has physiological, emotional and mental components. When the physiological is brought under control, then rational responses can be invoked. In the case of long-standing anger, you might also need more intensive work such as anger control groups or individual therapy, but the deep breathing is always a good place to start. It works!

"We'd Know Something Was Wrong"

People who grew up in a family where differences were denied or kept hidden are likely to experience communication difficulties. They don't know how to work out disagreements, so the problems that inevitably arise are never dealt with and therefore can never be resolved. Conflicts just seep out in undercurrents of resentment, sarcasm and withdrawal.

Ben, a professor of Jewish studies in a large urban university, grew up with a mother and father who both came from homes torn by alcoholism and strife. Because their early experiences of parental arguments were so traumatic, they vowed that they would never quarrel in front of their own children.

"Most of the time," Ben said, "they were very affectionate with each other. But there were times when there was tension in the air, and you knew that something was wrong, even though they never talked about it in front of us. It's given me a lot of apprehension about bringing things into the open.

"My father really worshiped my mother. He always said she was the most beautiful woman. He opened doors for her, made her laugh, bought her gifts. He would do anything to please her. My father also admired her education—she had earned her master's degree in English. He always regretted that he couldn't go to college because he had to help support his brothers and sisters. I was always bookish, and I think that seeing how much he valued my mother's education made me want that kind of admiration for myself.

"I find that I'm also attracted to women of intellectual achievement, but it's caused some conflict because I want to be the one who's recognized as intellectually superior. That was obviously very hard to talk about, because I know it's an unacceptable view and I'm somewhat embarrassed by it. Between wanting to be the leader, feeling chagrin at having this view and my inability to communicate, there was no chance for a relationship.

"Fortunately, I finally realized what a no-win situation I had placed myself in. Last year, I started dating one of my associates whose company I enjoy and whom I also respect very much. Even though it's been a struggle, I'm going to counseling and learning to communicate more openly. Probably the most important thing I've learned is that it's much more important to listen than to talk. For the first time, I'm really able to understand where my partner is coming from. It's turning into the best relationship I've ever had. It's an equal relationship, and we're starting to talk about marriage."

Being unable to speak openly about fears, desires and needs is a very common problem among couples. Few partners have the ability to articulate thoughts and feelings clearly, listen without prejudging and allow the other person to speak without interruption. The fear of possible misinterpretation, worries about hurting the other person's feelings or about how they will react, and the desire to avoid confrontation—all can make the right words at the right time very hard to come by.

"I Don't Know the First Thing About How to Be a Good Husband"

Sean, whose dark good looks could qualify him for a career as an actor rather than an insurance agent, recognized that the interactions he saw between his parents were poor preparation for his own marriage. "I don't know the first thing about how to be a husband," he admitted. "All my parents ever did was fight. My father worked long hours as a small-town newspaper editor. When he came home my mother would try to engage him in conversation, but it seemed all he ever wanted to do was hide behind a book or go down to his workshop. When she couldn't get a response, she'd usually get so mad she'd start screaming at him.

"No matter what she did to get his attention—even a couple of times throwing something at him—it didn't seem to make any difference. Most of the time he'd just ignore her or go downstairs and work on his 'inventions.'

"Sometimes, he'd start yelling back, and then they would go on for hours. I could never figure out what the point was; they never settled anything. It seemed like all we ever had in our house was a truce or a fight. There was never a happy medium. I hated it when they argued. I'd go to my room and shut the door and try to drown them out by listening to my stereo.

"I wish my mother and father could have gotten along better. I really can't remember very many good times. I swore the same thing wouldn't happen in my marriage; but when something starts to bother me, I clam up. It drives my wife wild. She tries to pull it out of me, but even though I know she means well, I feel like I just don't want to be bothered. I've got enough to worry about at work without coming home and having to explain myself. Last week, my wife said she wanted a divorce, and it's making me crazy. I know I love her. I'll do anything to get her to stay."

Sean is like many men who grew up in homes where there was little or no communication, or where communication became mired in endless arguments that trapped both partners in a continual state of siege. Upset by the constant altercations, Sean tried to protect himself by retreating to his bedroom and tuning them out. While this was a useful strategy when he was a youngster living under his parents' roof, tuning out was a poor method for resolving problems in his own relationship. In addition, because of the emotional trauma connected to his parents' shouting matches, Sean often suppressed views he thought might lead to disagreements. He had no idea how to reach an acceptable agreement.

As Sean retreated, so did his wife. Their uneasy silences led to still further problems, and gradually, they stopped sharing the thoughts and feelings that originally brought them together. Each began to feel increasingly isolated in their marriage. Now that a crisis has occurred, there is an opportunity to turn things around. For the first time, Sean truly understands how desperately his wife wants a connection, and he's willing to change. He and his wife have joined a couples' group at their church and are learning how to communicate with each other openly. After only a few weeks, they are already using their newfound skills to bring out into the open the fears that were *really* bothering them, and they are beginning to reach an entirely new level of understanding. "We're making a whole new start on our marriage," Sean reported with satisfaction recently.

If communication is difficult for you, find a communications class or couples' group to attend. Community colleges, businesses, learning centers, churches and community organizations all offer workshops. If the problems caused by communication difficulties have caused a serious rift between you and your partner, consider a few counseling sessions to acquire the basic skills you need. Books can help you understand the principles of good communication, but you need others to practice with.

Recommendation

One of the reasons arguments get out of control is because they have a habit of rapidly spreading beyond the original issues. In the resulting recriminations, nothing gets resolved, and each person feels increasingly misunderstood. The following set of problem-solving steps provides a structure that you can use to keep any discussion within bounds. Agree that you will stick to one topic only, and pick something relatively easy to practice on that does not have much emotional "heat" involved.

Consider your first few uses of this method a dry-run. Although it may seem artificial at first, you will find that you can use this approach to defuse many situations and reach solutions that you can both agree on. Writing down your answers to the steps will keep you on track and help the process even more.

PROBLEM-SOLVING STEPS

1. Decide

Decide what the problem is. Limit it to one *specific problem only.*

2. Brainstorm

Brainstorm possible solutions. Don't judge whether they will work or not—the more possible solutions, the better.

3. Select

Select the solution you will try by a process of elimination.

4. Know

Decide how you will know that the solution was a success.

5. Evaluate

How did this solution work? Would you like to try another?

JOURNAL SUGGESTION

In your journal, describe what this experience was like for you. How did the process work for you? What were the results? Do you need to do anything differently next time?

Fear of Intimacy and the Distant Father

While some people learn to retreat from strife by tuning out, others learn to retreat from the pain of their father's rejection by not letting anyone get close to them. Sometimes they have experienced overt rejection—perhaps their father has pushed them away when they approached him seeking affection. More often, a father simply holds himself aloof and does not respond. Whatever form it takes, rejection by a parent is one of the most painful experiences a child can have. It gnaws away at their security and leads them to believe that they are unworthy of love. Though they search for love, they are afraid to let themselves experience it.

Not getting your dad's love and attention often leads to painful conclusions early in your life that still affect you today. Maybe you decided that you were unlovable and that you could never trust that a relationship would be permanent. Perhaps you felt that you would never be good enough, no matter how hard you tried. Or you feared that if you got close to someone they would reject you when they found out what you were "really" like.

Any number of self-defeating thoughts may keep you from experiencing the fulfillment and happiness you deserve. They may even have caused you to actively end relationships rather than run the risk of losing them.

Relationships: Breaking Up to Avoid Rejection

"I'm Always Afraid that the Men I Get Involved with Will Leave Me"

Pauline, an extremely attractive and vivacious woman in her mid-thirties, struggled with this burden. As a youngster, she experienced continual criticism from a father who actively rejected her overtures for affection, leading her to conclude that she was unworthy of attracting love. She was always afraid that the men she had attracted would find some reason to leave her. The thought was so devastating that after she reached a level of intimacy with a new partner that provided the possibility of a real commitment, her anxiety would rise to such levels that she inevitably caused a breakup rather than take a chance that she would be rejected and her partner would leave *her*.

"I'm always afraid that the men I get involved with will leave me the minute they find out what I'm really like," she said. "A lot of people have told me I'm attractive, but I just don't believe it. I usually set my sights on somebody I think is way out of my league and couldn't possibly be interested in me. That makes it safe for me to flirt with them and try to get them involved. But if they respond to me, I back off right away. I don't want them to get too close because I'm positive that they only *think* they know me—they don't know the *real* me.

"I know I come across as confident, but I'm actually very insecure about myself. My father was always criticizing my weight and how I looked. I'm afraid that when men find out I'm not who they think I am, they'll stop liking me. When they get serious, I find something to start a big fight about so that I can leave them first— before they leave me. That way it doesn't hurt as much. I really want to have a relationship, but I'm too scared."

Pauline's dilemma is not uncommon. Like so many others who come to therapy, she wanted love but was afraid of the vulnerability that being in love might expose her to. Despite her attractiveness, good personality and intelligence, deep down Pauline was still not convinced that she was good enough to retain love. But by facing her fears, Pauline could free herself from old, limiting beliefs and adopt new ways of thinking and relating.

As a first step, I suggested that Pauline start doing an affirmation. Every morning when she got up, and every night before going to bed, she was to look in the mirror, gaze directly into her eyes, and speaking with full conviction, she was to say the following words three times:

AFFIRMATION

"You deserve to be loved."

I instructed her to keep doing this for one month and notice her changing reactions. I told her that it might feel silly or be difficult to do at first, but that if she would keep looking into her eyes and saying the words every day, by the end of the month there would be some major shifts.

It is common to fear being unworthy of love. If you feel you do not deserve to have the kind of relationship you want, you might want to try the exercise I gave Pauline.

"I Never Got the Feeling There Was Love Between Them"

Philip, a highly respected scientist who has worked in the space program for most of his career, grew up with parents whom he described as having a "functional relationship." In their household, little emotion was displayed.

"We had a routine that operated like clockwork," Philip said, "but there was never any affection in our family. I can remember a couple of times when I was really young, running to my dad when he came home so he would pick me up, but he just pushed me away.

"My parents were held together mainly by their need for financial security. I never got the feeling that there was any real love between them. It's made it difficult in my own relationships, because I tend to push women away before they get too close. I have problems showing any affection, feeling or emotion. All my girlfriends have complained about the same thing—that I'm not loving and open enough. I'll live with a woman for two years, and she'll say, 'You know, I really don't know much about you.' I don't express myself; I hold things in. I'm a very affectionate person inside, but I'm just not able to show it on the outside."

If your father displayed little affection toward your mother, if problems were avoided rather than worked through or if communication centered mostly on the necessary exchange of information rather than the expression of deeper feeling, you may have similar difficulties in your relationships. Even if you've decided that you don't want to repeat that pattern in your own marriage, you might find, often to your horror, that you do—usually because although you know what you *don't* want to do, you don't know what *to do*.

Suggestions for overcoming fears of intimacy in relationships could fill an entire book. Self-help sections of bookstores are stocked with a wide variety of titles covering every aspect of relationship problems. Classes abound and newspapers, community organizations and churches all have announcements about what is available. Once you start checking, you will be surprised how many resources are available to help you.

INTIMACY EXERCISE

One important factor in achieving intimacy is the ability to speak the truth about how you feel, ask for what you want and respond genuinely. In this exercise, complete each sentence as honestly as possible. Your partner will sit and listen carefully and empathetically. When you are finished, your partner will complete the sentences while you listen.

It's natural to be hesitant to reveal yourself at first, but as you do the exercise and are listened to empathetically, it will become easier. Do the exercise three times every night for at least one week. No response is necessary from your partner. You are simply practicing revealing your feelings.

"I want _____."

"I need _____."

"I doubt _____."

"I prefer _____."

"I believe _____."

"I'm afraid _____."

"I hope _____."

"I appreciate _____."

Recommendation

Write down your reactions to this exercise in your journal. What were your feelings? Were you able to speak openly? What reactions were you aware of in your partner? What did you learn from this?

Adoption and Divorce

"Are You My Real Dad?"

The deepest wounds are sometimes caused by the best intentions. Adoption is a subject that was long shrouded in secrecy. When a child discovers a long-buried family secret, it can destroy their trust. Shirley was shaken by a deep sense of betrayal when she found out that the man she thought was her natural father was actually her stepfather. The information came in a particularly traumatic way.

"I was about ten years old," Shirley confessed, "and I was teasing my cousin about having a stepfather. He said, 'Well, you do too!' Of course I got very upset and told him he was crazy and a liar. That night at dinner, I said to my "father," 'Johnny told me that you're not my dad!' It was a very intense moment—everyone suddenly got quiet and the meal stopped. I was crying, my mother was crying, my stepfather was crying. I think something shifted in me at that point. I really felt like the odd man out. Although I used to ask him for things before that, I never went to my stepfather again for anything I wanted.

"My aunt told me that my biological father cared about me and that he used to send Christmas presents. But if he did, I was never told they were from him. When I was fourteen, I was finally legally adopted by my mother's husband. My mother said that my dad sent a letter saying, 'Give me money, and I'll let her go.' It was only then that my stepfather was finally able to adopt me. "I know it doesn't make sense, but the feeling I got was 'I wasn't good enough for my natural father, and I'm not good enough for my stepfather.' Because I wasn't really his, I felt like I wasn't good enough.

"Trust is the biggest issue of my life. I don't trust anybody. First, my biological father left me, and then they withheld the fact that I was adopted. After that, I always felt that I was the one who had to take care of me, because I couldn't trust anyone else. My relationships with men get crazy because I'm so afraid they'll leave me.

I wish they had told me, because deep down there was a part of me that always knew he was my stepfather."

Like many adults who felt abandoned, Shirley has spent a great deal of time resolving her father issues. Now, she knows that despite having been adopted there were many things that could have helped her feel connected to her stepdad. Her wish that she had been informed is good advice that many children who were adopted or gained a stepparent early in life might want their parents to know and to heed.

At some level, children usually know. Even at an early age they sense there is something special about their status. When a father has left, mothers should discuss it with their children in an age-appropriate and sensitive manner. Even if another man enters the family, it is best to continue talking about the absent father and about how the new husband is going to fit in. If parents are loving and gentle in their presentation of the facts, even very young children can hold the love for both fathers. Being informed by their parents protects them from the trauma of finding out from someone else—a shattering experience that destroys their ability to trust.

For the stepfather, the hardest fact to accept is that the child's biological parent is never completely absent. There is a natural tendency to want to eliminate him from the family's memory and start afresh, especially in cases of abandonment. But despite the desire to remove all traces, the absent father will linger in the child's mind, creating doubts, fantasies and "what if's." The healthiest solution is to acknowledge the existence of the other father and allow the child to hold a place for him in her or his heart.

"It Seemed Like He Stopped Caring About Us"

When a divorced father who has been emotionally distant remarries, children feel even more abandoned—a reaction that can lead to serious consequences in their relationships as adults. This was Kelly's painful experience. "I know that the reason I jump from relationship to relationship is because I've got such abandonment issues," she stated. "My father was never too crazy about having kids. He liked excitement and preferred being with his friends. He was also a real womanizer. My mother had the full responsibility for taking care of us.

"Even though we weren't that close, my world was rocked when they got a divorce when I was thirteen because my mother couldn't take his infidelity anymore. Until then, I was able to get at least some of his attention by being a good student and winning in sports competitions. He liked having a daughter he could brag about. But after the divorce, he made it very clear he didn't want anything to do with any of us. It's given me a lot of anxiety about finding the right relationship. I'm always afraid that the man I find won't be able to commit to me, or that no matter how well things look, he'll end up walking out on me anyway. It's made keeping a healthy relationship very difficult because I don't trust myself to know if I've made a good choice or not."

Adults who felt rejected or betrayed by their parents often extend that expectation to others who become significant parts of their lives. Fearing that, once more, those they love will turn their backs on them, they repeatedly question whether the relationship will last and often place demands for reassurance on their partner that eventually become burdensome and may even lead to the very thing they fear most—their partner starts to feel overwhelmed by their needs and backs away.

The fact that Kelly is cognizant of this pattern, however, means that she can change it. By recognizing that projecting her fears of abandonment onto her partners may bring about what she fears most and deciding to change her habitual ways of thinking and acting, she has started to take charge of her life. Instead of being at the mercy of her emotional needs, she is learning how to fill those needs for love successfully.

One thing she has started to do is to write down a list of goals for herself—goals like resolving her anger at her father and preparing herself for a new relationship based on mutuality. By breaking down her goals into small, manageable steps and setting a target date for their accomplishment, she keeps herself on track and gets the satisfaction of viewing her progress. Small goals lead to larger goals, taking her on the path to reaching her ambition. Put your goals in writing. Each step, no matter how tiny, leads to your ultimate fulfillment.

Getting to the Summit: A Goal-Setting Exercise

One way to break down the steps to your goal is to imagine that your goal is at the top of a mountain with a trail that leads up to it from where you are now standing. The summit is your ultimate goal, where you are now is your base, and the camping areas are the in-between steps that will get you there.

In your journal, describe "Base Camp"—where you are now in your life. Put all the important facts about you and your life in here. What are your inner strengths, ambitions, doubts, fears? How will you overcome them? This is what you will build on.

Then describe your ultimate goal, the "Summit." Be very specific. Is it to have a more loving relationship in which both you and your partner feel fulfilled and valued? Do you want to maintain a strong family life, raising a happy family with healthy children? Are your desires for a fulfilling career in which you both can grow? Your ultimate goal is what will determine the steps in between—so although all the steps are important, this is the most important part of the exercise.

Now tear up some sheets of paper until you have a pile of approximately fifty 2-by-3-inch paper slips. (People really love to do this in therapy—it breaks every rule of adult decorum.) On each slip, write down a step you need to take to get from where you are to your ultimate goal. These steps can be tiny or large—it doesn't matter. It also doesn't matter what order you record them in. Approach this as a brainstorming session—the idea is just to get all the steps out. Don't judge—just write!

Once you have all your steps written on the slips of paper, it's time to start shuffling. Go through all the steps and arrange them in sequence from the first step you must take until the summit. You might decide a short break will be needed after some steps before you continue your journey. These are the "Camping Areas."

You can create a ladder from your slips of paper. You might want to glue each one to a separate page in your journal so you can record your progress. Or, you might want to create a collage from photos and other materials to track your progress. Have fun! Life is a journey, and you can help it unfold in the way that is most satisfying to you.

A goal-setting exercise for resolving anger at your father might work like this:

Base Camp (Where I am now in my life): Unresolved feelings of anger at my father for the hurt, criticisms, rejection or other painful memories from the past.

List your strengths and weaknesses, and state how you will overcome weaknesses such as doubt, fear and self-criticism. For example, "I will keep a list of affirmations by my side"; "I will visualize a positive thought every time I start to criticize myself."

Ultimate Goal/Summit: Set a goal such as "a loving, mutually respectful relationship with my father."

Intermediate Steps: Tear up paper until you have a stack of 2-by-3-inch paper slips. Brainstorm. Let yourself go into free-flow, and for ten minutes write down every sane, outrageous, trivial, ridiculous, logical, funny or impossible idea that comes to mind about how you could reach your goal. Write as quickly as possible without stopping until the ten minutes are over. Among your steps, list techniques you have already learned in this book, such as using affirmations of your intent, visualizing yourself achieving your goal, substituting positive thoughts when you begin to doubt yourself and reading the books in the Bibliography. If the situation is severe, a few sessions of psychotherapy might help you get started in the right direction. Do not judge or analyze what you're writing—you want to tap into your creative thinking. To paraphrase Einstein, "Solutions do not arise from what is already known."

When you're done, take a ten-minute break. Take a walk, listen to relaxing music or sit quietly. Then come back, take a few deep breaths to center yourself and look through your slips of paper, putting aside those ideas that are not practical and sorting the others into groups from the simplest steps that you can implement now to those that are more difficult and will take more time.

Track your progress in your journal, noting how it feels to take those steps and the changes you observe occurring in yourself and in your father.

Processes such as guided imagery, writing exercises and the rituals described in other chapters as well as the workbook section can also be modified to deal with anger or other specific needs.

Learning About Love and Marriage

We all want a "marriage made in heaven." If you grew up in a warm, loving household, you were given an incredible opportunity to absorb the abilities essential to create one of your own. You witnessed firsthand how marriage and family bonds are cemented by attentive gestures, ready laughter, spontaneous demonstrations that say, "I love you," open communication and the ability to clear the air quickly of any potential problems. You also saw the power of nonverbal communication: the relationship-enhancing qualities of courtesy, dependability and freely expressed affection.

Great marriages also illustrate the importance of *attitude* to a gratifying relationship. The spouses in these relationships are conscious of what so many married couples forget—that romantic love is a living organism that must be nurtured by playfulness, humor, spontaneity, consideration, lots of affection, courtesy and respect. The thoughtfulness that these partners show to one another keeps the original romance alive and allows love to grow and deepen during a lifetime of marriage.

Too many individuals believe or have been taught that romance is for courtship and marriage is serious business. It *is* serious. It's the most life-shaping decision anyone can make. But it needs to be lighthearted and joyful too. If the fun goes out of marriage, so does the romance and the passion—leaving only an empty shell.

If you missed out on watching a great relationship, you can still create one for yourself by acquiring the needed skills now. The good news is that there are numerous ways to obtain these capabilities besides growing up with them. There have never been more resources available to help you master relationship competence. Seminars, books, tapes, civic organizations, religious institutions and marriage counseling professionals can help you gain the expertise to create the deeply satisfying and loving marriage you deserve. And they can give you the tools to improve relationships in every area of your life.

Appreciate yourself for being willing to learn and grow in your relationships. Imagine the kind of relationship you want, and go for it. Your efforts will make your life infinitely richer and more filled with joy.

CHAPTER 8

In My Father's Footsteps:
Career Choices and Work Attitudes

We put our love where we have put our labor.
—RALPH WALDO EMERSON

How Fathers Influence Career Choices

Whether Dad was a blue-collar worker, executive, professional or small businessman, his opinions and experience influenced your education and career goals. Before women became a major factor in the workforce, it was your father who usually had the knowledge and practical experience to guide you into the world of work; his perspective most often shaped your own attitudes and aspirations. How much importance he placed on job security, monetary reward, professional prestige or independence were significant factors in your own career views and decisions.

The closer the bond, the greater the influence. If economic circumstances prevented your father from pursuing the higher education he desired, perhaps his love of learning and respect for scholarship prompted you to seek a career in which academic achievement was prized. Spirited debates around the dinner table in which you were expected to defend your views might have fostered the same challenging stance in business meetings. Or your father may have shared his plans for business expansion during your quiet moments together, leading you to incorporate that same far-ranging vision into your own future career plans.

A father who started work on a production line after graduating high school and spent most of his working life with one employer might place emphasis on steady work, good benefits and a pension plan. A management-oriented dad might emphasize the opportunity for advancement and financial benefits afforded in a large corporation. If your father was in one of the professions, you might have admired the prestige that was accorded to him and been inspired to enter it yourself. A dad who started his own business might have inspired you to take calculated risks in order to work independently.

One of my father's favorite sayings was "Better to own a peanut stand and it's yours, than to work for somebody else." Although I didn't realize it at the time, his independent, individualistic stance has definitely colored my life and made me strive for self-reliance. The rewards of autonomy and the ability to choose my own direction have outweighed the hazards and uncertainties of self-employment.

Your father influences not only your career choice but also your attitudes toward the role work plays in your life. This can take the form of assuming his habits and ways of thought or of concluding that you will do things differently. If your father stressed that the family came first and turned down career opportunities because they interfered with family life, you too might opt to forego advancement in order to ensure that you can devote more time to your home life. If his career consumed most of his energy so that little time was left for his wife and children, you may also find yourself struggling with maintaining balance between career and family obligations— or, because you saw the negative effect his career had on the family, you may deliberately have chosen a field where such conflicts would not exist. Alternatively, Dad's discontent with his employment might have led you to view work as a necessary impediment to more fulfilling activities.

If you were not encouraged to pursue career aspirations, you may have doubts about your abilities that led you to curtail your ambitions. Rather than aiming for what you want, you might have settled for what you thought you could attain—holding back from pursuing opportunities because you believe others will judge you unqualified.

If employment is a source of dissatisfaction in your life, be aware that it is never too late to develop new skills or refocus your current ones. Work and work-related activities consume approximately 40 percent of your existence. It is possible to create a satisfying career. An excellent way to start opening new avenues of thought is to read books and attend seminars to help you discover where your true interests and talents, lie. Adult education classes at community colleges offer courses ranging from art to zoology. Try something new. See where your creativity leads you!

JOURNAL EXERCISE

To put you in the right frame of mind for your journal exercise, start by sitting quietly for a few moments. Take a deep breath in order to center yourself. This quiets the "chatter" in your brain and allows your nonverbal, intuitive wisdom to arise.

Write down the five things you most want from work at this moment in your life. Which of these is your *most* important priority? Which item would be *easiest* to accomplish at this time? What would be the first small step you could take to achieve it? When will you take that step? How? Make a written contract with yourself that you will take that step.

Contract

I, _____ , hereby contract to take the first step toward achieving a satisfying career. The step I will take is

_____

_____

I will take the step on the date of _____ with the following action: _____

_____

_____

In Witness whereof, I sign my name: _____

"My Dad Is an Attorney"

Male college freshmen studied by C. E.Werts in the 1960s reflected the influence of their fathers. Werts found that more than 40 percent of physicians' sons went into medicine, and almost 30 percent of attorneys' sons went into law. Blue collar workers' sons also followed in their fathers' footsteps, often going to work in the same factory as their fathers, unless greater educational achievement directed them to more prestigious occupations. Today, of course, these trends would apply to daughters as well as sons.

The respect and admiration he saw his father receive inspired Stuart, a public relations consultant who is active in many professional organizations. "My dad is an attorney who belongs to many organizations and has always been very active in community affairs," Stuart said. "He's very humorous, so he's always asked to speak whenever one of the groups has a special function. I didn't want to be an attorney, but I did want to be a good communicator and get the recognition from others that he did.

"I also wanted to be around the kind of people he associated with, people who were influential and involved with the community. In my job, I work with powerful people and frequently speak in public. I'm comfortable with it because I used to watch my father and imagine myself doing the same thing."

Stuart's father served the function of a personal effectiveness coach. Taking Stuart along as he mingled with community leaders was an extremely effective way to teach his son to be comfortable in public and not be intimidated by meeting a wide range of people. Whether you are the heir to a throne who early on learns to respond to public adulation, the child of a president who meets heads of state or the son or daughter of a local official who attends numerous events, watching your father function in public gives you a valuable preview of what is possible and helps shape your plans for your own future career.

Women also aspire to follow in their fathers' footsteps, although historically, daughters were treated quite differently than sons. In the past, boys were expected to be the primary breadwinners for the families they would eventually raise. They were groomed to follow in their fathers' footsteps, taking over the family farm or business, or educated for a trade or profession. Girls were trained to become mothers, wives and housekeepers. The skills they were taught related primarily to those of maintaining a home and family. During World War II, "Rosie the Riveter" went to work in factories and performed the jobs formerly done by men. But at the end of the war, as the GI's returned home, so did Rosie. Women were once more relegated to being either housewives or secretaries, nurses and elementary school teachers.

Today, the situation is dramatically different. Present-day fathers are much more likely to encourage their daughters to strive for the ambitions once exclusively directed to their sons. In fact, many fathers conscientiously expose their daughters to experiences and expectations that were formerly only a male province. They value their daughters' abilities and want to develop them to their highest potential. They also acknowledge the economic reality that today's family usually requires two incomes and that a family's standard of living may depend as much on a woman's education and earning power as on a man's.

"My Dad Was a Genius Even Without a Formal Education"

There have always been some fathers, even in the past, who were far ahead of their time and prepared their daughters for jobs that were once considered "men's work," encouraging them to follow their ambitions regardless of traditional gender restrictions.

Sally, a dynamic woman whose trademark is her bright red pickup truck, has long played an active role in women's business organizations. Her immigrant father's faith in real estate, emphasis on independence and hard work, and example of "fixing up" and "making do" were a direct channel to her own career choice.

"My dad was a genius," Sally declared. "Even though he had no formal education, he could figure out how to fix or build anything. In fact, he once built a boat in our backyard so he could sail to Hawaii. No one showed him how—he just bought the plans and worked out how to do it.

"My dad was a firm believer in real estate. He would buy old houses, remodel them and then sell them. My brothers and I helped him repair every house he bought as I was growing up. I also helped out in his used furniture store, which is where I think I picked up some of his business skills.

"I learned a lot of things from my dad, but as far as my career goes, the main thing I gleaned was his belief in real estate. I bought my first house when I was twenty-one, got my broker's license when I was twenty-four and have been buying, selling, and fixing up houses ever since. Because of my father, I am independent and know I can succeed."

Her father's lack of distinction in his treatment of her and her brothers gave Sally invaluable training about home construction and real estate that directly led to starting to her own business. His maverick attitude bestowed an additional benefit. By dreaming big, her father taught her that she could draw "outside the lines" and not be deterred by preconceived restrictions. In addition to practical skills, she received a mind-set that laid the foundation for lifelong financial independence.

"He Treated Me Like a Son"

When a family business is involved, some fathers have their hearts set on its being taken over by a son. In the absence of sons, they must look to their daughters to carry on the tradition. Barbara's father, owner of a large construction company, also exposed her to nontraditional career training. When he realized he would never have a son, her father decided that Barbara would carry on the business and trained her as his heir apparent. Today, she is as much at ease wearing a hard hat to climb around a construction site as sitting in a conference room to meet with a finance committee.

"My father was very anxious to have a son to carry on his construction business," Barbara stated. "But my mother was told she couldn't have any more children after I was born. My dad decided to treat me as if I was a son and make sure I had all the same opportunities. He encouraged me to go out for sports, and he was very proud when I became captain of the girls' soccer team. He used to come to all our games and cheer me on.

"Saturdays he would take me to the office, or take me with him while he drove around to different job sites. That's one of the most special times I remember with my dad, riding with him to look at property he wanted to buy. To me it looked like just an empty field with weeds, but he would share with me his visions of houses and people living in them.

"When I was fourteen I started working for my dad, helping out at the office or running errands. I learned how to read plans and do estimates. He expected a lot from me, but it was fun too. My father's going to retire next year, and my husband and I will take over the business. I really hope that one of my kids, either my son or my daughter, will want to get involved. My dad would be thrilled to have three generations of our family working for the company!"

Today, more and more young women are exposed to their father's work and follow Dad's footsteps into similar careers. Sally learned about buying, selling and remodeling old homes by working side by side with her father. Barbara was purposefully groomed to take over her father's business. Both received an enormous advantage from the informal training and early encouragement to follow their career interests. But even those fathers who are unable to provide such direct experiences can discuss their work or take daughters and sons to visit their workplace in order to expand their horizons.

"If You Ever Fish for a Living, I'll Break Your Hands!"

Some fathers would do almost anything to *prevent* their children from following in their footsteps. The hardships they have encountered have fueled their determination that their offspring aim higher when planning careers. Andy's father supported his family by working on fishing boats most of his life. He felt so strongly that his son should accomplish more that he told him, 'If you ever fish for a living, I'll break your hands!'

"He was only half joking," Andy commented. "I knew that what he really meant to say was 'I didn't have the chance to get an education, so I had to work with my hands. But you have the opportunity, so use your head.' Education was very important to my father. He couldn't go to college because he had to drop out of school and support the family when my grandfather died. That made him all the more set on my getting the education I needed. He was really proud of me when I started my own business consulting firm a few years ago. It was like a wish come true for him. He enjoys my success as much as I do."

"My Dad Couldn't Help Me"

Some fathers are unable to provide any guidance at all. They may lack the knowledge of available opportunities, have lost touch with their children, be too involved in their own affairs or simply believe that they do not have adequate information or expertise. If you missed out on having a father who could give you career guidance, you probably feel a sense of loss and believe that things would have turned out better if you had been given direction earlier in your life.

Terry, who manages a popular catering business, was relaxing after a morning of delivering orders. Her enthusiasm, high energy and dedication to satisfying her customers have helped Terry succeed in a highly competitive business. But she spoke wistfully about how much she had yearned for a father who would "sit me down like my friends' dads did and say, 'Okay, you're in your third year of high school now. If you want to go to college, you'd better start saving money. Let's look at some programs you could apply to.' But that's not where he was coming from.

"I saw my girlfriends' dads doing that for them. They were all in professional fields and were able to advise them. They could map out a plan for them about where they were going. Like, 'Okay, you're going to do this, then you're going to law school, here are some choices about college.' Basically, everything was set up for them. My dad's a blue-collar worker and he worked long hours and sometimes two jobs to support five children. He didn't have any information, and he didn't know what to tell me. He really couldn't guide me to the goals I wanted.

"Actually, when I look back, I gained my independence because of that, although I regretted it a lot at the time. My parents always just lived paycheck to paycheck, and I realized at a young age that

I didn't want my life to be a struggle like theirs. I went to work at fifteen and I haven't stopped since."

Career choices can be made from knowing what you *don't* want as well as what you do. Andy's father was adamant that his son not follow him onto the fishing boats. Terry was equally determined that she would have a better life than her parents did. Being thrown onto her own resources early played a powerful role in motivating her to be independent and career successful.

Fathers and the Work Ethic

As is true of the general population, fathers' attitudes toward work vary widely. Some grudgingly accept it as a necessity of existence that must be complied with; some have developed close relationships that make otherwise routine employment enjoyable; some are loyal workers who are proud of their spotless record of performance; some find their work a major source of satisfaction.

How your father approaches his occupation, how he carries out his job and the value he places on the concept of work itself has an enormous bearing on how you look at it. If Dad disliked his position and often expressed the desire to be doing something different, you might react by carefully selecting the field that you enter. If your father felt that work was a rewarding avenue for creating a product or service that benefits others, then you too might have chosen an occupation that allows you to help people. Pride in fine craftsmanship, the ability to run a department smoothly, or gratification in serving the needs of patients or customers are the kinds of examples that can influence where you find satisfaction in your own work life.

"Is Your Hair Shirt Scratching?"

The work ethic can be carried to extremes. When it is, you are likely to bear the brunt of Dad's obsession with keeping busy in gainful labor. You might even unwillingly carry this trait over to your own adult life.

Constance, whose family has lived in New England for generations, grew up in a home where the Puritan ethic still ruled. Work was considered to be a religious duty, and in the rare moments when Constance was not busy with some chore, her father invariably asked her, "Is your hair shirt scratching?"

A hair shirt is a shirt woven of extremely coarse, scratchy hair—usually horsehair or boar's hair—that is worn over the bare skin to prick and irritate it. It was worn by monks in medieval times in order to achieve self-discipline and spiritual elevation. Her father's comment was a reminder that ease and comfort were to be avoided at all costs.

"It was a very stern attitude toward life," Constance said. "It was very clear to me that anything that felt good or was pleasurable was considered wrong. If it was enjoyable, it was bad. If you were having fun, you weren't working hard enough. Leisure was to be avoided at all costs. The message I got was that duty has to be onerous and burdensome. The way it's affected me is that no matter how much work I load on myself, I never feel I'm doing enough."

As professor and department chair in a small New England college, Constance regularly finds herself taking on more responsibilities than she really wants or can handle. "Everybody's problems seem to land on my desk," she said, "but I've finally decided that I'm not going to be a workhorse anymore. Life is too short—I'm going to start taking time for the things I enjoy!"

There's a huge difference between having a strong work ethic and not being able to say "No" when it's appropriate. A strong work ethic is inner-directed: You enjoy your work, carrying out your responsibilities gives you a sense of gratification and you find personal satisfaction in honoring the implicit bargain between employer and employee—"an honest day's work for an honest day's pay."

Taking on more work than you can handle because you feel compelled to try to cope with whatever is assigned is an altogether different matter. When you attempt to do more than you know is reasonably possible, you are probably driven by fear of punishment. You fear the negative consequences you have come to associate with disobeying authority—an attitude formed early in life, as in Constance's case.

To cope with this problem, you need to do two things: First, realize that your present behavior is based on anxieties that might have been valid in the past but no longer reflect your reality today; and second, reevaluate your priorities—actually make a list of what you value in your life and, like Constance, make a decision about where you will draw the line.

Constance found the following two exercises very helpful. The first is a mini-relaxation exercise that she was able to do at her desk during lunch to help her unwind and clear her thoughts. The second assisted her in discovering her true values and then setting priorities that would allow her to express them.

RELAXATION EXERCISE

This exercise will help you relax quickly and easily. You can easily do it at your desk, or in any quiet place, whenever you have about ten minutes. Or you can do it when you get home as a way to unwind.

Just sit comfortably, allowing yourself to relax in a favorite chair, or lie down if you're sure you won't fall asleep. Rest your hands in your lap. Uncross your legs and let your feet rest flat on the floor. Take a few deep, slow breaths, let your eyes close, and allow your body become more relaxed. Imagine the outside world drifting away, and focus on your breath going in and out.

Continue your easy, relaxed breathing, and imagine that the tension in your head and neck are flowing down and away. Take another deep breath and feel the tension in your back, your chest and your stomach flowing out as you exhale. Now, feel your legs becoming very relaxed and all the tension flowing out through your toes. Continue to breathe in and out a few times, slowly and rhythmically. Then breathe deeply, and as you exhale, feel any remaining tension flowing out of your body.

Stay in this comfortable space for a few more minutes. Then imagine a ball of golden energy surrounding you and filling you with a deep sense of well-being. The golden energy is flowing all through you and filling you with vitality. Absorb this energy, and feel it spreading throughout your body—a warm, radiant, liquid glow of energy. Absorb as much of this radiant energy as you want. Then, remember this feeling of well-being and slowly move your head, then your arms and shoulders. Feel your back against the chair and open your eyes. Notice how much more refreshed and energized you feel.

VALUES AND PRIORITIES EXERCISE

Ideally, priorities are values in action. Values are the components of our internal belief system, and priorities are how we actively manifest them in daily life—they are the reflection of our values. But the priorities that most of us follow in our lives are not true to our values. They are there by default, happening almost by chance. This exercise will help you discover your true values and use that knowledge about your most deeply held beliefs and desires to organize your priorities.

Rank order the following values, with 1 being your highest values, 2 the next highest, and so forth. There are no right or wrong answers.

Values

_____ *Comfort and prosperity*

_____ *Equality and opportunity for everyone*

_____ *Excitement, stimulation and change*

_____ *Family*

_____ *Freedom and independence*

_____ *Happiness*

_____ *Peace of mind*

_____ *Mature love, including sexual and spiritual intimacy*

_____ *National security*

_____ *Pleasure and leisure*

_____ *Self-respect*

_____ *Achievement, sense of accomplishment*

_____ *Status, prestige, admiration*

_____ *Friendship, companionship*

_____ *Wisdom*

_____ *Good health*

_____ *World peace*

_____ *Nature, the environment*

_____ *Financial security*

Use your journal to record your discoveries about yourself. Were you surprised at your preferences? Were some choices hard to make? What do you have to do to put your values into action so that they are expressed in your life? Discovering what you truly want is a process. Add to your journal entry as new insights occur.

"My Dad Is Very Meticulous . . ."

Alex, a tile setter who has worked in many celebrity homes, prides himself on adhering to the high standards and fastidious approach to his work that he acquired from his father. "My dad is very meticulous, very structured in how he does things," Alex said. "He's very complete, very precise—a real craftsman. He doesn't leave anything to chance. He takes the extra time to make sure the job is done right. There were plenty of times that I got chewed out for not putting tools away or leaving his workbench a mess. It had a big effect on me as I grew up and understood the reasons for what he did. I have the utmost respect for my dad because he's the epitome of the honest, hard-working person.

"I have people who call me twice a year, even if they don't need any work done," he boasts, "just to make sure I haven't moved and they can still get a hold of me if they need me."

Alex learned a craftsman's pride in excellence that gives his work integrity and makes him much in demand. Many interviewees spoke of how the work ethic their fathers passed on shaped their behavior: coming in to work on time, not engaging in personal business during work hours and doing a good day's work, whether working for someone else or self-employed.

"My Father Was a Man of His Word . . ."

Robert, a contractor who specializes in building custom homes, is another craftsman who spoke with pride of how greatly he was influenced by his father's integrity.

"My dad was a man of his word," Robert said. "He set an example that I still live by. If he said he would do something, you could count on it. I try to keep my word too.

"In the contracting business, a lot of things can happen that are out of my control. But if I promise to have something ready by a certain date, I'll bend over backward to make sure my customers get it. Like my dad, I like to seal agreements with a handshake. I know that things are different today, but I want people to know that my word is as good as a contract."

Example is the strongest teacher. Whether you accept an ever-increasing workload that never allows you time for leisure, take pride in maintaining high standards of craftsmanship or honor your commitments to perform as you have promised, what you observed in your father's daily performance and his attitude toward work made an indelible impression that is reflected in your current life.

Even if you didn't learn good work habits and attitudes, however, it is not too late to acquire them. Look around at co-workers and notice those who enjoy their work and excel at it. They can be your mentors. You can observe their attitudes and choose one or two traits that you would like to incorporate into your own behavior, then practice modeling yourself after them. If you feel close enough to them, you can also ask what gives them satisfaction about their job. For example, you might say, "I notice you have a real upbeat attitude about your work. How do you maintain that?" They might answer something like "I really like working with people," or "I like solving problems." Their answer will give you a clue that can give you direction about some part of your job that you can start to find satisfaction in.

Competition Between Father and Son

Not all fathers encourage their children, however. Sometimes children want to follow in their father's footsteps but are denied the opportunity by a father who is determined to remain in a superior position relative to his son. Competition between equals can be a spur to achievement. But if a father is driven to compete against his son and defeat him, instead of fostering his growth so that the son can eventually take the father's place, the struggle can destroy more than their relationship.

In the best of all worlds, the old pass on their skills to the young, and as their own powers wane they gain satisfaction from the younger generation who rise to take their place. Such fathers take pleasure in training their offspring for adulthood and rejoice in their maturing abilities. The baton gets passed gracefully from one generation to another.

Competition between a father and son stems from a father's fear that he will lose power and that his son will outdo him. To keep his control and prevent his son from becoming an independent adult, this type of father is likely to place restrictions that deny his son the ability to act effectively, belittle his efforts or exert so much pressure on his son that he feels he can never meet his father's demands.

"Everyone Knew I Was the Boss's Kid"

Raymond is typical of men whose fathers are unwilling to share power with them and do everything to ensure that their sons will never surpass, or even equal, them. "Right after I graduated from high school, I started working for my father in the family building supply business," Raymond said. "Everyone knew I was the boss's kid and had never worked there before a day in my life. I wasn't like a kid who knows his way around because while growing up he worked with his father on weekends. I felt like a fool. The employees would ask me to get things, and I didn't have the slightest idea what they were talking about. So after two months, I told my father, 'I don't need this business. I don't need this aggravation.' I went into the army, but a few months later I was discharged for medical reasons and went back to live with my parents.

"I got experience from a few other jobs and then went back to work for my father again. I stayed there for the next twenty-four years. After about sixteen years, he made me president of the company. But I was president in name only, because he became chairman of the board and still gave all the orders. I was the president, but he was the boss.

"The business was his whole life; he lived and died for the business. On the weekend, you had to be at the office at least till 2:00 P.M. on Saturday and sometimes even on Sunday. That was how you showed you cared. I did that for years and years because I felt that he expected it of me.

"My kids got used to my not being there on Saturdays, and my marriage was disintegrating. I started going to the office just to get away from my wife. Finally I said, 'This is ridiculous!' I felt like my life was falling apart and I would die at my desk like my father. So I went into therapy, and it took me a long time, but I finally realized that my father tried to keep me from being successful because he was so used to being the leader in his field. He was known throughout the region, and he couldn't bear sharing the spotlight with anyone. He always had to keep me off-balance. For years and years, he threatened to fire me, for all sorts of reasons. I finally figured out he never would. How would it look to all his friends if he fired his own son?

"I'm starting all over again at a time when most of the guys I know are planning their retirement. But I finally understood that I would never have any control over my life as long as I was working for him. He would never give up that power. So I resigned and moved across the country and have started a business here with one of my sons. I'm trying to give my son the responsibility and support I didn't get. I want to make sure I don't make the same mistakes with him that my father did with me."

Raymond has struggled for years with the feelings of powerlessness and frustration that came from being put in a position in which he was nominally in charge but lacked any real authority. His experience is a textbook example of the double bind, a situation in which no matter what you do, you lose. Raymond was given one message verbally—"You're the president of the company, and you're responsible if anything goes wrong,"—and a completely different message from his father's behavior, which clearly said, "I'm still the boss. I control the information, and you can't make a move without me."

This situation kept Raymond feeling helpless and frustrated until he finally became aware of how much he was losing both self-respect and the respect and love of his wife and children. As he progressed in therapy, he began to see the workings of the psychological web that imprisoned him, and he made the decision to escape. The inner strength he gained helped him not only to break free but also to realize that he had to stop the cycle of power and dependence that would rob his own son of his manhood. Personal experience taught him how vital it is to treat his son as an equal and build a true partnership.

Psychological webs such as the one Raymond struggled in become ever more confining and unendurable. The victim increasingly loses confidence in his ability to act independently and eventually gives up. At some point, as in Raymond's case, there is usually a life-saving realization that the break must be made; but because the emotional binds are strong, this can be very hard to achieve without support.

The complexity of the psychological dynamics involved, and the guilt and shame such individuals feel, mean that professional assistance is often the most effective method for extricating oneself. Such assistance can be found by looking in the Yellow Pages under Psychologists or Counselors, or by calling your local or state Psychological Association.

Bosses and Mentors: Father Figures on the Job

A male boss is the workplace equivalent of Dad. He has prestige, authority and the ability to direct your actions. Any issues you might have with your father almost invariably come to life in your relationship with him. If you had a good relationship with your father, you are likely to get along well with your boss and be tolerant of his flaws. If you had a poor relationship with your father, for whatever reason, the same issues that plagued you in your relationship with your father are likely to carry over to your relationship with superiors and create problems at work.

Just like fathers, bosses run the gamut from supportive and nurturing to distant or hostile. Some have good leadership skills and direct their employees in ways that lead them to feel ownership of their work. Others undermine their employees' confidence by holding back information, refusing to delegate authority or not backing them up when necessary.

Mentors, who help promising newcomers up the ladder, are

another workplace equivalent of Great Dads. Historically, they were powerful older men with senior status who took an interest in up-and-coming executives and groomed them for important positions. Today, the definition has expanded. A mentor is any person, male or female, who takes you under their wing and gives you the benefit of their experience and expertise. They are the on-the-job coaches whose interest and acumen are invaluable aids to success.

"He Was a Good Role Model"

Early in his sales career, Scott had a mentor who inspired the same admiration as a Great Dad. He treated his subordinates with respect, empowered them to do their best and gave them an example to strive for. "He was the only boss I ever had who treated me and the rest of the guys like equals," Scott said. "He was democratic, not autocratic. He socialized with us and had us over to his house for barbecues. He was a good role model; he was young, owned a very successful business, had a nice house and had a beautiful wife and two adorable little girls. I looked up to him. I knew he was my boss, yet he never held that over my head. He didn't need to; he earned my respect, and I got the job done for him.

"Since then, I've managed other people in most of my positions. I've always remembered his example and tried to do the same for those I was in charge of. We were inspired to work hard for him, and I want the people who work for me to feel the same way."

Great mentors, like Great Dads, teach by example and encourage employees to emulate their strengths. Scott was inspired by the excellent role model he found so early in his career. It was very useful training that showed him the power of respect in motivating others, and it gave him real-life experience with principles that he now uses to instill confidence in his own employees.

Great bosses, like Great Dads, often develop an intuitive sense about those they manage. They are able to pinpoint problems an employee is unwilling to admit but that are serious handicaps to career development. Their ability to call attention to problems so they can be corrected can literally save an employee's career.

"I Was Expecting Him to Chew Me Out"

Personality problems can sabotage the most promising career. Peter, a rising scientist for a government agency, developed a reputation for being hard to get along with. He regularly became entangled in skirmishes with managers, co-workers and support staff. "I have a lot of distrust for authority because when my dad got angry he would yell at me. Sometimes he would slap me in the face or slam me up against the wall," Peter said. "That might have something to do with the fact that I don't trust anybody who tries to control me.

"I've always been something of a maverick. The best boss I've ever had understood that. I remember one time I got into a big fight with one of the maintenance supervisors. It was about something really stupid, but it got back to my boss. I was expecting him to chew me out, but after he asked me what happened, he just said, 'Did you have trouble with your father?'

"It really blew me away that he would say that! It made me stop and think about how many of my actions, especially my anger, might stem from the way I felt about my father. I never felt like I was loved at all. I remember how much I wanted his respect and affection. Instead, I always felt defeated and humiliated. As soon as I could, I moved as far away from home as possible.

"Since that talk with my boss, I've become a lot more aware of how I react to people. I don't want to be carrying this monkey on my back forever. I've made a conscious effort to be more accepting of people and not immediately think that somebody's going to start finding fault with me or criticizing my work."

Peter's boss's insightful intuition that the relationship with his father was at the root of his problems shocked Peter into recognizing how damaging his automatic reactions were. The sudden flash of recognition was the wake-up call he needed to put the past behind him and start learning new ways of relating to others. It was certainly unusual that his boss recognized that Peter's poor relationship with authority figures was due to troubled relations with his father. But he was right on target in his shrewd realization that a reprimand would be counterproductive and that identification of the true nature of the problem was what Peter required.

COUNTERING AUTOMATIC REACTIONS EXERCISE

This exercise is similar to the Automatic Thought Log in chapter 2. Whenever you notice that you are having an automatic reaction, use this exercise to check out the reality of the situation so that you can act appropriately. Write down the five steps, and fill in each with the automatic reaction you are having. The following is an illustration of how this works, using Peter's story as an example.

1. Incident causing automatic reaction

Being confronted by maintenance supervisor about having car parked in the wrong lot.

2. Automatic negative reaction

Anger.

3. Automatic negative thought

"Who does he think he is? He can't tell me what to do!"

4. Reality check

"I shouldn't have parked there. He's just doing his job."

5. Reality-based action

Move car to employee parking lot.

Use this five-step process in your own daily interactions to give yourself a reality check when you get angry. A volatile temper usually stems from events that occurred long before the present situation. Practice counting to ten and breathing deeply between each step to calm yourself down, as suggested in chapter 7. Carrying an index card in your pocket listing the five steps is a good way to remind yourself to use them.

Recommendation

Write an account in your journal when you do this exercise. You'll notice that the more you do it, and the more aware you become of reality versus your irrational reactions, the less often those reactions will occur.

The Workplace "Family"

It is not uncommon for people to spend more time with the people they work with than with their immediate family. Relationships with people on the job can become second in importance only to those with your loved ones. You might get together after work, meet for activities over the weekend, help each other out with projects, support each other during difficult times and celebrate achievements together or commiserate over disappointments.

The job and your co-workers become like a second home with various people taking on different family roles. There is a father figure—the boss or supervisor—who sets the tone and whose approval everyone vies for; a mother figure—the boss's assistant or support staff—who plays a secondary but powerful role in making sure things run smoothly; and the kids—employees who make up the rest of the department and count on "Mom" and "Dad" to be fair about assignments and rewards and oversee the department's well-being. In today's workplace, father/ boss or mother/ nurturer roles can be assumed by either men or women.

"I Have a Lot of Very Bright People Working for Me"

Some managers make excellent workplace "fathers." They are firm but fair, lead by example, set achievable standards, enforce rules consistently, listen to those under them and help their employees to do their best. They encourage employees' growth, find creative ways to remunerate them if the budget doesn't have room for raises and help them advance in their careers. Keith, a senior manager for a large electronics corporation, is an excellent example of the "Great Dad" manager.

"I have a lot of very bright people working for me," Keith proclaimed, "so I don't really 'supervise' in the traditional sense. I think of myself more as a facilitator who keeps the group on task and motivated, and if they run into problems, I'm here to help them. In my position, I have to make sure top management is aware of what we're doing so that we get the funding we need to carry out our goals. Then I have to carry that message down to the people under me and be certain they understand where we're going and how their particular project ties into the overall picture.

"Sometimes personal issues come up and I have to be sensitive to individual needs. I remember one young man who had a lot of potential, but he'd had some previous problems that could have interfered with his work. I decided to take a chance on him, and although it was touch and go for a year or so, he finally got his life straightened out and has become one of our best performers.

"I also like to encourage people to continue to develop themselves," Keith went on. "One of our support staff, who has gotten a divorce recently, wanted to go back to college to finish getting her degree in accounting but had some fears about returning to school after such a long absence. She was also concerned about a possible conflict with work because of her class schedule. We talked about her future and where she might go in the company if she got her degree, and I encouraged her to move forward in what seemed to be a better direction for her."

Keith is the "Great Dad" at work. He provides leadership and acts as the interface between his "family" (his department) and the "outside world" (upper management). When problems come up, he helps resolve them. He also takes the time to get to know his "kids" on a personal basis and is confident enough to be flexible and supportive when it is in everyone's best interests.

"My Boss Never Even Says 'Hello'"

Managers who do not possess these skills and are unable to communicate with their subordinates create a very different result. A manager who is afraid of personal contact, discourages questions and refuses to hear feedback inevitably finds that employee morale and productivity suffer.

Barry, a highly skilled machinist who takes great pride in his work, says, "I bet I pass Carl in the hall a dozen times a day, but he has never once said 'Hello' or 'Good morning.' The only time he talks to me is when he's giving orders. He never gives me a chance to tell him what's going on. I might be in the middle of a rush job for somebody else, but he doesn't want to hear about it.

With everybody telling me what to do, he leaves it up to me to straighten things out. All he cares about is looking good to the higher-ups.

"Carl never even looks at you when he talks to you," Barry continued. "When I first started here I gave the job everything I had, but no one ever noticed. Now I do my job but I don't go the extra mile. Maybe that's not the right attitude, but I figure, 'Hey, if you don't care about me, why should I care about making you look good?'"

Carl is typical of managers who have never developed people skills, perhaps because of strained relationships with their own fathers. His curt manner clearly says, "You don't matter," and discourages both improvement of current operations and the prevention of future problems. This is a situation in which everybody loses.

Most people rank job satisfaction, work friendships and employment security as even more important than salary. Wherever we go, we have a natural tendency to create a "family," taking along with us whatever habits and values we learned early in life.

Those who have had problems with their father often transfer that attitude toward superiors and other authority figures or have difficulty exercising responsible supervision of subordinates. Some workers shrink into the background because they fear being criticized; others rebel against direction or silently resist and don't perform up to expectations. Employees who had good relationships with their father and view authority figures as benign are much more likely to take on new assignments, communicate progress to their boss and maintain a positive attitude toward their responsibilities.

The boss or Workplace Dad sets the tone for the entire organization—the "family" of employees that follow his lead: Some departments or businesses are known for their high morale and innovative employee suggestions. In others, workers are gripped by apathy or fear of making a mistake. Workplace Dads who understand their role will try to be positive models. They realize that their task is to bring everybody together so that the organization functions as a coherent whole. They make sure that all employees know what the expectations are, there is consistency in enforcement of rules and workers are encouraged to cultivate their skills and develop increasing autonomy. Like a real father, the Great Dad at work knows that his main job is to nurture his people's skills and confidence to the point where they can function without him.

| | | |

Whatever your concepts of work, your father was an important influence. If his influence was positive, you acquired a host of favorable impressions that swayed you to follow his lead. You may have admired the respect he was accorded, the fulfillment he found in his work, the dedication with which he pursued excellence or other job satisfactions that he exemplified and that affected your own career plans. If he voiced dislike of his job and found no enjoyment in it, you might have put extra effort into finding meaningful employment for yourself.

Dad's influence might also have been very subtle. Perhaps you are only now realizing how his views have shaped your own work outlook and aspirations, and you are deciding what to do about it. Many perspectives that are molded in childhood are unconscious and come into awareness only later in life. You might find that you are quite happy with many of your attitudes about work, but there might be others that you wish to change. Remember that you have the power to do so.

CHAPTER 9

Fathers as Guardians of the Flame:

Values, Beliefs and Community

*The need for devotion to something outside ourselves
is even more profound than the need for companionship.
If we are not to go to pieces or wither away, we all
must have some purpose in life; for no one can
live for themselves alone.*

—ROSS PARMENTER,

The Doctor and the Cleaning Woman

The values you live by and the world view you hold form your life. They determine your goals, influence your behavior, shape your relationships, sustain you during tough times and determine your level of involvement in the community. Traditionally, fathers, as heads of the household, were the major arbiters of family values, and even today, his beliefs regarding work, family, government, religion and other key elements of existence often play an important role in setting your own moral compass.

Teenage pregnancy, drug and alcohol addiction, school dropout and youth crime are often attributed to peer pressure, poverty, graphic depictions of sex and violence in the media, antisocial rap lyrics and other external factors. However, all these reasons fade in comparison to family influence. In the most comprehensive study ever done on teenage behavior, the National Longitudinal Study on Adolescent Health found that the single most important predictor of risky behavior was the degree of emotional closeness a young person had with their family.

Confirming what most parents intuitively know, the study concluded that a strong, loving family is *the* most important formative influence in a child's life—fortifying their child's moral and emotional immune system and instilling the ethical principles they will live by.

The reasons behind this finding are simple. Despite all the external pressures, children still want and need their families. An infant is neurologically wired to learn. The first years, when neuronal connections are still developing and every bit of information—every sight, sound and action—is absorbed in a burst of learning, are the most critical. Throughout life, but especially during early childhood, the actions that are witnessed, emotions that are conveyed and words that are spoken form the foundation for a child's world view. Is it safe? Is it consistent? Can it be trusted? Or is it violent? Unpredictable? Chaotic?

During the earliest years, words are useful, but a parent's actions speak infinitely louder. Children have not yet mastered language. They cannot express themselves as adults do. But they observe and react and store their feelings away. When fathers and families demonstrate caring, affection, responsibility, honesty, respect and trustworthiness, children absorb these qualities and express them in their own lives. When these elements are missing, due to lack of family bonds or a troubled home environment, a vacuum is created for other, more destructive influences to enter.

Psychologist Lawrence Kohlberg stated that children pass through six stages of moral development. In the first two stages, generally until age three, they have no sense of right or wrong. They simply try to avoid pain and gain rewards. In the next two stages, starting around age four, they strive to be "good" in order to avoid disapproval from parents and other caretakers; they also learn to obey rules and respect authority. In these first four stages children learn about the dictates and constraints of society.

Internal moral guidelines are developed in the last two stages. In the fifth stage, children start to base their actions on community standards and opinions, rather than fear of punishment by authority.

In the sixth and highest stage, individuals are guided by their own conscience to live a life based on moral principles.

The parent who spends the most time with the children generally exerts the most influence in the formation of moral character. However, fathers who have close relationships with their children and demonstrate desirable moral behavior themselves exercise a powerful influence on ethical development, instilling values that help children develop an internal moral compass, their own inner sense of right and wrong, that will guide them in their decisions and actions.

"My Father Stood Up for What He Believed In"

Tom's father, a judge who believed in putting his principles into action, passed the same passionate commitment on to him, particularly his battle against the mistreatment of animals. "I've always admired my father for standing up for what he believed in," Tom said. "Even when I was angry at him, I still wanted to be like him. As an adult, I've consciously modeled myself after the things I liked and respected about him.

"For example, my dad loves animals. I remember one time, he heard about a man who was abusing horses. He went out to the man's farm to investigate and saw that the reports were true. It was a horrendous scene. The horses had been tied up and left to starve to death. Some horses were dying, others were already dead and just lying there on the ground.

"My dad had this guy arrested. One of the things I admire most about my dad is that he doesn't just talk about things, he takes action. Whenever my dad felt he had some ability to right a wrong or do something about an injustice, he would *do* something about it, and I do too. I volunteer for Project Wildlife, which rescues animals that have been hurt and cares for them until they can be returned to their own habitat or to the local animal shelter. It feels good to help animals, because they really depend on you."

Tom received from his father not only a love of animals and desire to care for them but also an example of how to do so. Values he learned from his father of custodianship and compassion for helpless creatures moved him to alleviate their suffering—these are legacies that Tom treasures and that provide him great inner gratification.

"I Never Stole Again"

Honesty is another value that fathers pass on to their children. Dean, a flight engineer who grew up in the rural South, remembered an example of his father's honesty that left an indelible impression.

"I started hanging out with some local 'bad' kids," Dean said. "We used to steal cigarettes and go out in back of the barn and smoke them. One time, when my friends and I were at the store, I wanted an ice cream bar, but I didn't have enough money to buy it. So I thought, 'What the heck. Why don't I just take it?' The clerk caught me and I tried to play innocent. I insisted that I didn't steal it, but they called my father anyway.

"When he got to the store, my dad stuck up for me and said, 'If my son said he didn't take it, he didn't take it.' But all the way home, he kept questioning me. First, I told him I had found some money. Then, I said I thought I had paid for it. Then I said one of my friends gave it to me. I made up all this stuff, but I knew he knew I was lying, so I finally told him the truth.

"The next day, my dad got up extra early and drove forty-five miles to apologize to the clerk and tell him what really happened. It made me feel terrible! I never stole again. It wasn't his yelling at me that stopped me. It was his example of integrity that impressed me. He was the kind of man who would turn around and drive all the way back if you gave him too much change. He was just a really honest person."

Dean's story is a compelling illustration of the power of example to teach values. Nothing his father could have told him or done to him could have come close to matching the impression made by driving almost one hundred miles to apologize to the clerk and pay back the small amount owed. The value that his father placed on making amends for mistakes, being honest regardless of the amount involved and taking responsibility for one's actions was indelibly inscribed on Dean's conscience.

His father demonstrated one more thing: that Dean's moral development was more important to him than any possible inconvenience or embarrassment. And Dean responded by never stealing again.

"A Lot of Men Would Have Walked"

Some fathers take on such heroic proportions in their children's memories that these children find it hard to limit praise to a single example. Everything their dad did seems exemplary, from his smallest actions to his largest sacrifices. "A unique man, tremendously principled, who never shirked responsibility," is how Calvin summed up his father's personality.

"I have tremendous admiration for the way my dad lived his life," Calvin said. "A few years after my parents married, it was discovered that my mother had diabetes, which was a very serious illness in those days. A lot of men would have walked, but my father stuck by her and paid all the hospital bills, sometimes working six different jobs to keep the family together. It was the Depression, and by today's standards we were a poverty-level family, but we had a lot of love and laughter. He was a wonderful example of doing whatever it takes to make things work. If one job didn't do it, get two —whatever you needed to do to keep things going.

"My father walked like he talked; he had great integrity. One of the important things I learned from him was that whatever you do, and whatever your attitude is, it affects others. He owned a small machine shop where I worked for him one summer. I remember that he never yelled at any of the men. He was a real gentleman.

"I remember one day we had to go to Denver, which was about a one-hundred-mile drive. The roads were bad, and the car and tires were old. We had three flat tires on the way there. Each time, my dad had to get out and repair the tire because we didn't have a spare. It was hard, sweaty work. You'd scrape your knuckles, bump your head, drop things, but my father never lost his temper. My grandmother, who was in the car with us, finally couldn't take it any longer. She said, 'Henry, will you use some profanity! If you don't, I'll do it for you!'

"My Dad also had a wonderful sense of humor. On my twenty-first birthday he gave me a big box. When I opened it up, there was a wooden shoeshine stand in it with twenty-one silver dollars and a note that said, 'A very happy twenty-first birthday. I know you're going to college, but a man should always have a backup business—and here's your backup business and a little capital.' I've tried to follow his example as much as possible."

Fathers and Spiritual Values

Spiritual values give meaning to life and to the events that occur in it. Without spiritual values life has no hope, no purpose, no substance. They provide the faith and trust that sustains us during difficult times. They are the inner resources that guide individual existence and inspire full participation in life. Above all, spiritual values expand awareness beyond personal ego to the humbling vastness of the universe, the preciousness of life on earth and the underlying interconnection of all that exists.

Lacking spiritual values, an individual may drift, looking for something to fill the hollowness. Addictive relationships, substance abuse, excitement, even cults—all are methods of searching for meaning and some way to feel purposeful and alive.

Spiritual values you grow up with are the most powerful determining guidelines you inherit. Whether they are grounded in traditional spiritual practice, limited to nominal religious identification or a unique expression of your own personal philosophy, the closer you felt to your father and the more you admired him, the more likely you are to have adopted his spiritual beliefs as your own.

My first spiritual teaching came to me from my father at age five, during one of our Sunday walks. We stopped to rest at the top of the hill when I suddenly turned to him and asked, "What happens when you die?" He inclined slightly toward me, touched the area between his eyes with his forefinger, and said, "Your soul is here. When you die, your soul goes to heaven," and he pointed up to the sky. His simple, direct answer was reassuring and satisfying. It answered my question and has stayed with me to this day.

Other fathers also teach spiritual lessons using methods other than traditional churchgoing. These lessons can be taught in many ways. Acting against established tradition and custom is sometimes the most effective way to do so.

"Our Farm Was Too Deep in the Mountains to Get to Church"

MaryJean, a minister in a metaphysical church, has been involved in pastoral work and spiritual teaching for years. "I grew up in the 1930s, in a very rural corner of Tennessee," MaryJean said. "Our farm was too far out in the mountains to go to the church in town on Sundays. We only went to church once a year, on Mother's Day. But my father loved to sing. So sometimes, when we were young, he'd take my brother and me to the small black churches nearby, where we'd get up and dance while he sang for the congregation. I think that's where I got the idea that we're all God's children. My father always practiced the Golden Rule and showed his beliefs by his actions. 'You treat people right, and you show respect for others,' he'd always say."

MaryJean's father took her to places where whites did not venture in those days. Segregation kept the races strictly apart in separate churches, schools, movie theaters, restaurants, hospitals, housing and all other public facilities. But her father told her that everybody had to be treated with the respect due a fellow human being. He took his children to share in the religious services of people with whom the customs and legal restrictions of the era forbade such contact. He taught not only with his words but with actions —instilling the concept that despite the prevailing laws and traditions, a higher law existed according to which each person was inherently equal.

"I Often Dreamed He Was Telling Me Not to Be Afraid"

In contrast to some people who grow up with relatively unstructured principles, Leah, a marketing representative for a hotel chain, was raised in the Conservative Jewish faith.

"My father was a very devout man who was proud of his Jewish heritage," Leah said. "He saw to it that I went to temple every

Saturday and on all the major Jewish holidays. Even though once I became a teenager I wasn't as observant, it was that early religious training that kept me going when my older brother, whom I adored, was diagnosed with multiple sclerosis.

"At the time of his diagnosis, I was nineteen and had just started college. Neither of my parents could afford to stop working, so I dropped out of school and took care of Morris for the last three years of his life. During that time, I often dreamed that he was telling me not to be afraid.

"I'll never forget the night before he died. His eyesight had been gone for a long time. I took him outside for some air, and he told me, 'Leah, I can see the stars! They're so real. I haven't seen them in years!' And he told me he knew he would be leaving soon.

"I don't talk about my religion a lot because I haven't really kept up with it," Leah stated. "But I believe in God, and I'm glad that my dad made sure I had some kind of religious training. I don't think I could have handled Morris's death and other things that have happened to me without it."

Spiritual values can be expressed in many ways. Some find their appreciation of life by placing themselves amid nature's awesome splendor; others are filled with reverence by the wonders of the cosmos; still others feel their spirits respond to magnificent music. There is no "right" way to experience spiritual wonder. Whether participating in a worship service, working in the garden, gazing at the face of a child or feeling an intangible presence, spiritual experiences present themselves through a wide range of phenomena.

"My Faith Made Me a Better Officer"

Most religions emphasize assisting the less fortunate. For some families, giving becomes part of the family heritage, honoring religious ties maintained for generations that emphasize sharing good fortune with the community.

David's family has a missionary tradition that has made them civic leaders for more than one hundred years. Their religious and ethical beliefs were instrumental in preparing him for military leadership and coping with the losses in his life.

"Religion was always a very large part of my family's life," David said. "They were always strongly supportive of the church. When I was young, my dad made a real effort to go to church with us every Sunday, in spite of the fact that he worked six days a week. He and my mom also saw to it that we went to Sunday school. Even though I go to church only about once a month now—I call myself an 'occasionally religious' person—I've always had a very strong sense of faith. It's an important part of my life.

"The way I was brought up left no doubt that belief was a central part of our way of life. I couldn't have gotten through the ordeal of losing my lover to AIDS without my sense of faith. During times of crisis in my life, such as when I left home the first time to go away to prep school and was desperately homesick, it was a great comfort to have the familiarity of the chapel. When I entered the marine corps and was stationed in Vietnam, it gave me solace to be secure in my faith.

"Without question, my faith made me a better officer, but I was not a moralistic officer. I feel that letting people know you have a spiritual side, and that you recognize God, enhances your stature. It keeps your rank from putting you up in an inaccessible position. Your faith turns you into an approachable human."

"I was also taught that privilege entailed responsibility to those less fortunate. Giving to schools and to the church was an ongoing example. There was a continual focus on how being fortunate gave you an obligation to help those less favored by circumstances. That ethic—the sense of obligation to the community—was an integral part of my growing up.

"The result has been that my main focus is out in the community. I'm very lucky that I have the resources to be able to volunteer my service and to work for the programs I believe in. My conviction about the responsibilities that go with privilege are very strong—it's inconceivable to me that I wouldn't use the assets I've been blessed with to help others."

David's father instilled a deep, strong current of religious faith that has directly guided his entire life. All his experiences—his duty in Vietnam while in the marines, the devastation of losing his lover to AIDS, and his continuing sense of obligation to those less fortunate—have been shaped by this faith. His father consistently emphasized the importance of religion, made it a point to go to church with his family as often as possible and made responsibility to others an integral part of family life. David's deep love and admiration for his father has inspired him to embrace those values and live out the moral heritage that was bestowed.

"My Dad Would Leave Food on People's Doorsteps"

For others, "giving back" is more personal. They act to provide immediate, essential assistance to those who are struggling to survive. Whenever hard times strike friends or family, Sherman follows his father's example of personally lending a helping hand.

"My dad was very actively involved in the community," Sherman said. "He served on the board of supervisors, he sponsored the local athletic teams, and he contributed to the cost of the town's yearly pageant. He was a 'silent giver,' too, anonymously giving to many charities.

"He came from a large family, and during the Depression Era when there was no work, he had all his brothers and sisters come to work for him in his grocery store. A lot of people in town were hurting then and couldn't afford to buy food, so my mother and father would make up food packages at night with chicken and canned goods and go around and drop them off at people's houses.

"My dad was the kind of man who had dozens of friends and no enemies. When he died, hundreds of people came by the house to pay their respects and tell me, 'Your father did this for me' and 'Your father helped me with that.' I don't think I'll ever be able to match him, but I've tried to do the same in my own life. If I know anyone who needs help, I'm ready to give them anything I've got."

The principle of the Great Dad doesn't stop at home. It extends from the family out into the community. Whatever the need, these fathers contributed. Some had the means to provide financial support for civic improvements; others had the background to be leaders in community organizations. Still others assisted by providing for the basic needs of survival. Whatever their contribution,they saw themselves as part of an interrelated whole in which the welfare of each individual or family was dependent on the well-being of the entire community.

Standing Up and Being Counted: Fathers' Influence on Political Expression

Until the recent past, fathers set the tone for the family's political, religious and social beliefs. Politics was considered to be "men's business," and women generally followed along. Now, women make up 52 percent of the voting population. But for many adult women and men, memories of Dad's predominant influence in forming political convictions are still fresh. Most often, their beliefs and actions have been similar to his. In some cases, children have found Dad's convictions were abhorrent and have worked against them.

The following two stories illustrate the power of a father's beliefs and actions to inspire similar views and endeavors in his children. Each is about women who were spurred to enter politics because of their fathers—but their motivation arose from two diametrically opposite impulses. In one instance, it was to carry on her father's work—in the other, to combat his ideas. But both were activated by their father's unflagging zeal.

"My Father Got Environmental Laws Passed"

Constance, who teaches business and ethics, was not only imbued with her father's work ethic, as described in chapter 8, but also inspired by his civic involvement and efforts to protect the environment. A tireless community activist, Constance has provided shelter to political refugees, participated in a women's prison visitation program and organized business groups in undeveloped areas.

"My father was very active in governmental affairs," Constance stated. "He contributed a lot. For example, he was instrumental in getting our State Environmental Protection Act passed so that our natural resources would be safeguarded. He also initiated agricultural research on maple trees in order to make maple syrup products a more profitable crop for our farmers.

"It was direct modeling for me. It has always seemed important to me that whatever I did was of some public service. I believe that knowledge is useless if you don't help people with it directly. One of the ways I've put my business training to use is by getting very involved with the Small Business Institute that helps new enterprises develop.

"I also want my students to see that business can play an important role in making communities better. One of the things my husband and I are planning to do when we retire is to go into undeveloped areas and help start small community businesses that will generate enough income to improve the quality of life of the people living there. Helping people bring in clean water, put in sewers and build schools, for example."

Her father's example inspired Catherine to utilize her talents in her own field to carry on the kind of work he did. His efforts to preserve the environment and help farmers produce more profitable crops is echoed by her economic development work to bring in clean water and sewage disposal to improve people's lives. She is a prime example of how, when fathers turn their views into actions, that legacy of translating opinions and words into actual deeds can also be handed down.

"My Father Was a Reactionary Bigot"

However, not all children accept the values and traditions that their fathers espouse. Children react to a father's views on a continuum from complete acceptance to complete rejection. Sometimes, when they react against views they find extremely offensive, they are even motivated to launch political movements that are in direct opposition to their father's principles.

Janet, who grew up in coal mining country, has combined a social service career with political activism fueled by revulsion at her father's oppressive views. "My father was a reactionary bigot," Janet stated. "I grew up inundated by his political tirades at the dinner table. We always heard political talk at home—who was running, what they stood for, why that wasn't right. He was always saying that if the elected officials would just ask his opinion, they would know what to do. Finally, he decided to put his ideas into action and ran for local office. Later on, he had larger ambitions and ran for Congress. Although he didn't win, he later served two terms in the state legislature. My father felt that taking charge of the governing situation was an important part of being a man—it was asserting the patriarchal role on a much wider scale.

"When I became a social worker my dad disowned me because I was working with black people. He didn't think anyone should help them because, in his opinion, 'You pull yourself up by the bootstraps like I did, and if you can't, you're lazy.' His views were strictly Darwinian.

"The effect was to drive me into politics, because I figured out that was where the rules were being made. Everything else was just going along with the system. Working for the welfare department and seeing the problems firsthand gave me a desire to have an impact on legislation. I started corresponding with various congressmen and state legislators proposing changes that would improve the delivery of services such as child care, job training and collection of child support payments.

"If my Dad had been kind and loving, I probably wouldn't be out agitating for women's rights because I wouldn't have needed them. But his attitude about women was very limiting. He believed women should not leave home until they were married. He viewed women strictly as inferior beings. My father showed me how to agitate, and he gave me everything to agitate against."

Janet's father exerted a profound influence on her political views. His reactionary tirades and prejudices against women and minorities drove her to take up political arms against the repressive ideas he represented. Driven by the same zeal for putting her ideas into action, she too entered the political arena, but on the opposite side— fighting to right the wrongs that she felt he stood for and fueled by his often-stated conviction that a man defined himself by participating in governmental power.

| | |

The moral values, spiritual principles, community involvement and political opinions you grow up with are among the most powerful legacies you inherit. Whether they are grounded in traditional religious practice, ethical principles, the Golden Rule or your own personal spiritual faith, many of these beliefs can be traced to your father.

If you admired your father, you probably have adopted his ideals and express them in your own life. His compassion, commitment to family, integrity and honesty have been linchpins for your own moral standards—governing your behavior, the causes you embrace and the obligations you feel to the community. Religious and spiritual beliefs he exemplified have become the foundation for your own spiritual values—sustaining you through difficult times and providing a beacon to guide yourself by.

As a citizen, whether he regarded politics and politicians as evils to avoid, mechanisms to bring about change or essential structures for governing society, your father also influenced your view—even if you disagreed. Whether you agreed or disagreed, his opinions made an impression that influence how you view your role as a member of society today—a mental record that continues to affect important aspects of your life.

Perhaps spiritual teachings and political ideals were missing in your childhood. Or perhaps former practices no longer are satisfying to you. You may be searching for your life purpose, or seeking some meaning to hold on to. One way to start this quest is by looking within—the answers have always been there and are waiting for you to discover them.

SELF-DISCOVERY EXERCISE

This is a self-discovery journal exercise inspired by James Redfield and Carol Adrienne's *The Celestine Prophecy*. To start your inner process, as always, begin by taking a deep breath and allowing your body to relax. Breathe in and out slowly a few times until you become centered.

These are some questions for you to ponder and answer in

your journal. They will take you back to earlier days when your world view was beginning to form. As you write, you may be surprised at some of the insights you develop.

What was the dominant motif in your family?

The following are some examples of dominant motifs: "We're one big, happy family, and we all look out for one another." "We share everything equally." "If I don't watch out for myself, no one else will." "There's never enough to go around."

How was that motif played out, and what was its effect on you?

How did you express this motif? Describe the actions of various other family members that illustrate how this theme played out. What was your reaction to them? How does that continue to affect you today in your relations with others?

What major motif do you really want to express in your life at this time?

Write about the motif you would ideally like to express in your life. Some examples are unconditional love, acceptance, faith, loyalty, trust, generosity, openness, spirituality, hope. You might want to choose more than one motif.

How would you express the motif you have chosen? How would your life be different if this way of living was a major factor? What could you do as a start?

AFFIRMATIONS

"I am able to learn and grow."

"My awareness expands daily."

"I am open to new experience."

"I am at peace."

"The awakenings I seek are given to me."

"Love surrounds and protects me."

"Answers are given as I need them."

"I am open to growth."

"My purpose is being revealed to me."

SECTION III

It's Never
Too Late

CHAPTER 10

Healing the Bond with Your Father:

Stories of Inspiration and Hope

Forgiveness is another word for letting go.
—MATTHEW FOX

No matter how painful a father-child relationship has been, most adult children want to work through past hurts and achieve resolution with Dad. They yearn to be able to express their love and establish a new connection that is free from the burdens of the past. Even after years of estrangement, they often want to gain the love and acceptance that was denied and to heal wounds caused by the rift. In fact, even following a father's death, unresolved issues may continue to linger and cause pain.

Without coming to terms with the man who was probably the most formative male figure in your life, it is nearly impossible to come to terms with yourself. Regardless of the nature of the relationship, your father is a vital part of you. Without resolution, you may end up denying a major part of your own identity. So much of who you are is tied up in the father-child relationship—either as talents you absorbed from your father, strengths you developed to cope with difficulties or traits in yourself that you dislike and want to disown because they remind you of him. You might even react to others in habitually negative ways because of problems that are rooted in that relationship.

To free you from past demons and finally feel at peace, you can embark on a healing process to resolve these issues and develop a new relationship based on love and respect. If it is impossible to effect a reconciliation or strengthen the existing ties, then individual work to mend past hurts can help you get on with your life and heal old wounds.

Resolution can be accomplished in a number of ways. The ideal is making personal contact to set the stage for removing old communication barriers and long-standing resentments. Such contact does not always come easily, however. Fathers who have matured and mellowed are often reluctant to be confronted by adult children with reminders of a past they would rather forget. Many have great difficulty dealing with feelings of guilt or inadequacy and dread having these emotions brought to the surface. Other fathers still refuse to acknowledge or examine what has happened in the past and vehemently reject any attempts at resolving such issues.

Most adult children do not want to confront their fathers in anger. They just want to bring the painful issues out into the open in order to receive validation of their experience and then move on to a more fulfilling relationship. However, in most cases these fathers have had little or no experience in dealing with deeply held emotions. Initiating and participating in the process takes tremendous courage on both sides.

The adult child requires courage because of the fear that if Dad is confronted there will be a final rejection and the relationship will be forever destroyed. Dad might just find it easier to shut the door one last time than acknowledge painful actions and apologize. If nothing is done, however, the relationship will remain as it is.

Dad also needs inner fortitude in order to admit feelings of guilt that may have haunted him for years and concede that his behavior caused pain to his child. Fathers show tremendous inner strength and maturity when they can listen to an adult child say, "This is what I experienced . . . this is what I felt . . . ," and respond, "I wish I hadn't done that . . . I'm sorry I hurt you."

Even thinking about addressing the past can create so much anxiety that attempts at healing are frequently delayed for years. Not until a life-threatening illness or other crisis occurs does the need to come to peace with the past while it is still possible precipitate a reconciliation.

"I Knew He Was Dying"

Resolution is sometimes delayed until a father's last breath, when an adult child, holding Dad's hand, says "I love you" for the very first time—and receives gentle pressure back, indicating Dad has heard and returns that love.

Carla grew up in absolute terror of her alcoholic father's rages. Only when her father was near death with cancer was she finally able to heal their relationship

"When I was younger, I went through a long period of hating my father," Carla said. "But while he was dying, I saw a father I never saw before—someone who showed me that he cared—and I went after every crumb I could get.

"I remember feeling him watching me as I was leaving the hospital one time; I looked up and saw him standing in the window, waving good-bye at me. I knew then that he knew he was dying.

"Even though my father changed a lot during his illness, the real resolution happened after his death. The counseling I got played a major role, because I realized I had to take a good look at his background to understand him.

"I would advise anybody who wants to resolve their relationship with their father to buy a pad of paper, go off by themselves and think about where he came from and how he got to be the way he was. Then, if you decide he's not going to change, detach and take yourself out of the conflict. Counseling was really the answer for me, because it helped me look at myself in relationship to him. Even after examining my parents' families, and knowing their background of abuse and alcoholism, I wouldn't have been able to understand my childhood without a therapist's help to gain perspective."

Carla's father changed when he realized he was dying. But his reversal of attitude alone was not enough to allow Carla to come to terms with her past. By getting professional help and finding the time and solitude to write down everything she knew about her father's parents and his childhood, Carla was able to sort out her dad's own traumatic experiences growing up in an alcoholic household. His childhood had sown the seeds of the raging, alcoholic parent he eventually became. Writing down and thinking about all the information she had about her dad's early years gave Carla insight and compassion, so she could finally place the past in perspective and put it away.

"I Finally Understood He Was Doing His Best"

Not all adults have to overcome a traumatic childhood when they reconcile with their father. Many find that simply by maturing and looking at their father with more tolerant eyes they gain an understanding of him as a human being, rather than seeing him as a larger-than-life figure of intimidation and awe.

Like many young men, Ken went through a stormy adolescence. He and his father battled constantly until he finally moved out on his own. Adulthood gave him new insight into himself, however, enabling Ken to resolve difficulties with his father.

"My dad and I weren't so far apart that we couldn't establish better ties," Ken said. "But our relationship improved a lot when I stopped having to win every argument and feel that I always had to prove myself to him. That's when I started to feel closer to him, and a lot of the anger and resentment went away. I didn't feel the need to fight with him anymore to prove that my way was the right way.

"It took a lot of soul searching, but I finally understood that he was doing his best. He wasn't a perfect father; he was a person just like me. I started to have empathy instead of resentment. In the last couple of years, I've become so much less judgmental of my father. When I looked within, I realized that I was judging him for problems, weaknesses and faults that I began to see I had myself. We've all got weaknesses in one form or another.

"What's good about the relationship now is that we're more like friends than father and son. We talk about anything and everything on an equal level. We can just hang out together, and I don't feel the pressure that I used to feel around him."

Like many adults, Ken understood his father better when he gained greater understanding of himself. When he learned to judge himself less harshly, he could also accept his father as a man with human frailties. As children, we want our fathers to live up to our ideals and can become extremely critical if they don't. As adults, we understand that we each struggle within ourselves and that good intentions are often sidetracked by conflicting needs.

How to Resolve Conflict with an Absent Father

People seeking resolution with their father often ask, "What if my father is no longer alive?" Active participation by your father, although desirable, is not required in order to resolve the relationship. There are circumstances in which this is simply not possible: Contact may be refused, communication may have been cut off for so long that your father's whereabouts are unknown or your father's death may make reunion impossible. Yet even if reconciliation through personal contact is no longer feasible, healing can still take place. Your father's involvement in the process, while ideal, is not necessary. The most important goal is to cleanse yourself emotionally—discharging the grief and changing your outlook so that you are no longer burdened by painful memories.

"I Could Finally Feel My Father's Humanity"

Gabrielle is an example of someone whose relationship with her father was resolved *after* his death. When she looked at him through the eyes of an adult rather than a child, she saw a man struggling with his own demons, rather than a father who withheld the love she longed for.

"I was five years old when World War II started and we went into hiding," Gabrielle explained. "My father was in the French Resistance, so everything had to be kept secret. We were very isolated, and I spent the whole day alone under strict instructions to stay out of sight and not to talk to anyone. For the next four years, until I was about nine and the war ended, I had very little contact with my father. Even when he was home, he was too preoccupied to be present for me emotionally.

"When the war ended and he returned for good, he had gone through such hell that he couldn't adjust to normal life and be a husband and father. He was mentally "lost," and because he couldn't deal with the everyday world, I decided he was weak and despised him. I looked to him to supply my need for approval, but because he was shell-shocked he couldn't give me anything.

"I finally went into counseling to improve my relationship with my husband. The insights came fairly quickly, and I decided that even though my parents were both already dead, I had to resolve the pain from my upbringing before my marriage could work.

"I went back to France and went to the hiding place where we had concealed ourselves throughout the war years. It had an enormous effect on me. I could feel my parents around me and come into contact with their feelings—their hurt, their vulnerability, their fears for me.

"It was overwhelming. I started crying and apologizing out loud to them, as I felt what they had gone through. I had steeled my emotions for years, but I could finally feel my father's humanity and my own. I had to forgive him and myself because I had been so harsh in my judgment. I could finally let go of all the sadness and hurt."

As a child, Gabrielle could not understand the devastating effects that living in constant fear had on her father or how his focus on survival made it impossible for him to fulfill her needs. When he developed the classic symptoms of Post-Traumatic Stress Disorder, an emotional disturbance that left him unable to cope with the normal pressures of everyday life, she felt abandoned and betrayed.

Revisiting the isolated hiding place where she had spent the war years opened the way for all the pent-up memories to come flooding back. But now, she had an adult's understanding and was able to feel her parents' emotions as if they were her own. Realization brought compassion, and with that came the release of the pain she had carried for so many years. Gabrielle came to peace with her father when her understanding of him released the needs that had haunted her.

Letter of Release

Another approach to resolution is to write a letter to your absent or deceased parent in which you express all the regrets and disappointments that you still carry with you. There is great power in simply acknowledging the truth of your feelings. After all the anger and sadness is released, you may find that the tone of your letter changes from anger and grief to one of understanding and forgiveness, or perhaps acceptance and detachment. Allow your emotions to flow, and then put the letter away.

Later, when the time feels right, read your letter. You may be surprised at how your feelings have changed. Take the letter to a special place and burn it. As the fire consumes the letter and you watch the smoke drift away, imagine that it is carrying away the last vestiges of your grief with it and freeing you. (Please make sure that the embers are all safely extinguished before leaving.)

Regrets Letter

In his book, *Making Peace with Your Parents*, psychiatrist Harold Bloomfield suggests a "Regrets Letter" in which you list all the regrets you have about the relationship. After writing "Dear Dad," start each new line with "I regret that. . . ." Let all your misgivings about your relationship with your father come out. You may want to do this several times, because each time you will be accessing a deeper level of feelings. When all your regrets have been expressed, put the letters away or dispose of them in a way that is meaningful to you, such as burning it, as the final act of letting go.

"I Visited My Father's Grave"

Raelene's traumatic past seemed almost impossible to heal. As a six-year-old, she watched her mother kill her father in self-defense after years of abuse. At midlife, she decided she needed to go back to her old hometown and confront ghosts she had long ago fled in order to come to peace with herself.

"It was a long time coming," Raelene said. "I was in and out of abusive relationships like my parents, until I finally went into therapy ten years ago. In order to understand my self-destructive life pattern, I knew I had to go back and face the shame that I feel even today. When I was growing up, when you met people, they always asked you, 'Who are you?' 'Who's your family?'; they wanted to put you into a little cubbyhole. I never wanted people to know who I was. "I knew the only way to resolve it was to go back and confront my roots. I visited my father's grave and met some of his relatives who could tell me about his early years. I spent a lot of time with my mom talking about him as a person—not the pain of their relationship but just seeing him as a human. That was tremendously healing, because the things that happened between my father and his dad have always been a family secret. I still have a lot of mending to do, but I'm going to stay here and make a new life for myself. This is where my roots are."

Going back to her childhood home gave Raelene the opportunity to face the fear and shame she'd felt as a child with adult strengths and understanding. When she listened to her father's relatives talk about his youth and his relationship with his own father, she gained a very different perspective—one that turned him from a monster into a human being.

It took exceptional courage for Raelene to return to the place where she had been so shamed as a child; but it was especially healing to confront the townspeople who remembered her history as an adult. Years of work had succeeded in resurrecting her spirit. Her unflinching willingness to know the truth strengthened her resolve to finally dispel the shadows of a violent past and show her true being to those who had once known and judged her.

True understanding brings compassion, release and wholeness. It can come through direct communication, letters, self-exploration or actually making a pilgrimage back in time—returning to the place where significant events occurred in order to revisit the places and people who shaped your life. Whatever method you choose, the most important work is done by *you*. Your father's participation is not necessary—*you* are the force that empowers and heals yourself.

How to Heal When Healing Seems Impossible

"I'm Not Here to Rage at You"

Jed, who finally reached an understanding with his father after years of disappointment, speaks for many adult children when he says, "I love my dad. It used to break my heart when he wouldn't talk to me. I wanted to resolve things once and for all. I offered to go to a psychologist with him, join a support group, pay for private counseling, whatever would make it easier for him to get through it. But he refused everything because he was scared to death.

"I wanted to tell him, 'Dad, I'm not here to rage at you. You didn't invent this stuff. But we have to call it by its name—the abuse that happened to me and my sisters. I've thought about what it must have been like for you to be Grandpa's son. It must have been hell to live there.'"

Jed desperately wanted to heal the old wounds. He wanted to share his feelings and have them acknowledged. He longed for the emotional release that would follow validation of what happened. He even hoped his father might say, "I'm sorry."

But Jed is a child of today's knowledge and attitudes, and his father is a captive of the past. Jed views therapy and support groups as invaluable resources that enable him to let go of negative emotions and gain understanding of himself. His father grew up in an era that stressed hiding abuse and other family secrets. Expressions of emotional pain or anxiety were ridiculed as admissions of inadequacy.

Jed's father's fear of acknowledging his failings kept him from accepting any offers of help. Support groups, joint counseling, even private, individual therapy were all too threatening. His father had a tremendous fear of being judged—by himself perhaps even more than by others—and so he built ever higher walls to keep Jed out.

Finally, Jed decided to move beyond confrontation and to place himself on the other side of the emotional abyss—the side of nonjudgment and acceptance. At that point, he was finally able to start building a bridge.

"I Looked for the Light Inside Him"

Finding the light, the essential spirit of any person, is *the* key to healing. It connects your higher awareness with the soul of another human—the part that is detached from events in the past and transcends the concerns that roil human emotions. When you are in touch with that part of yourself and able to see it in another, you experience the redeeming power of agape, or universal love.

"I went to see my father the day before Father's Day," Jed said, "hoping against hope that there would be some kind of movement. But he didn't want to hear anything. He raged at me and then turned his back on me and stood there with his arms folded against his chest—he was totally closed off.

"So I did what I've learned to do in my meditations. I sat there in silence and looked for the light inside him—the presence of God that I've learned is in every person. I just sat there in silence and tuned into that.

"After a long while, my dad dropped his arms and turned around and faced me and said, 'Why did you wait so long?' I said, 'Because I was frightened,' and I held up my hands to show him that they were shaking. We didn't say much, but his attitude was softened.

"The next day, I took my two daughters to church for Father's Day, and as we listened to the sermon they each lay their head on my shoulder. I felt like a dragon slayer—scarred, singed, strong and victorious. That moment with my father was a miracle."

Years of abusing his children filled Jed's father with so much guilt and shame that it made any acknowledgment of the past unbearably frightening. In order for Jed to heal the relationship, he first had to find the spark of humanity in his father and start the healing process from there. When he touched that spiritual core—the part of his father that wanted love and acceptance—the barriers fell and they were finally able to take the first step toward reconciliation.

"I Stopped Blaming My Father for Everything"

Lucia, a curator of prehistoric artifacts, spent years rebuilding her relationship with her father. "I was always working on understanding my father," Lucia said. "I decided that the core of every problem I had in my life was due to him and the relationship between us. Growing up with my father was a *lot* of work because of his alcoholism and out-of-control rages. It was really different from having a functioning father. I used to love going to my friends' houses; I never wanted to go home. I had really low self-esteem because I never felt that I knew what to do; I didn't know where I fit in. I was mad at him for not teaching me the things I thought I needed to make it in life.

"At age eighteen, I got out of there but ran into a *lot* of problems and went to my father for advice. It was crucial that he listen to me, but he didn't want to hear anything, so I got away from him again. The only problem was that I landed in a relationship with an alcoholic man who was twenty-five years older than me. I thought I needed someone to take care of me. I hated my father and always thought, 'One day, he'll die, and then I can return to be with my mother and get all her attention.'

"Instead, my mother was diagnosed with a fast-growing cancer and died. It threw me into a completely different relationship with my father. I told my mother after her death, 'I know you always loved me. I'm sorry I never understood that coping with Dad took so much of your energy that you had nothing left for me,' and I made a vow to myself that I would clear up all the anger and my father would get the benefit of that.

"Soon after, I went to an intensive weekend seminar where I realized I had to stop blaming my father for everything. I had to acknowledge what had happened to me and then get on with my life and heal my relationship with my father.

"I'm much more mature now, which is definitely the result of all the money I put into seminars, psychology, counseling—anything I think will help me. I still have a ways to go, but I'm much better off now than I was before. My life is so much better now. There's nothing and no one more important than my father is to me now. Now I listen to him, console him, cry with him, go on trips with him. I'm the closest to him of all the children. He loves everyone equally, but I'm the one he can talk to.

"Of everything I've done, having my dad in my life is the biggest accomplishment. It seems like the only way to be at peace is to just let the past go and start over. He's a happier person now because of it, and I am too. I know I won't have regrets when he goes. I can say I've done as much as I can. There was *no* relationship before, and now there is. I'm doing much better on accepting myself now, too. For the first time, I'm in a really good relationship, and my life is finally going in the direction I want it."

Lucia was determined to establish a good relationship with her father and was willing to do the work that would allow that. She knew that her poor self-image, which stemmed from early experiences, created situations in her life that were completely against her self-interest. She also realized that she had to resolve her anger and stop blaming her father for her unhappiness before she could mend their relationship. These were not easy realizations to come to, and Lucia did a tremendous amount of work on herself before she was able to start reconnecting with her father. But when her newfound ability to communicate led to a closer bond with him, Lucia felt that all her efforts had been validated.

"My Father Said, 'I've Never Felt So Loved Before'"

Julius had an equally powerful healing experience during the two years he cared for his heroin-addict father before he died of AIDS. "My father died of AIDS last year," Julius stated. "He was missing most of my life—sometimes there physically but never there emotionally. I call him a 'functional heroin addict' because he always held a job, but there was no room for anything else. Once I hit my teens, I saw him only about once a year—just to borrow a suit or a car to go to a prom. Each time, we got into a big fight because he always had to control everything, so eventually I stopped seeing him completely.

"My last year of college I took Spanish, so I went to visit him, thinking he could help me practice. When I saw him, I was shocked. He was in this little room with just a bed and a side table. It was so empty, so vacant; he had nothing to live for. I thought, 'His life is over.' This was a man who won the Salesman of the Year Award every year like clockwork. He owned expensive suits, drove fancy cars, played golf at the most exclusive clubs—and now he was down to this. He couldn't work anymore because his legs were completely shot from the needles. He *was* nothing and *had* nothing; it was pathetic!

"The difference between the image I used to have of him and what I now saw was so extreme, I had a flash of insight. I thought, 'I want to know this man's story. I want to know *why* he is the way he is. I'm not going to judge it, I'm just going to take it the way it comes.' He had full-blown AIDS, so I moved nearby and took care of him until he died two years later. Every answer I got from him was also an answer for me. When I understood why he did certain things, I could understand those actions in myself

I was told 'You're just like your father' so many times. I acted just like him. I'd keep it all in and then let it out physically. When I saw my father get violent, I thought, 'I'm just the same,' and I'd get violent too. Here was a handsome, bright guy who was filled with shame and always felt he had to prove himself. He thought he was nothing, and I thought I was nothing too.

"Every night, I picked his brain to try to understand him. What I realized was, *'It wasn't his fault!'* My father was a victim in the truest sense. He didn't believe he was worthy of love because *his* father had disowned him and claimed he wasn't his son. That was always rubbed in his face. He ran away from home at age eleven and was on his own ever since then.

"When I realized it wasn't his fault, I thought, 'Maybe, it's not my fault, either.' Maybe some of my pain about who I am isn't rightfully mine either. I knew his negative habits in the present belonged to him, but they didn't start out that way. So I realized I didn't need to blame myself, either, anymore. When I released *him*, I released *me*.

"Before my father died, he told me, 'I've never felt so loved before.' I would do it again a thousand times, only I would ask more questions. Those were precious times when I lived with my father."

| | |

It is of paramount importance to heal the bond with your father—not for his sake but for yours. Otherwise, you will continue to struggle with the effect the relationship had on your behavior, emotions, world view, intimate and professional relationships and self-concept. Because every part of your life is affected, freeing yourself from this burden is hard work—but it is the greatest gift you can give yourself.

Healing starts when you decide that the rewards of a new relationship with your father are worth the effort of letting go of anger, pain, resentment or blame and opening the door to love, compassion and acceptance. Even if your father has died, or personal contact is not possible for other reasons, issues can still be put to rest and wounds healed. His participation is not necessary. Unlike in the past, when you felt helpless, now you have the resources to shed old habits and emotions and find *yourself* in the process.

CHAPTER 11

The Path to Healing:
Exercises and Success Stories

Letting go is not to regret the past;
But to grow and live for the future.
Letting go is to fear less and live more.

—TWELVE-STEP PROGRAM

Healing involves a paradox: In order to heal the relationship with your father, you have to heal your own wounds first. It is impossible to mend a relationship when you are still full of anger or pain. These feelings will spill out and destroy any attempt to establish communication, clear up past misunderstandings or build bridges back to your dad. Even if your father has passed on or is unavailable, so that direct reconciliation is not possible, as long as blame, resentment and hostility still exist, there can be no resolution. You will still be stuck in the old relationship and the problems it causes in your present life.

When you think about this rationally, it may not seem to make sense. But emotions are separate from rationality, and what is true for you emotionally is what runs your life. These feelings must be approached on another level of understanding that allows you to see your father from a different perspective. Therefore, all the exercises in this chapter involve your own inner work. They are designed to be done alone, with the support of a trusted friend, or with a therapist, so that you can finally reach that new outlook and come to peace.

When healing does occur, it frequently comes so quickly that it seems like a miracle. Yet this "miracle" requires the patience to stay with a process that takes place over time.

Seven Steps to Healing

The following are the seven steps that usually occur during the process of healing your relationship with your father. They do not necessarily occur in this order. You might find yourself working on more than one step at one time, or you might do a single step for a while and then go back to a previous one; however you encounter these steps, they are the ones that most people go through in reaching resolution.

1. *Intention*

2. *Investigation*

3. *Understanding*

4. *Nonblaming communication*

5. *Reconciliation*

6. *Acceptance*

7. *Release*

Intention

Everything starts with intention. Whether you decide to commit to a relationship, start a business, move to a new location or improve your golf score, nothing happens until you develop an intention. When you make the decision to heal the relationship with your father and affirm out loud to yourself, "I'm going to mend my relationship with my father," or "I am going to face my father without blame or judgment," you are starting the process.

Investigation

Just as you were shaped by your upbringing, your father became the man he was in response to his own family background. Find out about your father's parents, grandparents, aunts and uncles. Who was he closest to? How many children were in his family? Was he the youngest? Oldest? The middle child? How did that affect him? Did he have to take care of all the other children?

Were there any serious illnesses or accidents in the family? Did someone close to him die? Were there other major losses or disappointments? For example, was he unable to accept a college scholarship because he had to help support the family?

Was there alcoholism or another addiction in your father's family? Did your father grow up with both parents? A single parent? A stepparent? What was that relationship like?

The more you know about your dad and his early life, the more you will be able to understand why he acted in the ways that he did.

What about if you can't find out any information about your father? What if he left you early in life and no one knows anything about him? What should you do if his family history, likes and dislikes, and personality traits are all unavailable? Now matter how little you know, you usually have some clues: a name, the circumstances under which your mother met him, where he was from, what his occupation was, his age during the time your mother knew him or perhaps something about his other family members and background.

Even scraps such as these can tell you something that allows you to construct an imaginary portrait of the man that feels right to you. It may not be complete, but you can imagine him as he was, his relationship with you and what personal or physical traits he may have passed on to you. Factual accuracy is not the goal here—emotional connection is.

Understanding

When you have gathered all the information you can about your father and given yourself time to absorb it, he will emerge in your mind as a real person rather than the one-dimensional figure who intimidated or rejected you. When you know more, you will probably see that given the time, the place and the conditions that he grew up in, combined with the limited knowledge and means available then, he coped the best way he knew how.

The mental health and other support systems we now take for

granted were almost nonexistent for many of our fathers. Depending on the time and the place they lived in, Alcoholics Anonymous or other support groups, psychological counseling, self-help books or medications to control depression or anxiety were either unavailable or inaccessible.

When you realize that your father is human, and that he had to survive his own pressures as best he could, with far fewer resources than you have now, you will understand how it was almost inevitable that he became who he was and acted as he did. It is possible that you will still be unable to understand your father's actions. Even if this is the case, you can still accept that they did happen, realize that the question "Why?" may never be answered and move on.

Nonblaming Communication

Nonblaming communication means that you communicate your experience compassionately—without blaming, accusing or expecting any specific outcome. Because this is impossible to do if you still carry anger or resentment within, it is essential that you deal with these emotions in such a way that you relate your truth out of a desire for resolution and healing, rather than a need to punish in retaliation for the pain you experienced in the past.

Your father may respond in a variety of ways. He might listen in silence so that only his body language or facial expressions give away his reaction; he might turn his back on you; he might let you know he's sorry, either verbally or nonverbally; he might shut you out and refuse to discuss it. The most important factor is not his response, because that only reflects the degree of his own inner turmoil. What's important is taking an action that empowers you and releases the pain.

What if communication is impossible? Some fathers may no longer be available because of death or other circumstances. Although it is extremely healing to join in the mutual release brought about by telling your story and having it acknowledged, it is not necessary to do so face to face. If your father is not physically available, you can try one of the other methods of resolution that are described at the end of this chapter.

During the fourth and fifth stages, communication and reconciliation, it is especially important to go slowly and carefully. Having done the work of the previous stages, you may feel anxious to resolve your relationship as quickly as possible. However, bear in mind that your father has not gone through the lengthy inner preparation that you have. You want to proceed sensitively so that he does not feel threatened and close himself off to you further.

Reconciliation

When you open your heart to your father and accept him without blame or judgment as a fallible human, reconciliation becomes much easier. It is possible that he had been wanting to reconcile with you but was uncertain how to do so. He is undoubtedly aware of the shortcomings in your relationship, but he might not have known how to go about repairing them.

This is where the work you do on yourself bears fruit. Jed looked for the light in his father when all else had failed. When you approach your father from a place of love, you touch the part of him that is capable of returning it. It is the part that lies beyond his guilt and the protective barriers he has erected that push you away. When this contact is made, he is much more likely to respond to you.

Just be aware that discomfort with intimacy, fear of losing control, inability to articulate feelings, guilt over the past, unresolved anger stemming from his own background or any number of other factors have kept him at a distance all these years. Holding to your intention to approach him from a place of compassion is the best way to bridge that chasm. When you feel the change that has taken place in your father, you will know that the reconciliation process is in motion. But sometimes, even when you approach your father out of a place of love, it may appear that your efforts have failed. In this case, know that your father's actions and decisions reflect his inability to respond; it is not about you.

Acceptance

When you examine and understand your father's history, it becomes easier to understand how his early experiences influenced him as a parent and the effect those influences had on you. You see how relationships reach from one generation to another to form the person you are now. As the larger picture forms from the pieces you assemble, events in your life start to make sense, and you enter the next stage—acceptance.

Acceptance simply says, "This is the way it was," without anger or blame. It flows naturally from the stages that have gone before. If you find that hurtful emotions persist, and this understanding is not yet complete, return to the previous steps and continue working on them.

Acceptance is a process that comes quietly and has no timetable. You simply wake up one day and realize you're there. It may seem like a long journey, but it is definitely worth the effort.

Release

Release allows you to move on. After having gone through all the other stages—acknowledging the courage and determination that were required and realizing the greater meaning of these events for your life—the release and renewal you experience constitute the last step in your healing process.

Once you understand how all the pieces fit together, you will realize that you couldn't be who you are, with the wisdom and depth that you now possess, without the tempering experiences that you have gone through. Release allows you to bring all the strands of your life together and weave them into a tapestry of deep, personal meaning. It enables you to transcend the past—leaving behind old burdens and opening up to the new vision you create for yourself.

The seven steps do not have to happen in exactly this order. You may find yourself skipping a step, combining steps or going back and forth between them. You can work on more than one step at the same time. Be gentle with yourself and take as much time as you need on any step. There is no set schedule or "right" way to do them. Everyone is different, and everyone's needs are unique. Just know that in successful reconciliations, these seven steps will have taken place.

Starting the Healing: Inner Work

When you're ready to start, begin by stating your intention. A very effective way to do this is to write down your intention and then stand in front of the mirror and tell it to your image. This makes it real; it becomes a promise to yourself. You might write something like, "I am going to heal the relationship with my father" or "I am going to contact my father and start mending our relationship." Write whatever feels right and comfortable for you.

MY INTENTION STATEMENT

_____

_____

_____

_____

After you have stated your intention, the most essential factor in achieving resolution of your relationship is the inner work you do. Inner work comes first because it is impossible to have a successful outcome if you approach your father in anger. If your father harbors feelings of guilt or shame, he is likely to respond to your overtures with anger, denial or counteraccusations. In fact, he may initially respond this way no matter how you approach him, and you need to be emotionally centered to deal with that.

People in our society are so heavily invested in avoiding blame that it is extremely difficult for anyone, especially a man raised in a traditional environment, to say "I'm sorry" or "I was wrong." Resolving your own issues allows you to move beyond focusing on your own hurts from the past to being able to empathize with the pain in your father's life that led to his actions. Once you have developed empathy, you are able to approach him with compassion —often because you see your own pain echoed in his life.

A question people often ask is "Why should I have to empathize with him?" or "Shouldn't he have to take responsibility for his actions?" or "Why do I have to be the one to do all the work?"

The reason is that you are the one who has something at stake.

You are detaching from the hurtful memories that are controlling your life in order to take back your own personal power. Your father is responsible for his life. You are responsible for yours. If you delay your healing until your father sees the error of his ways and apologizes, your burdens may continue for a very long time.

In complete contradiction to what you may believe is right, it is *you*—the adult child who suffered in the past and wants the healing—who must go to your father and offer him your love and acceptance. You have to offer compassion and understanding of *his* pain in order for him to trust you enough to be open to you. Compassion is a state of mind. It does not have to be expressed in words; it can be conveyed by your attitude. However, it is possible only if you have done the work to heal your own wounds first.

You might be able to deal with these issues on your own, or you might need the more structured professional assistance offered by a therapist. Even just a few counseling sessions can be very helpful in assisting you to gain perspective and get started on the right track.

Write down information sources you could turn to in order to locate support groups, workshops or a therapist. Some places to start looking are your company's employee assistance program; your minister, priest or rabbi; professional associations for psychologists or other therapists; or local listings of self-help groups.

RESOURCES

_____

_____

_____

_____

To begin the process, buy a notebook that fits easily in your purse or pocket so you can jot down thoughts about your father as they occur.

SELF-EXAMINATION FOR FATHER-CHILD HEALING

Here are some areas for you to explore. Use as much extra paper as you need.

What are your earliest memories of your father?

_____

_____

_____

What happy memories do you have of your father?

_____

_____

_____

What painful or sad memories do you have?

_____

_____

_____

Which of your father's traits do you dislike the most?

_____

_____

_____

Which of his traits do you admire the most?

_____

_____

_____

Which of your own personality traits do you dislike the most?

_____

_____

_____

Which of your personality traits please you the most?

_____

_____

_____

Which of your and your father's personality traits cause the greatest conflict between you?

_____

_____

_____

In what ways are you like your father?

_____

_____

_____

In what ways are you different?

_____

_____

_____

Find a quiet place to relax and close your eyes. Imagine your father as a child and notice the feeling you get with that image. Is there anything missing? Is there anything he needs? Imagine yourself providing him what he needs.

_____

_____

_____

_____

If you were more tolerant of your dad, which of his habits would you learn to accept? What would you have to do in order to develop that tolerance?

_____

_____

_____

What would enable you to reach out to your father and let him know you accept him just as he is?

_____

_____

_____

What have you found out from exploring these areas? Give yourself time to sort out the implications. Having gone through this process, you now have a much better picture of your father and where you stand in relation to him. You are now ready to take a deeper look at your father's family history.

Investigation: My Father's Family History

You are tracing your roots now. Go back to the people who knew your father and discover as much information as you can. (If your father has disappeared, and you know little or nothing about him or even if he is alive or not, go to the section later in this chapter entitled "Resolution: If Reconciliation Is Not Possible" to help you deal with the loss and bring closure to this issue.) Some things you may already know; other details may take you by complete surprise. Keep an open mind. Evaluation comes later. Here are the questions you want answered:

When and where was your father born?

_____

_____

Did his parents welcome his birth, or was it a problem?

_____

_____

_____

How old were his parents at that time? Were they married? What was their living situation?

_____

_____

_____

_____

What was the education level of his parents? Their income level?

_____

_____

_____

Were there other children? How many? Was your father the oldest? Middle? Youngest?

_____

_____

_____

Was either of his parents an alcoholic? Did either suffer from depression or any other mental disability? If so, what were the effects?

_____

_____

_____

_____

What were the major events of your father's childhood? Any major losses? Divorces? Moves to another location?

_____

_____

_____

_____

Were there any serious accidents, illnesses or traumas in your father's family? Did someone particularly close to your father die?

_____

_____

_____

_____

How much education did your father get?

_____

_____

At what age did your father leave home? Under what circumstances?

_____

_____

_____

_____

How old was your father when he married your mother? What was their relationship like? How did that affect him as a father?

_____

_____

_____

_____

What were your father's main hopes and dreams? What goals did he have for himself?

_____

_____

_____

_____

_____

What were his major disappointments, frustrations or failures? What did he regret the most?

_____

_____

_____

_____

What were his most important successes?

_____

_____

_____

_____

Where is your father now in his life? Physically? Emotionally? Financially? In relationship to others?

_____

_____

_____

_____

_____

_____

You have learned a great deal about your father from this exercise. Now you are ready to write his life story as if *he* were writing the letter to *you*. Pretend that you are your father when you write the letter and that you are telling your child the story of your life. Use the information you have gathered and write the letter as your father might write it to you if he wanted to tell you all about himself.

Begin the letter any way that you like. For example, you might start by writing, "Dear Judy, I know we haven't gotten along well over the years, and there are things you've been angry at me for. I'd like to tell you about myself in the hope that you'll understand more about me. I was born in. . . ."

Take a deep breath to get comfortable, let your body become more relaxed, and allow whatever words come out to flow. Don't worry about spelling, grammar or punctuation. Let your hand write, and keep writing without any interference from your mind as long as the words keep flowing. You'll be amazed at what comes out.

Some space has been provided here just to get you going. You can continue in your notebook, or you may prefer to write the entire letter in your journal so that your thoughts can pour out freely without interruption.

"LIFE STORY LETTER"
from My Father to Me

Dear _____
             (Your Name)

_____

_____

_____

_____

_____

_____

_____

_____

_____

_____

_____

_____

_____

_____

_____

_____

_____

_____

_____

_____

_____

_____

_____

I love you,
Dad

You now have a much better picture of the events in your dad's life that formed the man he became. You also have a greater understanding of how your two personalities meshed or clashed, and how the relationship between you affected other decisions you made in your life. At this point you are ready to start the joint healing work with your dad. Each situation is different, depending on the amount of communication there has been between you, how far apart you've grown, whether he is in the same geographic location, his age and health condition and other factors.

Regardless of your situation, now that you have done the groundwork and feel ready to start the process, here are some ways to start building bridges. Use the space provided for notes about how you could apply these suggestions in your own situation to begin opening the door to your father.

JOINT WORK FOR FATHER-CHILD HEALING

Write a note to your dad just to say "Hello." To start communications again, tell him about some activity you're involved in. Enclose a picture of yourself.

_____

_____

_____

Write a letter to your father telling him about a positive trait that you admire in him. Mention a time when that trait inspired you and helped you in your life.

_____

_____

_____

_____

_____

Write a letter to your father telling him about a positive trait that you *both* share. Describe a time that you admired it in him and then realized that you had it also.

_____

_____

_____

_____

_____

_____

Write a letter to your father and tell him about a pleasant memory you have of him. This can be anything—even a very small, seemingly insignificant remembrance. Describe what it means to you.

_____

_____

_____

_____

_____

_____

Tell your father about something he did for you that you remember and appreciate.

_____

_____

_____

Call your father once a week just to say "Hello." Ask how he's doing, and just listen for a few minutes. You don't have to stay on the phone long. The contact is what's important.

_____

_____

_____

Spend some time with your father on a regular basis. For example, invite him to dinner once a month, play golf with him once a month, or go over one Saturday morning a month, for a couple of hours, to help with the yard work.

_____

_____

_____

Attend a workshop with your father. Choose something that will get you talking, such as a communication workshop, a stress management seminar, or a hobby workshop.

Hug your dad and tell him you love him every time you see him. It's catching! Remember, the greatest gift you can give your father is to let him know you love him and that you're glad he's your dad.

"I Wrote My Father a Letter and Told Him How Much I Loved Him"

Floyd characterized both his parents' families as "crazy, violent drunks, completely infested with alcohol." At age forty-two, after his mother's death, he decided to reconcile with his father. Floyd started the healing process using the letter-writing approach.

"After college, I started drinking so heavily I finally went to AA," Floyd said. "I realized I had been harboring tremendous anger at my father and that I had to process that anger in some way, or I would never be happy being sober. Being angry at my father was like being angry at myself. I wanted to be more loving, but in order to do that I knew I had to understand *his* perspective—I had to know what it was like for *him*.

"I also realized how much I was like him. It was a scary thought, but I decided I could turn those traits around to be positive.

"After my mother's death, I wrote my father a letter and let him know how much I loved him. That started a process through which our relationship has gradually gotten better. My father has had some heart problems and will probably pass away in a few years. But he has more peace of mind knowing that he's been understood by at least one of his children; and I continue to reassure him so that he can feel that his life *did* count."

When Floyd realized that his anger at his father prevented him from being at peace with himself, he decided to take whatever steps were needed for healing. By developing empathy in order to understand his father's perspective, he could also be more accepting of himself. Showing his love at a time when his father needed emotional support was the final step in an ongoing process that has deepened their relationship and enriched both their lives.

"I'm Glad I Made the Effort to Contact Him"

Even if a father has been missing for most of an adult child's life, it may still be possible to find him and resurrect the relationship. Marie Louise saw her father only a few times during a childhood in which she was shunted back and forth between relatives and the orphanage. By the time she was forty, she had completely lost track of her father, but a few years ago, she was finally able to find him and reconcile

"I love my father very much," Marie Louise said, "and I'm glad I made the effort to establish contact with him and communicate with him regularly. I'm sorry that we never had the opportunity to live together as a family. But despite the fact that we live so far apart, we have really bonded over the last years. I call him every week. It's easier for me to talk to him now than it's ever been. We have good conversations—they're very uplifting. I feel like a daughter toward him now, and I know he feels like a father toward me."

Marie Louise found her father and created a relationship where there had been none before. Although she was in her forties before they were reunited, the relationship steadily took root and is now a source of deep satisfaction for both of them.

Healing Your Relationship with a Deceased Father

"Suddenly, My Heart Released the Pain"

Sometimes, it's not possible to reconcile in person. Your father may have died, leaving you feeling shut out with a finality that is absolute. How do you deal with the hurt when the memories still linger but the person you need to resolve them with is not available anymore? How can you find resolution when you can't express your feelings to him or be told the words you need to hear? How do you find peace when there's only you?

Fortunately, there *is* a way. Even if your father is no longer physically accessible, his spirit still lives on in your memories. The information you receive by tuning into a deeper knowing evokes a recognition of the truth at a level of healing that is possible only when your conscious mind and automatic reactions are put aside.

Simone discovered this when she attended a spiritual retreat deep in the mountains of New Mexico. "We were sitting in a circle around the fire participating in a healing ritual," she mused. "It was a beautiful evening—the sky was so incredibly clear you could see hundreds of stars. Everyone was taking turns sharing something personal that they wanted to release from their lives.

"I had no idea what I was going to say, but when the feather was passed to me, and I held it in front of my face and closed my eyes, an image of my father suddenly appeared in my mind. I could feel his presence so strongly that there was no doubt. I had a sudden rush of realization that I was the one in the family who understood him, despite how difficult he was. I realized he was far ahead of his time: showing us survival skills, telling us about native ways, trying to make us self-sufficient. He even bought a little nature preserve so we could learn to be in harmony with the natural world.

"As I remembered these things, suddenly my heart released the pain I had been carrying around for years. I knew that my father really loved us and had given us a great gift in the way he taught us to look at the world. I felt so much love from him—I only wanted to say, 'I love you too, Dad.'

"When my father came to me that night in the circle, I realized how much he had given us. I saw how his spiritual beliefs had affected my own life, and I felt lucky to have been given that knowledge. It was a tremendous gift, and I was overcome with emotions of gratitude.

"It was a very important night for me. After years of doubt and lack of self-confidence about living up to his expectations, the doubts were dissolved. I knew I loved him always, and he loved us. I felt really peaceful about my dad and myself. When it was all over my mind was really put to rest."

Simone had no conception that in a few moments, the pain of years of rejection could be swept away. But when you open yourself to receive the information that is available through other ways of knowing, then you can access knowledge that is outside your conscious mind but that shows the larger truth of your relationship with your father. You can gain an awareness that can free you from the pain of years of rejection and reveal the love that was always there.

Healing After a Loss

"Reconciliation Came After My Brother's Suicide"

Martin, a writer, was also in midlife when a family tragedy prompted him to make use of his writing talent to come to terms with his father. "My father was a 'rageaholic' who had many extramarital affairs," Martin said. "Our reconciliation finally came about after my brother, who was a tremendously gifted musician, committed suicide while he was on tour.

"The whole family was in shock. As a memorial, I wrote a story about him and sent a copy to everyone. The next year, my father sent us all birthday cards for the very first time. Since then, we've been trying to get beyond all the things from the past and put our relationship back together. We write each other letters, and I'll send him copies of some of the things I'm working on. He actually makes some favorable comments about my work now, as well as con-structive suggestions.

"I agree with the principle that in order for a man to fully mature, he has to first bond with and then separate from both his father and mother. What I've seen is that a lot of men can separate from their fathers, but they can't take the second step and experience the grief and *bond* with their fathers."

Martin is right. There are three steps to reaching full maturity. In the first, children identify with their mother or father and wish to be like them. In the second, which comes during the teenage years, they separate from their parents so that they can prepare for independence. This is the basis for adolescent rebellion, because teens must demonstrate that they are *not* like Mom and Dad. The third stage is reconnection. In this stage the child has reached full independence and is confident in his or her own identity. The parent-child bonds are renewed but at a new level; and the parent and child now relate to each other as respected equals. This is the ideal.

In order to achieve fully maturity, separation alone is not enough. Separation is a necessary first step—it removes you from both the problems of the family and the security it provides, and it gives you the time and space to grow and become an independent adult. However, unless you use the separation not only to become autonomous but also to confront past pain and work through it, it is impossible to free yourself from past emotional attachments. Denying your pain keeps you a prisoner of unresolved grief and anger and interferes with all your other relationships.

Many men have stated, "I saw myself in my father, and it scared me." Being able to acknowledge the part of yourself that you reject allows you to work with it and transform it into something positive.

Despite the fear of pain, reconciliation or resolution is an indispensable element of maturing—whenever it takes place. When we learn to either forgive or detach, in order to make peace with one of the most important people in our lives, our father, we also learn to forgive and make peace with ourselves.

Sometimes, it is not possible to forgive. If this is the case, then it is still possible to detach. Even though no reconciliation can take place, resolution is still possible. For any number of reasons, including death, not knowing where your father lives, his refusal to have anything to do with you or your desire to avoid him, detachment may be the most effective route to resolution.

How do you detach from someone you still hold such strong feelings about? It's important to understand what detachment is, since this is a concept people often have difficulty with. Here are my definitions of detachment.

DETACHMENT IS . . .

Detachment is not being uncaring but letting go of a desired outcome.

Detachment is doing what you need to do without worrying about the others person's reaction.

Detachment is knowing what is within your control and what you can't control.

Detachment is accepting the facts of the past.

Detachment is when your feelings from the past don't influence your feelings in the present.

Detachment is when the hurt of the past fades away.

Detachment is when you can't be manipulated anymore.

Detachment is reclaiming your power.

Resolution: If Reconciliation Is Not Possible

No matter how hard you try, sometimes it is impossible to reconcile. You've called, you've written, you've begged and pleaded, but no matter how many tears you shed or how many phone calls you make and letters you write, your father remains adamant. He will not listen to you, hangs up on you, rages at you, makes unfounded accusations and completely refuses to acknowledge you in any way.

Perhaps the last time you saw your father, hurtful words were said that have stayed with you and cannot be undone. But he is no longer available because of death or other circumstances, and that painful event is the last recollection you have of him. Or, your experiences were so bad that you don't want any contact with him, but you want to be rid of the pain.

When reconciliation is impossible, through your own decision or because events are beyond your control, the only solution available is to focus on your inner work and detach. Your goal is the peace of mind that comes with disengagement and resolution.

EXERCISE: IF YOU CAN'T RECONCILE

Rejection is something like death. A person whom you love has turned their back on you and is no longer available. To detach and heal from the pain of rejection, you have to allow yourself to go through the grieving process until you come to the moment of insight—the place where you gain the profound understanding that there is no longer any relationship.

Although you may still feel obligated by family ties, the emotional connection you seek simply cannot be had. Writing a letter of release often helps when you decide that it's time to detach from the relationship and let go.

LETTER OF RELEASE

Write a letter to your father releasing him from any ties to you and wishing him whatever is necessary to fill his needs and bring him peace. Since you are releasing him, it can be simple and short. You are not blaming him and you are not expecting anything. You simply want to thank him for whatever gifts he has given you, and release him so that he can go on his way with your love and blessings. This letter need not be mailed; it is written for *you*, so that you can bring closure to this part of your life. If you do mail it, be sure that you are doing so with no expectations. The following is a sample letter of release.

> Dear Dad,
>
> I want to thank you for giving me life and bringing me up to adulthood. Despite our problems, I've always loved you as my father and hoped that one day we could straighten things out. I know now that is not possible. You have your own desires, and I respect them. I hereby release you from any expectations on my part and gently place you in the hands of life.
>
> Your daughter/son,
>
> _____
>
> (Your name)

YOUR LETTER OF RELEASE

Dear Dad,

_____

_____

_____

_____

_____

_____

Your daughter / son,

_____

(Your name)

GUIDED IMAGERY MEDITATION TO
RELEASE YOUR FATHER

Find a quiet place where you can experience this process undisturbed. You can read the following script into a tape recorder, pausing between phrases to give yourself time to fully experience the imagery. Remember, you are always in charge and can stop at any time. Extraneous thoughts that come into your mind are natural. Simply notice them and let them float out again. It's not necessary to actually "see" anything. Just imagine what might be there. Whatever you imagine or sense is right for you.

To begin, allow yourself to relax comfortably in a favorite chair, or lie down if you're sure you won't fall asleep. Rest your hands in your lap. Uncross your legs and let your feet rest flat on the floor. Take a few deep breaths, and as you exhale, let your eyes close and your body relax even more. Imagine all your worries and concerns flowing outward with each breath.

Now, breathing slowly and rhythmically, imagine that you are standing on a bluff overlooking a large body of water. As you look down, you notice a man who looks just like your father standing at the water's edge getting ready to board a boat of some kind. You can see that he is going on a very long trip. It is uncertain whether he will ever return to this shore again. There is an air of finality about his departure. But as he leaves, you have the sense that the captain of this ship knows where he is going and is an expert seaman. Your father is in good hands and will arrive at his destination safely.

From your place on the high ground, raise your hand in a final farewell and give him your blessings. Your prayers for his safety will protect him on his journey.

Watch the ship cast off and slowly sail away, getting smaller and smaller until you can barely see the mast or smokestack on the horizon. All the feelings you have about your father are also on the ship. As you watch it disappear, your emotions about him will also start to gradually fade, getting fainter and fainter until they completely disappear and the ship vanishes over the edge of the horizon.

When the ship has completely left sight, go down to the shore and look around for the gift that has been left for you. It is something that you can always have with you, and it will give you strength whenever you need it. Pick it up. Feel its weight, examine its surface, feel its degree of warmth or coolness, hold it with both hands to your heart and see or sense what is inside. This object contains wisdom and love that you can tap into whenever it is needed. Sense or imagine what it feels like and how you will use it. Then, holding your gift gently, bring it back with you and put it in a place of safekeeping.

Remember, there are no "right" or "wrong" images. Whatever presents itself to you is right. You can enjoy this experience as a symbolic release, or you might find additional meanings that are highly significant to you. Write down what you experienced in this visualization—everything you saw, felt, heard or perceived, so that you can read it later and remember the feelings. This experience can be repeated whenever you like. Each time it will lead to further understanding. If you wish, you can also use this experience to release other elements of your life that you want to detach from.

NOTES: IMAGERY TO RELEASE MY FATHER

_____

_____

_____

_____

_____

RITUAL FOR LETTING GO

Ritual is another powerful method for letting go. In ritual, you symbolically divest yourself of something or someone that is no longer a part of your life. You create a sacred act for letting go and direct the person with your blessings into the safekeeping of a greater power.

One effective letting-go ritual is to take the letter you have written to your father and burn it in a natural setting that represents beauty and tranquillity to you. This might be the beach, a lake shore, a mountain area or any other natural environment where you feel at peace. When you have found the appropriate setting, burn the letter and bless and release your father as you watch the smoke drift away.

As the smoke dissipates into the air and disappears, imagine the bond with your father dissolving and disappearing until it is completely gone.

Spend as much time as you like in the nature spot you have chosen, and allow the beauty and healing properties of the outdoors to fill you. (Of course, you will make certain that there are no smoldering ashes and that the fire is completely out.) Later on, you may choose to talk about your experience with a trusted friend who will listen in a supportive manner. Write down your experience here so that you can read it another time.

NOTES: "LETTING MY FATHER GO" RITUAL

_____

_____

_____

_____

_____

The Legacy of Fathers and Families

Families are the nurseries for society. Within the social microcosm of mother, father and children, expectations are developed for the social roles and rules expressed in the larger world. When families are strong, with the active and equal participation of both fathers and mothers, children have the security of knowing that they are valued and that there is an unbreakable bond between two loving adults who have pledged commitment not only to each other but to their children. The knowledge that their parents care about them and are invested in their future is the best guarantee of the children's own eventual happiness and success—as individuals, parents, and members of the community. In this microcosm, the presence of fathers makes a critical difference.

"To Have Family and Friends Gathered Around Is God's Greatest Gift"

The following moving statement is a loving remembrance of a wonderful father by his fifty-three-year-old son, Carl. As the other stories in this book demonstrate, it shows that a father's legacy is never lost. The father-child bond, whatever form it takes, is an influence that lives on in memory forever.

"What am I to say about my father?" Carl began. "I remember

only the presence of the man and his quiet and enduring strength. He was always there—a good and consistent provider whose character lent stability to my childhood and permanence to my relationships.

"What do I remember learning from my father? Always carry your own weight, and help the other guy if you can. Take care of your mother, and your brothers and sister. Show respect for your elders, and keep yourself and your home neat and clean. And one thing more—to have family and good friends gathered around a bounteous table is perhaps God's greatest gift.

"I have an immense regard for my father, who was a largely silent man . . . but I read in his silences all the patience and dependability that made up his character—along with the love, the kindness and the unending concern for his family.

"If I could speak to my father, perhaps nothing would be more adequate than a heartfelt 'Thank you.'

"I can hear his response now: 'Thank me? What for? I didn't do very much.'

"Yes, you did, Dad. Oh, yes, you did!"

| | | |

We all desire a father's love, affection and guidance. Neither schools, television nor peers are adequate substitutes—fathers remain essential. Whether he is a traditional father in a two-parent home, a divorced father with weekend custody, a stepfather or a surrogate father, youngsters want a close relationship with Dad.

Men and women who had a strong bond with their fathers expressed enduring appreciation for the support, counsel and affection they received. Those who had poor relationships voiced disappointment, anger and pain at being deprived of male nurturing during their growing-up years.

Mothers have performed heroically as heads of single-parent households and by contributing to the family's financial welfare through their efforts in the workplace. Yet most adults whose fathers played minor roles in their youth, especially men who grew up without any father or father figure in the home, decried the lack of a male presence and expressed a deeply felt need for masculine role modeling. Girls also stated strong desires for the opportunity to interact with a parent of the opposite sex and to observe a standard for male-female relationships,

Having a Great Dad as a role model is an enormous benefit when men become fathers themselves. But even men who did not have a Great Dad often deliberately changed the parenting style they had experienced as children. Knowing how important good fathering was, they committed themselves to developing those skills—thereby becoming for their own children the fathers they once desired.

We are at a critical point in the formation of families and the way children are nurtured into adulthood. Some will continue to grow up enjoying the advantages of a two-parent home—many others will not. In this equation, the necessity of fathers must not be forgotten. In a time of rapidly changing expectations, many men are discovering an almost forgotten truth—fatherhood can be endlessly demanding and challenging, but it is also infinitely rewarding.

The most enduring and meaningful legacy most of us will ever leave is the inheritance of love and values we transmit to our children and in so doing, transmit to their children and their children after them.

Bibliography

Recommended Reading

Appleton, William S. *Fathers & Daughters: A Father's Powerful Influence on a Woman's Life*. New York: Berkley Books, 1984.

Biller, Henry B. *Father, Child and Sex Role: Paternal Determinants of Personality Development*. Lexington, MA: Heath Lexington Books, 1977.

Biller, Henry B., and Trotter, Robert J. *The Father Factor*. New York: Pocket Books, 1994.

Blankenhorn, David. *Fatherless America*. New York: HarperCollins, 1995.

Bloomfield, Harold. *Making Peace With Your Parents*. New York: Ballantine Books, 1983.

Blos, Peter. *Son and Father: Before and Beyond the Oedipus Complex*. New York: The Free Press, 1985.

Bly, Robert. *Iron John*. Reading, MA: Addison-Wesley Publishing Co., 1990.

Borhek, Mary V. *Coming Out to Our Parents: A Two-Way Survival Guide for Lesbians and Gay Men and Their Parents*. New York: Pilgrim Press, 1983.

Bradshaw, John. *Bradshaw on the Family*. Deerfield Beach, FL: Health Communications, 1988.

——. *Homecoming: Reclaiming and Championing Your Inner Child*. New York: Bantam Books, 1990.

Byers, Kenneth. *Man in Transition*. La Mesa, CA: Journeys Together, 1990.

Clark, Donald H. *Loving Someone Gay*. New York: New American Library, 1977.

Colman, Andrew, and Colman, Libby. *The Father: Mythology and Changing Roles*. Wilmette, IL: Chiron Publications, 1981.

Corneau, Guy. *Absent Fathers, Lost Sons: The Search for Masculine Identity*. Boston: Shambhala, 1991.

Cosby, Bill. *Fatherhood*. Garden City, NY: Doubleday, 1986.

Fanning, Patrick. *Visualization for Change*. Oakland, CA: New Harbinger Publications, 1988.

Farrell, Warren. *Why Men Are the Way They Are: The Male-Female Dynamic*. New York: McGraw Hill, 1986.

Glennon, Will. *Fathering: Strengthening Connection with Your Children No Matter Where You Are*. Berkeley, CA: Conart Press, 1995.

Greer, Germaine. *Daddy, We Hardly Knew You*. New York: Knopf, 1990.

Greif, Geoffrey. *Single Fathers*. Lexington, MA: Lexington Books, 1983.

Hamilton, Marshall L. *Father's Influence on Children*. Chicago: Nelson-Hall, 1977.

Jampolsky, Gerald G., and Jampolsky, Lee L. *Listen to Me: A Book for Women and Men About Father-Son Relationships*. Berkeley, CA: Celestial Arts, 1996.

Keen, Sam. *Fire in the Belly: On Being a Man.* New York: Bantam Books, 1991.

Laikin, D. *Daughters of Divorce.* New York: Morrow & Co., 1981.

Lamb, Michael E., ed. *The Role of the Father in Child Development.* New York: John Wiley & Sons, 1981.

Lee, John. *At My Father's Wedding: Reclaiming Our True Masculinity.* New York: Bantam Books, 1991.

Levant, Ronald, and Kelly, John. *Between Father and Child.* New York: Viking, 1989.

McKee, Lorna, and O'Brien, Margaret. *The Father Figure.* London: Tavistock Publications, 1982.

Pruett, Kyle. *The Nurturing Father.* New York: Warner Books, 1987.

Scull, Charles, ed. *Fathers, Sons & Daughters: Exploring Fatherhood, Renewing the Bond.* Los Angeles: Jeremy P. Tarcher, 1992.

Wakerman, Elise. *Father Loss.* New York: Henry Holt and Co., 1987.

Wallerstein, Judith, and Blakeslee, Sandra. *Second Chance: Men, Women & Children a Decade After Divorce.* New York: Ticknor & Fields, 1989.

Wallerstein, Judith, and Kelly, J. B. *Surviving the Breakup: How Children Actually Cope with Divorce.* New York: Basic Books, 1980.

Winokur, Jon. *Fathers.* New York: Dutton, 1993.

Yablonsky, Lewis. *Fathers and Sons.* New York: Simon & Schuster, 1990.

Further Reading

CAREER

Bolles, Richard. *What Color Is Your Parachute?* Berkeley, CA: Ten Speed Press, 1981.

Campbell, David. *If You Don't Know Where You're Going, You'll Probably End Up Somewhere Else.* Niles, IL: Argus Communication, 1974.

Covey. Stephen R. *The Seven Habits of Highly Effective People.* New York: Simon & Schuster, 1989.

Scott, Gini Graham. *Resolving Conflict: With Others and Within Yourself.* Oakland, CA: New Harbinger Publications, 1990.

Shaevitz, Marjorie Hansen. *The Superwoman Syndrome.* New York: Warner Books, 1985.

Sher, Barbara. *Wishcraft: How to Get What You Really Want.* New York: Ballantine Books, 1979.

COMMUNICATION

Alberti, Robert. E., and Emmons, Michael L. *Your Perfect Right: A Guide to Assertive Living.* San Luis Obispo, CA: Impact Publishers, 1986.

Gottman, John, et al. *A Couple's Guide to Communication.* Champaign, IL: Research Press, 1976.

McKay, Matthew, Davis, Martha, and Fanning, Patrick. *Messages: The Communication Skills Book.* Oakland, CA: New Harbinger Publications, 1983.

INCEST

Bass, Ellen, and Davis, Laura. *The Courage to Heal: A Guide for Women Survivors of Child Sexual Abuse.* New York: HarperCollins, 1989.

Maltz, Wendy. *The Sexual Healing Journey: A Guide for Survivors of Sexual Abuse.* New York: HarperCollins, 1991.

Sanders, Timothy L. *Male Survivors: 12-Step Recovery Program for Survivors of Childhood Sexual Abuse*. Freedom, CA: The Crossing Press, 1991.

PARENTING

Biller, Henry B., and Trotter, Robert J. *The Father Factor*. New York: Pocket Books, 1994.

Clarke, Jean Illsley, and Dawson, Connie. *Growing Up Again: Parenting Ourselves, Parenting Our Children*. Center City, MN: Hazelden Publications, 1989.

Gordon, Thomas. *Parent Effectiveness Training*. New York: Peter H. Wyden, 1970.

Weston, Denise Chapman, and Weston, Mark S. *Playful Parenting: Turning the Dilemma of Discipline into Fun and Games*. New York: Putnam, 1993.

RELATIONSHIPS

Bilicki, Bettie Youngs, and Goetz, Masa. *Getting Back Together: How to Create a New Loving Relationship with Your Old Partner and Make It Last*. Holbrook, MA: Bob Adams, 1990.

Bloomfield, Harold, and Vettese, Sirah. *Lifemates: The Love Fitness Program for a Lasting Relationship*. New York: New American Library, 1989.

Gordon, Lori, H. *Passage to Intimacy*. New York: Simon & Schuster, 1993.

Notarius, Clifford, and Markman, Howard. *We Can Work It Out: How to Solve Conflicts, Save Your Marriage, and Strengthen Your Love for Each Other*. New York: Berkley Publishing, 1993.

Paul, Jordan, and Paul, Margaret. *From Conflict to Caring: An In-Depth Program for Creating Loving Relationships*. Minneapolis, MN: CompCare Publishers, 1989.

SELF-ESTEEM

Branden, Nathaniel. *The Six Pillars of Self-Esteem*. New York: Bantam Books, 1994.

Burns, David D. *The Feeling Good Handbook*. New York: Penguin Books, 1989.

Clarke, Jean Illsley. *Self-Esteem: A Family Affair*. San Francisco: Harper & Row, 1981.

Touchstones: A Book of Daily Meditations for Men. San Francisco: Harper/Hazelden, 1986.

SPIRITUALITY AND VALUES

Houston, Jean. *The Search for the Beloved: Journeys in Mythology and Sacred Psychology*. Los Angeles: Jeremy P. Tarcher, 1987.

Moore, Robert, and Gillette, Douglas. *King, Warrior, Magician, Lover: Rediscovering the Archetypes of the Mature Masculine*. San Francisco: HarperCollins, 1990.

Raspberry, Sally, and Selwyn, Padi. *Living Your Life Out Loud*. New York: Pocket Books, 1995.

Redfield, James, and Adrienne, Carol. *The Celestine Prophecy: An Experiential Guide*. New York: Warner Books, 1995.

Simon, Sidney B., Howe, Leland W., and Kirschenbaum, Howard. *Values Clarification*. New York: Warner Books, 1995.

STEPFAMILIES

Belovitch, Jeanne. *Making Remarriage Work*. Lexington, MA: Lexington Books, 1987.

Einstein, Elizabeth, and Albert, Linda. *Strengthening Your Stepfamily*. Circle Pines, MN: American Guidance Service, 1986.

Rosin, Mark Bruce. *Stepfathering: Stepfathers' Advice on Creating a New Family*. New York: Ballantine Books, 1987.

About Dr. Masa Aiba Goetz

Dr. Masa Aiba Goetz is a nationally recognized psychologist with a private practice in San Diego whose work with individuals, groups and organizations has earned her a reputation as a respected authority in the fields of interpersonal relationships, marriage counseling and personal growth.

A popular guest expert on national television and radio, Dr. Goetz has appeared on *Sally Jessy Raphael*, *Geraldo* and *Sonya Live*, as well as dozens of local television and radio stations throughout the United States. She is the coauthor of *Getting Back Together*, which has been hailed as a "must read" for couples who have separated and wish to reconcile successfully.

Masa's annual New Mexico retreat, Spirit Journey, a small-group self-discovery and renewal experience, is designed to heal spiritual, emotional and relationship issues in a supportive setting that intensifies the divine potential of each participant.

In addition to her private practice, Dr. Goetz is professor at the California Institute for Human Science in Encinitas, California, where she teaches courses in transpersonal psychology, clinical intuition and guided imagery. She was formerly director of psychological services at an AIDS clinic and a psychologist at a community health clinic and treatment centers for emotionally disturbed youth.

Dr. Goetz is on the advisory board of the San Diego Mental Health Association and is a past director of the San Diego Community Research Group. She is a member of the American Psychological Society, the Association for Transpersonal Psychology, the California Psychological Association and the California Association of Marriage and Family Therapists.